WESTERN EUROPEAN
PENAL SYSTEMS

WESTERN EUROPEAN PENAL SYSTEMS

A Critical Anatomy

Edited by
Vincenzo Ruggiero, Mick Ryan
and Joe Sim

SAGE Publications
London • Thousand Oaks • New Delhi

© Editorial selection and matter © Vincenzo Ruggiero,
Mick Ryan and Joe Sim 1995
Chapter 1 © Joe Sim, Vincenzo Ruggiero and Mick Ryan 1995
Chapter 2 © René van Swaaningen and Gerard de Jonge 1995
Chapter 3 © Vincenzo Ruggiero 1995
Chapter 4 © Ermanno Gallo 1995
Chapter 5 © Mick Ryan and Joe Sim 1995
Chapter 6 © Claudius Messner and Vincenzo Ruggiero 1995
Chapter 7 © Roberto Bergalli 1995
Chapter 8 © Karen Leander 1995
Chapter 9 © Mike Tomlinson 1995

First published 1995

SAGE Publications Ltd
6 Bonhill Street
London EC2A 4PU

SAGE Publications Inc
2455 Teller Road
Thousand Oaks, California 91320

SAGE Publications India Pvt Ltd
32, M-Block Market
Greater Kailash – I
New Delhi 110 048

British Library Cataloguing in Publication data

A catalogue record for this book is
available from the British Library.

ISBN 0 8039 7562–7
ISBN 0 8039 7563–5 (pbk)

Library of Congress catalog record available

Typeset by Mayhew Typesetting, Rhayader, Powys
Printed in Great Britain by Biddles Ltd, Guildford

Contents

Contributors

Roberto Bergalli is Professor and Director at the Oñati International Institute for the Sociology of Law, Oñati, Spain. His most recent publications include the editorship of the international collection *Sistema Penal e Intervenciones Sociales: Algunas Experiencias en Europa* (1993).

Ermanno Gallo is based in Paris. He has written extensively on penal systems and with Vincenzo Ruggiero has co-authored *Il Carcere in Europa* (1980, Verona: Bertani) and *Il Carcere Immateriale* (1989, Torino: Sonda).

Gerard de Jonge is Reader in Criminal Law and Penitentiary Law at the University of Limburg at Maastricht. He is former President of the Coornhert League of Penal Reform, and a practising lawyer who specializes in prisoners' cases. He has just finished a book on forced labour in penal settings, entitled *Strafwerk: arbeidsverhouding tussen gedetineerden en justitie (Impositions: Labour Relations between Prisoners and the Justice Administration)*.

Karen Leander is employed by the Stockholm County Council Department of Social Medicine to specialize in violence studies and prevention while also lecturing in the Department of Criminology, Stockholm University. She also leads a weekly seminar in a Swedish prison for women and for several years has acted as convenor for the European Group for the Study of Deviance and Social Control.

Claudius Messner lectures at the University of Saarlandes, Saarbrücken, Germany. He has published extensively on criminal justice issues and is closely associated with the Italian journal *Dei Delitti e Delle Pene*.

Vincenzo Ruggiero is Reader in Criminology and Social Studies at Middlesex University, London. He has written numerous articles and books on criminal justice issues, including *La roba: Economie e culture dell 'eroina* (1992, Parma: Pratiche) and most recently a co-authored volume with Nigel South, *Eurodrugs: Drug Use Markets and Trafficking in Europe* (1995, London: UCL Press).

Mick Ryan is Professor of Penal Politics at the University of Greenwich, London. He is author of *The Politics of Penal Reform* (1982, Longman) and co-author with Tony Ward of *Privatization and the Penal System: The American Experience and the Debate in Britain* (1989, Milton Keynes: Open University Press). He was Chair of INQUEST, the pressure group concerned with deaths in custody between 1992 and 1994.

Joe Sim is Professor of Criminology at the Liverpool John Moores University. He has written extensively on the English and Scottish penal systems. He is author of *Medical Power in Prisons* (1990, Milton Keynes: Open University Press) and co-author of *British Prisons* (1982, Oxford: Basil Blackwell) and *Prisons under Protest* (1991, Milton Keynes: Open University Press).

René van Swaaningen is Reader in Criminal Justice, Criminology and Penology at the Erasmus University at Rotterdam and board member of the Netherlands Society of Criminology (NVK). He has published in different languages on themes of critical criminology and penal reform. He is currently finishing a book on critical criminology in Europe (forthcoming, Sage).

Mike Tomlinson is Lecturer in Social Policy at the Queen's University of Belfast. He co-edited *Whose Law and Order? Aspects of Crime and Social Control in Ireland* (1988, Belfast: Sociological Association of Ireland) and *The Expansion of European Prison Systems* (1987, Belfast: EGDSC). A founder member of the West Belfast Economic Forum, he is a regular contributor to *Statewatch*.

Preface

This book on Western European penal systems came about for three reasons.

The first was that we became aware that in spite of our own sometimes quite detailed knowledge of other Western European penal systems there was no readily available introductory text in English for undergraduates or interested professionals on these neighbouring systems. This text is an attempt to put this right, albeit sometimes at a fairly descriptive level. That is to say, we genuinely want our undergraduates and professionals such as probation officers to discover more about the basic structure of the penal apparatus in other European countries such as France and Sweden, to learn about the agencies which constitute that apparatus and to reflect on the variety and distribution of penalties which are imposed on those who transgress the law.

But beyond mere description, and most important, we have asked each of our contributors to both contextualize the systems they describe and provide their own critical anatomy, though we must stress that we have not sought to privilege any particular approach in this respect.

The second reason for the book stems from our interest in diverting the gaze of British policy-makers from the American experience. Far too often we in Britain look to America to reflect on trends and possibilities when looking closer to home might arguably serve us better. In terms of penal policy what has happened in America, e.g. electronic tagging, private prisons, all too quickly happens here and with far from certain benefits. There are other systems, other processes we might conceivably learn from and we should at least begin to look at how some of these other, more proximate systems operate.

Third, while we stress the plural here deliberately since each chapter is a testimony to the very different historical and cultural traditions in which different European penal systems operate, there are nonetheless some broad trends and generalizations – including some disturbing ones – worth noting as we move towards the millennium and the pace of European unity quickens. The very fact that all the countries covered are now part of the European Union is itself significant. We pull some of these tentative threads together in the introduction.

Finally, two very practical points. Up-to-date statistics are not easy to come by for a number of European countries, and it is significant, for example, that even the HEUNI (European Institute for Crime Prevention and Control) report on criminal justice statistics in Europe and North America due to be published in 1995 will only cover the years 1985–90. We have done our best to be much more up to date than this whenever possible, and we are grateful to our contributors for badgering their respective national departments to secure this. In this context, we are particularly grateful to the Goethe Institute, London which held a timely Anglo-German conference on crime and punishment in the summer of 1994. Second, we have had to alter in translation certain usages as this text is intended mainly for an Anglo-Saxon audience. We ask for our readers' forbearance in this matter.

Acknowledgements

A number of people and institutions have helped us in the preparation of this book.

In particular we would like to thank: Biko Agozino, Anette Ballinger, Kristi Ballinger, Sue Barlow, Tony Bunyan, Angela Dell, Pete Gill, Gill Hall, Paddy Hillyard, Mavis James, Ken Pease, Marion Price, Pat Rosser-Davies, Joan Ryan, Anne Singleton, Edith Stollery and Tony Ward. Several librarians have lent their support to this enterprise, most notably Imogen Forster at the University of Greenwich. The Research and Staff Development Committee, School of Social Science, Liverpool John Moores University, provided Joe Sim with relief from teaching in the autumn of 1994 to pursue work on this book. Colourbytes provided technical support. Finally, our thanks to Gillian Stern at Sage for her forbearance. The task we set ourselves was far more complicated than we had originally thought and this led to delays which must surely have tested her patience.

1

Punishment in Europe: Perceptions and Commonalities

Joe Sim, Vincenzo Ruggiero and Mick Ryan

> The New Penology . . . is concerned with techniques for identifying, classifying and managing groups assorted by levels of dangerousness. It takes crime for granted. It accepts deviance as normal. It is sceptical that liberal interventionist crime control strategies do or can make a difference. Thus its aim is not to intervene in individuals' lives for the purpose of ascertaining responsibility, making the guilty 'pay for their crime' or changing them. Rather it seeks to regulate groups as part of a strategy of managing danger. (Feeley and Simon 1994:173)

> Of course we must make it easier for our people to travel throughout the Community. But it is a matter of plain common sense that we cannot totally abolish frontier controls if we are also to protect our citizens from crime and stop the movement of drugs, of terrorists and of illegal immigrants. (Margaret Thatcher 1988, cited in Gordon 1989:8)

In October 1993, there were 300,000 individuals confined in the prisons of the twelve member states of the European Union (EU). Eighty-five per cent of these individuals received no work or training during their detention. In four states – France, Italy, Germany and the United Kingdom – the prison population was over 50,000. These bare figures, published by the European Employment Group (*Guardian* 18 October 1993), are part of a much larger package of statistics and studies which have appeared since the mid 1980s comparing different aspects of imprisonment in Europe. The biannual statistical bulletins published by the Council of Europe, various United Nations surveys and a range of sociological work have raised a number of important theoretical and empirical questions about the place of the prison within nation-states and the differences between prison systems in terms of structure, organization, regimes and populations. The profound economic, political and cultural developments which have taken place in Western and Eastern Europe since the late 1980s have only added to the significance of the questions asked within the literature, particularly in respect of the complex relationship between crime, punishment, social change and the maintenance of order.

(See, for example, Downes 1988; Cain 1989; Whitfield 1991; Pease and Hukkila 1990; Muncie and Sparks 1991; Heidensohn and Farrell 1991; Smit and Dunkel 1991; Hudson 1993; Young and Brown 1993; Vagg 1994; Thomas and Moerings 1994; Tomasevski 1992; 1994; Pease 1994; Powell 1994; South and Weiss forthcoming).

However, despite the insights developed within this burgeoning literature there are still a number of gaps which remain to be filled. This collection of essays seeks to fill some of them by providing one of the first detailed studies of a range of Western European penal systems. The word 'penal' is important here for we have sought to ensure that contributors have focused on, and analysed, not only prison systems in their respective countries but also the various alternatives to custody which are available and the place of these alternatives in the business and distribution of punishment. The collection, therefore, provides a critical anatomy and empirical overview of the full range of penal sanctions utilized in each country and analyses how these sanctions are organized. Contributors have been asked to pinpoint the nature of the penal population in relation to sentence disposition, their class, gender and racial composition and the nature of the offences for which individuals have been confined. This last issue is particularly apposite when set against the (non) policing and (non) punishment of the crimes committed by the powerful in Western Europe (both economic and otherwise), a point we shall return to below.

Finally, we have also asked contributors to critically evaluate trends in the philosophy, practices and politics of punishment and to locate these trends within the broader processes of social change taking place within nation-states. Individual authors have identified a number of significant trends, many of which began in the mid 1970s, intensified in the 1980s and became institutionalized in the 1990s. In particular, the intensification and interpenetration of disciplinary discourses within the state and civil society, the drive towards authoritarian law and order solutions for social problems and the rolling back of national and international welfare states are key themes identified in this volume.

In the remainder of this introduction we shall elaborate on these points by focusing on a number of issues highlighted by different authors as important for the development and consolidation of the penal systems in their respective countries. These include: the processes of bifurcation and harmonization; the politics of crime and deviance; gender and penal systems; punishing the powerful; the impact of privatization; the deleterious effects of penal regimes on the hearts and minds of the confined; the place of the penal system in a changing political situation; and finally contradictions and conflicts surrounding the direction of penal policy. Detailed consideration of these issues provides the analytical starting point for the rest of this introduction.

Bifurcation and harmonization

In May 1992, the twenty-seven Directors of Prison Administrations in the Council of Europe held their tenth conference in the Palais de l'Europe in Strasbourg. In summing up the conference, William Rentzmann, the Deputy Director General of the Danish Department of Prisons and Probation, pointed to a number of general tendencies affecting penal policy in the member states of the Council. These included: an increase in the number of prisoners and in the length of sentences passed by the courts in the different jurisdictions; the expansion in prison capacity both through the construction of new buildings and in the utilization of existing buildings for prison purposes; the increasing use of community sentences in terms of the extension of those already in use and through the introduction of new sanctions; and finally the non-decline in the capacity of prisons despite the increased use of alternative sentences (Rentzmann 1992).

Each chapter in this volume confirms these points. The contributors note the expansion of individual penal systems; the rise in the length of sentences and in the time served by the confined; and finally, the increasing use of alternatives which have had little or no impact on the prison population. They also point to a process of international bifurcation taking place. The concept as originally developed by Tony Bottoms has been described in the following terms: 'put crudely, this bifurcation is between, on the one hand, the so-called "really serious offender" for whom very tough measures are typically advocated; and on the other hand, the "ordinary" offender for whom, it is felt, we can afford to take a much more lenient line' (Bottoms 1983:196). The majority of countries considered in this volume have experienced this process at work in the last two decades.

At the same time, a number of contributors also point out that the concept of bifurcation may need some theoretical modification to take account of the political and sociological fact that by the mid 1990s the idea of 'leniency' at the 'shallow' end of the system was looking increasingly problematic. As the contributors from Holland, Sweden and England and Wales make clear, those offenders at the 'shallow' end of the system were being confronted by regimes, both inside and outside in the community, in which surveillance, discipline and punishment had become the basis of their philosophy and practice. The punitive and disciplinary elements which had always existed in community sanctions have intensified in the 1990s to the point where those states such as Sweden and Holland which were regarded as reasonably liberal have become tied into a less informal, more regulatory network of disciplinary power. At the same time, this process is both incomplete and not without its own internal contradictions. Nonetheless, it is possible to perceive an intensification in the emphasis being placed on discipline, surveillance and punishment within different nation-states, underpinned by an internationalization of the concerns around crime and disorder and a concomitant internationalization of demand for a calibrated law and order response to these concerns. Within this discourse, expenditure on welfare oriented elements within different criminal justice systems has been challenged by the discourses of the new right and the strident demand not only for prudent austerity but also for an iron toughness in therapeutic and caring practices. The changing role of the probation service in Western Europe, which is discussed by some contributors, provides a good example of the intensification in the demand for punishment as opposed to welfare in the community, a process which is paralleled by, and reflected in, the restrictions and cuts in social welfare in general in Europe in the 1990s (Gibson 1993). René van Swaaningen and Gerard de Jonge's chapter on Holland and Karen Leander's discussion of Sweden provide two examples of this process. In the case of the latter, Leander develops a suggestive analysis of a country which despite deeply entrenched, positive, welfare policies has not been immune from pursuing a political strategy which emphasizes austerity in the provision of social services. This strategy has involved not only cuts in welfare provision but also the utilization of the prison to regulate 'the worst of the worst'. Drug users, in particular, have become the group used to legitimate an intensification in control both inside and outside the prison gates. She also notes how the Social Democratic Party, elected to government in 1994, refused to repeal the law and order measures introduced by the previous Conservative government. This process has been reflected in other countries such as Holland and England and Wales. In the case of the latter, the Labour Party opposition under the realist slogan 'tough on crime, tough on the causes of crime' has conceded crucial ideological and political ground to the Conservative government on a range of law and order, welfare and educational issues. More generally, it is worth noting that the ideological attack on welfare has also become apparent in the way that the EU has 'decreased its work on the treatment of non-Union citizens in employment and social services, which was its original mandate, while concentrating instead on migration control through "a previously unknown committee of officials"' (Tomasevski 1994:42). We will return to the question of migration control below.

Alongside the question of bifurcation is the question of harmonization and convergence. In other words, are European criminal justice systems in general and penal systems in particular pursuing a set of common goals and policies? This remains a controversial question as writers seek to avoid crude pan-European reductionism on the one hand while on the other attempting to avoid simplistic assertions that national penal systems remain immune from global economic, political and ideological trends and processes. As John Muncie and Richard Sparks pointed out in 1991:

> Given the diversity of practices and local experiences it is difficult to arrive at adequate global judgements: it may be unwise to seek to identify pan-European trends. Yet such provisos should not obscure a basic truth, namely that prison populations have risen sharply in most industrial societies during the last two decades. (1991:100)

In her introduction to the collection *Crime in Europe* which she co-edited and which was also published in 1991 Frances Heidensohn made the point that while there was 'considerable congruence in definitions of what constitutes crime problems and issues between different nation-states in Europe' there appeared to be rather 'less harmony . . . in the responses to crime among European nations' (1991:8–9). The introduction rightly went on to note that there was evidence of convergence and co-operation in some areas of criminal justice policy in Europe in the early 1990s, particularly in response to political violence, organized crime and drug trafficking. At the same time, penal policies 'differ[ed] markedly', a point reiterated in Jon Vagg's study of accountability in the same volume (Vagg 1991; see also Vagg 1994).

While we would argue that it is important to recognize the cultural differences that exist between different penal systems and the contradictions and conflicts that are still apparent between nation-states in Western Europe, two important issues tend to be either under-stated or missing in these earlier studies. First, there is little consideration given to the full implications of the particular definitions of crime and deviance which European states operate from. This has particular relevance for who is policed and as importantly who is not policed in relation to criminal and deviant behaviour. This in turn inevitably raises questions about the powerful and the powerless and the construction of penal populations across Western Europe comprising the latter rather than the former. As all of the contributions make clear, Western European penal systems confine the economically, politically and ideologically marginalized. It is a process which is not a natural event but the result of a definite convergence of discourses around who are defined as problematic in Western European society. We will return to this issue below.

The second problem with earlier studies is that they tend to ignore or obscure the structural links which have been established between different penal administrations in Western Europe. In the effort to avoid reductionism these links have been neglected. It is therefore important to recognize the different levels at which penal power operates if a full, analytical picture is to be developed with respect to penal systems in Western Europe (Hillyard 1994). Shining the searchlight of sociological scrutiny at different *levels* of state practices can uncover evidence of greater harmonization and convergence than previous studies have recognized. This may well be an embryonic process but as we noted above it is a process that has been happening with respect to the different meetings and conferences which have taken place between the Directors of Prison Administrations in the Council of Europe. Their tenth conference held in Strasbourg in May 1992 was convened after a series of seminars which had discussed various penal issues including the management and philosophy of regimes and the European prison rules. These seminars were themselves part of a Council of Europe inspired programme code-named 'Demosthenes' which was designed to 'encourage and develop links between the Council and the countries of Central and South-East Europe'. Consequently, the programme had arranged seminars for individuals working in penal systems in Hungary, Czechoslovakia, Poland, Romania and Bulgaria. These seminars took place between September 1990 and May 1991. One of the participants supported extending the penological link to former communist countries by maintaining that: 'communism should be seen as just an episode. The true perspective is of a pan-European tradition to which we are ready and able to return' (cited in Neale 1992:3). By 1994 eight former Eastern bloc countries had achieved their ambition and had been admitted to the Council of Europe.

In thinking about harmonization and convergence it is important also to recognize that the Council of Europe's role in penal affairs has been contradictory. On the one hand, its role in bringing together member states to explore the possible benefits of privatization in 1988 illustrates its position as a facilitator of the new managerialism which began to enter the prisons debate at this time (*New Statesman and Society* 13 March 1993). On the other hand the liberal programmes it has generated and supported over the years, such as the demand for international minimum standards within the context of the European Prison Rules, should also be acknowledged (Neale 1991), although this liberalism could well be superseded by the European Union's more hard-line, formalized approach to criminal justice matters. In his address to the Directors of Prison Administrations in Strasbourg, William Rentzmann complained about the fact that the meetings between the Directors were to take place every three years. Previously they had been meeting every two years. At one level this change appears to undermine the arguments about convergence and harmonization. However, as Rentzmann noted, the Maastricht Treaty extended the 'interest spheres of the European Community so as to include criminal justice'. While the Treaty did not lead to the creation of any supranational authority in the field of penal affairs it did institute 'general international co-operation within the framework of the community . . . this means that in future, the Council of Europe will have to envisage increased competition in this field' (1992:13).

Some indication of what future pressures might be brought to bear on European penal systems for greater harmonization can be gleaned from the developments in law and order policies in the EU since Rentzmann's speech. At the end of November 1993 the first meeting of the new Council of Interior and Justice Ministers of the EU was held in Brussels. This meeting came in the wake of the ratification of the Maastricht Treaty at the beginning of the month. The ratification brought the area of law and order into what was designated as the 'third pillar' of the Union. This meant that for the first time proposals, policies and strategies concerning law and order would go through the Brussels bureaucracy. Previously these issues had been dealt with by a web of secret *ad hoc* committees. The change was co-ordinated by the 'K4 committee' which was staffed by senior members of the justice and interior ministries of the member states. The new structure was built around three steering groups which reported to K4: asylum and immigration; police and customs; and judicial co-operation. The November meeting identified a number of law and order priorities including: establishing working parties on terrorism, organized crime, drugs and police co-operation; developing Europol, the embryonic criminal intelligence agency; harmonizing procedures for granting asylum; constructing a list of countries (129 of them) whose nationals would need visas to enter the EU; and, finally, transforming law and order objectives into a priority area for the foreign policy of the EU (*Statewatch* 1993; *The Guardian* 26 November 1993). As Tony Bunyan has pointed out, these developments can be seen as part of a qualitative shift in which:

> the move from *ad hoc* cooperation to permanent institutions and agencies – to the creation of a European state – is a quite logical development. But this state is different to those of the national states of the EC. The usual tenets of 'liberal democracy' cannot be applied to the new European state. The idea of the 'separation of powers' between the executive, the legislature – backed by an independent civil service – and the judiciary does not apply. The state has been conceived by governments, honed by state officials and passed back to governments to agree – only then have national governments been asked to ratify the whole package . . . No democratic accountability or due process of law to protect the citizen is built in (after all, people and parliaments played no part in framing the new structures). (1993:32–3)

It is important not to over-dramatize these shifts: there are still complex contradictory processes at work, as the meeting of the EU's justice ministers in December 1994 indicated. This was the twenty-eighth meeting to be held since July 1994 yet it still failed to reach concrete agreement on the development of Europol, rules for handling asylum seekers and tougher criminal sanctions for EC fraud (*The Guardian* 1 December 1994). At the same time European penal systems are unlikely to stand outside or above the processes of harmonization that slowly are developing whatever cultural differences, discontinuities and disjunctures exist on the ground in terms of the delivery of policy. In practice, as a number of contributors show, penal systems in Western Europe have already been drawn into these broader processes of harmonization by the fact that their expansion and extension have been legitimated by a very definite set of discourses around criminality and deviance shared by politicians, state officials, media organizations and an increasingly harmonized European popular culture. In pursuing this argument we are following Jon Vagg's point that comparative criminological studies 'need to recover a broader social, economic and political view of crime problems and policies if we are to address the topics of crime and crime policy in a realistic way' (1993:552). Vagg's argument is particularly relevant to the discourses surrounding criminality and deviance and the legitimacy that these discourses lend to the expansion of Western European penal systems. It is to a consideration of these issues that we now turn.

The piston of criminality and the drive for order

Since the mid 1970s it has become clear that the expansion and growing harmonization of criminal justice and penal systems in

Western Europe have been legitimated by the construction of quite explicit definitions of crime and deviance which have become mapped in with broader concerns and anxieties about the maintenance of order and stability. This is not a new revelation: the utilization of folk-devils within nation-states to legitimate often draconian strategies to maintain order has now become an accepted part of criminological wisdom (Hall et al. 1978). What is interesting is the internationalization of this process, the targeting and labelling of particular groups whose potential for chaos and disorder symbolically transcend national barriers and tax the collective minds of politicians, criminal justice personnel, media commentators and academics who have elided them into an apocalyptic vision of economic misery, political destruction and cultural degeneration. Throughout the 1980s those engaging in political violence, drug dealers and users, and organized criminals were key symbolic figures in this process. In a book published at the turn of the decade by the English academic and ex-soldier, Richard Clutterbuck, these themes were brought together under the revelatory title *Terrorism, Drugs and Crime in Europe after 1992* (1990). Chapter 17 was equally apocalyptic, 'Fighting the War in a United Europe'.

Since 1990, the shifting social arrangements in Europe in general, and the attempt to construct a new hegemonic order in Western Europe in particular, have intensified the targeting of not only traditional but also new folk-devils whose presence has been not simply understood in terms of the crimes they may or may not engage in but more symbolically read in terms of the politics of internal infestation, a threat to these new shifting social arrangements. As Stephen Gill has pointed out, order is not a neutral concept. Rather since it is 'a political concept we need to ask for whom and for what purposes?' (1992:158). The new configurations that have emerged since the turn of the decade, in Gill's view, have had a direct impact on the international state which has increasingly become central to 'the reproduction of a (disciplinary) neo-liberal order . . . [and] is concerned to police not only markets but also populations more generally' (1992:188). It is important to recognize that the internationalization of state power and the policing of particular populations that has followed this process are not necessarily coherent, nor are they guided by an invisible, conspiratorial hand. There are disjunctures and inconsistencies in this process which, as Bouventura De Sousa Santos has noted, lead not only to a 'decentering/recentering dialectic of state action' but also to an 'explosion of the unity of state action and its law, and the consequent emergence of different modes of juridicity, each one politically anchored in a micro state. As a result the state itself becomes a configuration of micro states' (1992:134).

It is possible therefore to situate penal systems within a network of power which operates both nationally and internationally with other micro and macro institutions of power in constructing, regulating, disciplining and punishing those groups whose lifestyle, behaviour and actions present a material and symbolic challenge to the hegemony of neo-liberalism in all of its economic, political and ideological manifestations.

This is not an instrumentalist argument, nor is it an argument which marginalizes the impact of crime on particular groups. The chapters in this volume recognize this point. However, as Mick Ryan and Joe Sim argue, it is possible to hold this position while at the same time link the development of changing levels of punishment to social structural change and in particular to the demand to manage what have been termed the 'aggregates of dangerous groups' (Feeley and Simon 1992:449). These late twentieth century equivalents of the historical rabble have become the material and symbolic property of both national and international state institutions. A number of different groups make up this 'rabble'.

The first is the unemployed, poor and homeless whose numbers increased steadily throughout Europe in the first half of the 1990s. By early 1994 they had reached 18 million, 52 million and 3 million respectively. In the case of the unemployed, this figure represented 11 per cent of the work force and by 1995 was expected to reach 20 million, a quarter of whom would be aged between 18 and 25 (*The Economist* 30 July 1994; *Independent on Sunday* 20 March 1994). Following Steven Box (1983) a number of contributors to this volume point to the role of the prison as a disciplinary regulator of the poor and unemployed. This marginalized and ill-disciplined detritus is perceived, both within and between nation-states, not simply in terms of its ascribed or actual criminality but more fundamentally as 'social dynamite', potential subversives undermining the good order and discipline of the neo-liberal collectivity.

The second group within this subversive 'rabble' is a toxic mix of immigrants, asylum seekers, 'undocumented aliens' and foreigners. Within the Council of Europe it has been recognized that there has been 'a disproportionate increase in absolute and relative numbers of foreigners in prison' (Tomasevski 1994:5). In the 1980s the rise in the number confined in some countries was spectacular: between 1983 and 1988 the increase was 297 per cent in Spain, 118 per cent in Portugal and 102 per cent in Luxembourg. The survey of the prison systems published by the Council in June 1990 indicated that in Belgium, France, Switzerland and Luxembourg they constituted more than one-quarter of the prison population. Many of these detentions were tied not to criminal behaviour but rather to breaches in immigration laws. For example, in Belgium more than one-third of foreigners who were incarcerated were detained for 'administrative reasons . . . as a measure of social defence'; in France '85.5 per cent of newly arrested prisoners' were charged with public order offences the majority of which involved 'infringements of the immigration laws' (Tomasevski 1992:56–9). In Tomasevski's view, the issue of migration has become central to the development of 'Fortress Europe'. In particular:

> because there are no legal opportunities for immigration, all attempts to immigrate are necessarily illegal. The suppression of illegal immigration has become prominent both in official pronouncements and in the conduct of law enforcement agencies. Official statements regularly link the suppression of illegal immigration with crime prevention. (1994:41)

In practice, this has meant that the intensification in restrictions on admission policies has created a Europe of 'concentric circles' in which 'rejected migrants are expelled from "Fortress Europe" to neighbouring countries, thereby broadening the geographical reach of migration control'. The twelve countries in the EU have signed migration treaties with East European countries and the additional five members of the European Free Trade Association to facilitate the return of rejected asylum seekers, leading to 'the creation of a *cordon sanitaire* around Western Europe' (1994:41).

Liz Fekete (1993) has argued that associating these groups with criminal activity also explains their disproportionate rates of detention. In the early 1990s, Germany, Greece and Holland released racialized crime statistics; in Denmark the media focused on refugees, constructing them as thieves, criminals and welfare freeloaders; in Switzerland and Italy immigrants have become associated with terrorism, which in Switzerland has resulted in all foreign groups including refugees being kept under surveillance; and finally, associating gypsies with crime has become a 'familiar stereotype' in both Western and Eastern Europe (1993:158). As a result, in Romania this group constituted between 40 and 60 per cent of the prison population while in Hungary between 40 and 45 per cent of all prisoners were gypsies, with women and juveniles disproportionately represented amongst them (Tomasevski 1992:59). The final twist in the positivist screw has come in France where individuals with a 'foreign physiognomy' have become targets for identity checks, detained and then expelled with little possibility for launching an appeal (Tomasevski 1994:41).

As a number of chapters in this volume make clear, penal systems in Western Europe are warehousing and managing not only conventional criminals but also a disproportionate number drawn from ethnic minority groups, foreigners and asylum seekers. With respect to this latter group, institutions are operating in much the same way as pre-modern houses of detention functioned up to the middle of the eighteenth century. In Holland, Germany, and England and Wales these contemporary houses of pain and punishment include prisons, detention centres, anchored ships and refugee camps. In Germany they are known as 'concentrated camps' and have been tied in with 'the introduction of measures designed to "reduce the country's attractiveness" including a compulsory period in camps, a prohibition on employment and restricted rights to movement and welfare benefits' (Carf 1993:8). The impact of the regimes has had devastating consequences for some groups; twenty-five asylum seekers from Nigeria died in the custody of the German police between 1991 and 1994 (*Statewatch* 1994:1). In England and Wales, the verdict of 'unlawful killing' in the case of the Zaïrean asylum seeker Omasase Lumumba raised a whole series of questions about the conditions in which asylum seekers were detained, the involvement of private security agencies in their detention and the denial of any form of natural justice in relation to those appealing against their deportation. Across Europe:

> asylum prisoners are quite literally incarcerated without committing a crime, without a trial, without even the right to know when they will be released. They are detained without a family to support them, to publicize any abuse of their rights, to ensure that international standards surrounding detention are upheld. (Carf 1993:8)

Avtar Brah (1993) and Kum-Kum Bhavnani (1993) have argued, it is important to recognize that such international state structures operate not only at the material level of physical detention but also at the symbolic level in terms of 'demarcating the boundaries of "them" and "us"' (Brah 1993:24). In Bhavnani's view the different agreements which have been entered into by EU nations:

> continue and expand on themes which form the underpinnings of racism – namely the simultaneous equation of citizen with desirable, and immigrant with undesirable. This undesirability is then apparently justified with reference to narcotics and crime. It is this European internationalism which is a racialized nationalism, in the sense that 'black Third World' people are always defined as immigrants, and therefore not citizens, and therefore not Europeans, and therefore not desirable. (1993:35)

It is also important to recognize that there are cultural and historical variations as to which groups become labelled and designated as problematic within the borders of nation-states. Since the mid 1970s, as a number of chapters illustrate, different groups have become focal points for vilification and regulation at different times: in Italy the drug taker; in France and Germany the illegal immigrant and asylum seeker; in Sweden the welfare scrounger and drug abuser; in England and Wales illegal immigrants, welfare scroungers, single parents and young people. This process may, at times, encompass powerful members of particular societies, a fact that is missing in the sociological literature. As Vincenzo Ruggiero points out in relation to Italy, corrupt politicians became important in the early 1990s in legitimating greater regulation and control in that country. These individuals became symbolic of the society's deeper anxieties concerning the breakdown in moral and political order. The key issue for Ruggiero is whether the clampdowns that follow are turned towards others at the pinnacle of the hierarchy of power or whether such clampdowns are oriented towards the powerless. In the case of Italy, it is the latter strategy which has prevailed.

One further issue should be noted. New groups may emerge to reinforce and legitimate the drive to maintain order. This point has been well made by Nils Christie who has argued that the policing, regulation and detention of particular groups has been central to the development of what he has termed 'Fortress Europe Western Division'. The cross-border co-operation that has been established, the new technical tools of internal control, the labelling of those with HIV/AIDS as the 'new untouchables' and the utilization of the war on drugs 'to control the dangerous classes in general' are all in Christie's view key elements in the ideology and practices of Fortress Europe. At the same time, this allows European states to pursue a policy of keeping those identified as the most dangerous elements outside 'this assembly of affluent societies'. The poor are locked out of Fortress Europe but for those who are locked in the prison facilites their regulation and control (Christie 1993:62–72). Such groups provide a fresh moral impetus to the demand for greater regulation and are, as a number of chapters show, increasingly well represented in penal institutions. The place of women in these institutions is the focus for the next part of this introduction.

Gender and European penal systems

All of the contributors to this volume highlight the importance of gender differentiation in relation to penal systems. It is a point that is still lost in many academic and non-academic texts despite the impact of feminism. As Maureen Cain has noted, the penal system for women and girls should be analysed and understood as one amongst a range of interconnected sites in which gender is constituted. These sites regulate, discipline and attempt to normalize women and girls, through forging and shaping their social identities. As Cain (1989) points out, it is a process which can be recognized across Western European nation-states. It is clear from the contributions to this volume that women still constitute a numerical minority within Western European penal systems and that prison regimes and alternatives to custody are built on a complex structure of patriarchal discourses oriented towards the normalization of deviant women. In that sense many of the contributors reaffirm the arguments developed in the critical, sociology literature in this area, namely that patterns of female crime can be understood in relation to the impact of gender socialization, economic and political powerlessness and social control in generating conformity and restricting the avenues of opportunity open to women to commit crime (Heidensohn 1985; Carlen 1988).

There are, however, some interesting and important cultural variations highlighted in this volume. Roberto Bergalli's chapter on Spain illustrates that in the mid 1980s *fewer* women than men were in prison for property offences but *more* women than men were incarcerated for crimes of violence. At first glance this appears to challenge much of the accepted wisdom in critical criminology. And yet, read another way, these statistics might be seen to reinforce the insights from this literature. It could be argued that the dynamics of social control and the operationalization of power, materially, culturally and ideologically, are such that the opportunities to commit property crime were even more restricted in Spain than in other countries. At the same time, those women who stepped outside their highly restricted roles were more likely to be classified as violent deviants and therefore in need of institutional normalization.

Karen Leander notes in her contribution on Sweden (where the patterns of crime conform to the model developed in the critical literature), not only are more women being imprisoned but the pattern of sentencing is changing. Women are beginning to 'catch up' with men so that by the end of 1993 women were receiving equally long sentences as men and more women were serving these sentences. Second, she points to the impact of drugs in particular on sentencing practices for women. Finally, she raises the question of gender segregation and the utilization of separate treatment facilities for women drug abusers. She notes how in the absence of men these women experience a more positive and empowering environment compared with the levels of harassment and exploitation that came with the presence of men in the shared facilities. René van Swaaningen and Gerard de Jonge point to a similar debate in Holland. The rejection of mixed regimes was due to the fact that a large percentage of women in Dutch prisons had a history of sexual violence committed against them and were fearful of further sexual exploitation in mixed regimes. The authors also note that some improvements in women's prisons have taken place after interventions by a number of women's groups. In this respect Holland may prove to be the exception to the patriarchal rule.

Two other issues have been identified by contributors in relation to gender and the penal system. First, as noted above, prisons are not the only sites in which the discourses of patriarchal regulation flourish. Other sites in the penal complex are also intimately involved in this regulation. For example, the availability of, and practices in, alternatives to custody for women have been much less discussed as a site of regulation and discipline. Yet as is made clear here, the alternatives which have been introduced in different countries are heavily restricted in terms of the number and range available, thus ensuring that women will be sent to prison because of this lack of availability. Furthermore, if women do receive an alternative to custody, they are often isolated amongst larger groups of men and pursue activities which have no direct relevance for them in terms of empowering them economically and ideologically.

Second, the disproportionate number of foreign women who are serving increasingly lengthy sentences is another clearly identifiable theme. In percentage terms these women come close to or outnumber men, while in some countries the rate of increase is faster than those of foreign men, a situation that is reflected throughout Western Europe (Tomasevski 1994:11). The gendered nature of economic power and powerlessness in their countries of origin provides the material context for the activities of many of these women (Green 1991). At the same time others are being confronted by various changes in different immigration laws, citizenship rights, asylum legislation and labour processes built on the back of 'a variety of racisms . . . [that] are being reconstituted into new configurations' (Brah 1993:20–1) which not only reinforce their economic powerlessness but also effectively criminalize them. Once inside, they face regimes which, because of the gendered operationalization of penal power, impact on them in quite specific ways in terms of social isolation, health and welfare arrangements (Cheney 1993).

Punishing the powerful

The treatment and punishment of these women and the other groups discussed in the various chapters in this volume can be contrasted with the treatment of powerful institutions and individuals in Europe. As Stephen Gill has pointed out, the macro-economic policy of the EU is based on 'the discourse of the "new constitutionalism" . . . the move towards construction of legal or constitutional devices to remove or insulate substantially the new economic institutions from popular scrutiny or democratic accountability' (1992:165). This lack of scrutiny provides a further contrast with the intense surveillance and targeting of the different groups discussed above. For example, it is worth noting that a four year investigation into police, crime and justice in the EU published in December 1993 found that fraud was 'an extensive and growing menace' while reports concerning a crime wave around political violence and drug trafficking had been 'much exaggerated'. The investigation argued that the real threat to European internal security lay in the areas of 'commercial fraud, credit card fraud, tax fraud as well as fraud against the European Commission itself' (*Times Higher Education Supplement* 10 December 1993). In November 1994, a report by the European Court of Auditors (ECA) indicated that out of the 55 billion pounds distributed in subsidies by the European Union (more than half of which was spent on food subsidies), 6 billion pounds was lost in fraud. The majority of those engaged in the fraud were never caught, principally because of the lack of commitment on the part of the authorities to pursue them ('The Big Story', ITV, 10 November 1994) and the small number of investigators involved in this pursuit. In 1994, the number was increased from 45 to 95 (BBC Radio 4, 15 November 1994). As Michael Clarke has pointed out, there are a range of 'problems' associated with the pursuit of fraudsters which do not exist in relation to the policing and punishment of the less powerful. The treatment of fraud as a non-issue and the lack of will in placing it high on the political agenda is compounded by the fact that:

> there is no EEC police force or inspectorate with legal and sanctioning powers; there are extradition problems and difficulties with compatibility of laws in different member states. The Court of Auditors has powers of enquiry and exposure but not of trial and sanction, and often finds it difficult to gain access to evidence. (1993:179)

In December 1994, EU justice ministers accepted British demands for a common system of community law to make serious fraud against the EU budget a criminal, extraditable and imprisonable offence. At the same time £4 million was removed from the anti-fraud budget which had been set at £100 million (*The Guardian* 2 December 1994).

The problems surrounding the non-policing of the crimes of the economically powerful are reflected in the non-policing of crimes in other sites of power in Europe. The desultory efforts made to police the wave of racist violence that has swept across Europe in the 1990s is a good example of this point. As Tore Björgo and Rob Witte have pointed out:

> More and more socioeconomic problems like unemployment, poor housing, crime and deprivation, are portrayed in close – if not directly causal – connection with the presence of ethnic and cultural minorities and with the growing numbers of asylum-seekers and refugees. The continuing marginalization and criminalization of minorities is apparent in several European countries, a tendency which seems no longer to be the monopoly of Neo-Nazi and right wing extremist movements and parties. It is within this context that racist violence is occurring frequently all over Europe . . . Most racist incidents . . . receive neither international nor even national attention. The majority of racist attacks against people, their property or places of worship occur without any mass media publicity or public attention throughout Europe – from Sweden to Italy, from Britain to Russia. (1993:2–3)

The routine violence against Czechoslovak gypsies is a good example of Björgo and Witte's argument. There have been calls for gas chambers to be introduced in Prague, and a Ku-Klux-Klan group has been established. There have also been a series of violent attacks on gypsies culminating in 12 murders between 1990 and 1991 (Powell 1994:9).

It is apparent, therefore, from the various contributions here that late twentieth century prisons in Western Europe continue to detain those whom penal institutions have always confined, namely the poor and dispossessed. Clearly they also hold a number of offenders who conventionally have been defined as dangerous, although as all of our contributors point out, this group is still in the minority in terms of national prison populations. Even here, however, the issues are obviously not clear cut because definitions of dangerousness themselves can be seen as social constructions. While comparative European research is still rare (Dobash 1994), we only have to observe the extent of violence against women in countries like England and Wales, the ongoing problems with the state's response and the continuing cuts in the funding of safe refuges to recognize that dangerousness is still defined and responded to in very conventional and reductionist terms. (It is also worth noting that international surveys still tend to collapse various forms of violence against women into general categories. Indeed, the six page summary of findings from the International Crime Survey produced by the Home Office in England and Wales in April 1994 failed to mention domestic violence while managing to mention theft from cars, robbery and pickpocketing, and *bicycle theft*. Sexual assaults were collapsed under a general heading of 'assault, threats and sexual offences' (Mayhew 1994).) As with the question of racial violence discussed above, European penal systems are not involved in a coherent or converging response to these crimes. Rather, behind the rhetoric of European harmony and harmonization lies the threat and actuality of violence (sometimes orchestrated) and conducted by those who hold power in macro and micro situations. These individuals and groups remain overwhelmingly untouched by the expansion in the penal systems in Western Europe described in the chapters below.

Other themes and issues

In the last part of this introduction we wish to focus on a number of other themes and issues which are developed in individual chapters and which are directly relevant for a full and analytical understanding of penal systems in Western Europe in the mid 1990s. There are four issues, in particular, that we wish to discuss: the development of private prisons and the emergence of the prisoner as customer; the question of internal regimes and their deleterious impact on the confined; the role of the prison in a changing political context; and finally, the contradictions and points of resistance which are still apparent in particular cultural contexts such as Italy and Germany.

Private prisons and customer services

The appearance of private prisons on the penal stage marks a significant step in the development of penal systems in the late twentieth century (Ryan and Ward 1989). This development has enormous implications across a range of different areas, some of which are touched on by different contributors to this volume. Four areas in particular are worth noting. First, there is the question of the relationship between private institutions and state run institutions. The danger of a two tier system emerging is discussed by Mick Ryan and Joe Sim in their chapter on England and Wales. Second, as Ermanno Gallo points out in relation to France, the emergence of semi-private prisons in that country has been built on the discourses of, and demands for, cost-effectiveness and on a technological-managerial axis in which prisoners become biological appendices to the machinery which controls them. The question of the prisoner as a customer of a service agency is the third dimension in this process. It is an issue which has been discussed more generally in relation to the impact of new right ideology on criminal justice institutions (Jones 1993). It has a particular resonance in prisons because of the way in which it fractures and atomizes the prison population still further and transforms the 'discourses of discipline and punishment which underpin penality into politically neutral and individually safe questions of satisfaction or dissatisfaction with the commodity or service on offer' (Sim 1994:41). René van Swaaningen and Gerard de Jonge point out in relation to Holland, the language of new managerialism, industry and commerce cuts through the Dutch prison system from 'result oriented offer' and 'product registration' through to 'unit manager' and 'result measurement'. As they note, the same kind of privatization with respect to the prison system is to be carried through to the probation service, again something which is also apparent in England and Wales. Finally, there is the question of the political accountability of these institutions, particularly as they are developing within a set of broader social relationships in which the public institutions of Western Europe appear to be increasingly free of democratic control. Given this scenario, what chance is there to maintain democratic control of private penal institutions when their activities are increasingly shrouded behind the veil of commercial confidentiality?

Internal regimes
Penal regimes and their impact on the confined remain a central issue to any analysis. As a number of contributors indicate, both prisons and alternatives to custody are becoming more austere and punitive in different countries. We have already pointed to the often appalling regimes used to detain asylum seekers in different countries. For the confined the experience of these regimes can be devastating in terms of suicides, self-mutilation and psychological depression. Vincenzo Ruggiero demonstrates in relation to Italian prisons, the majority of prisoners experience long periods of depression which cause many of them to develop ulcers as a result of their nervous distress and fatigue. Suicides in Italian prisons rose from 23 in 1990 to 61 in 1993. The intensification in internal control measures and the ongoing paramilitarization of prisons are unlikely to alleviate this situation. Rather these processes are more likely to generate further disturbances in West European prisons resulting in another turn of the prison screw so that a spiral of escalation is maintained. The disturbances in Sweden and in

England and Wales discussed in this volume have been paralleled by a wave of demonstrations and hunger strikes in immigration detention centres in Western Europe. At the same time, as Ermanno Gallo points out in relation to France, this situation extends to the private system as well. In February 1994 the private prison at Salon was destroyed by prisoners.

Political prisons
The contributions to this volume by Roberto Bergalli (Spain) and Mike Tomlinson (Ireland) discuss an area which has been neglected in debates about Western European penal systems, namely the politics of prisons in a changing political climate. Prison literature has quite rightly pointed to the role of imprisonment in overtly political situations such as South Africa, Russia and China, while Amnesty International has provided detailed accounts of the ongoing role of penal institutions for the detention, torture and murder of political detainees. Bergalli and Tomlinson provide accounts which also highlight the political uses of imprisonment much closer to home. As Bergalli notes, up to the mid 1970s prisons in Spain were locked in with the fascist regime of Francisco Franco. With the coming of democracy this situation changed as a democratic penal code was developed. Crucially, however, this democratization has resulted in Spanish prisons becoming 'normalized' in that the institutions are now detaining populations similar to those in other Western European countries. Tomlinson also provides a searching account of the symbolism and place of the prison in the politics of Ireland and considers its changing role in the development of the peace process on the island. Both of these accounts add a new dimension to the conceptualization of the prison in Western Europe.

Contradictions and discrepancies
The final (and most optimistic) issue we wish to highlight that comes out of a number of contributions is that the expansion of penal systems is neither an inevitable nor a 'natural' event propelled forward by a unified, homogeneous state. Within Western Europe there are clearly cultural variations with respect to penal policy. While we have pointed to the growing authoritarianism of the international state, the apparent convergence of different institutions, the intensification in internal controls and the concomitant rolling back of national welfare states, it is important to recognize that sites of difference and resistance remain. The chapters on Germany and Italy point to the key role of the judiciary in these countries in pursuing policies of decarceration and in placing

limitations on the use of imprisonment for particular groups of offenders. In the case of Italy, as Ruggiero notes, politicians were also involved in the early 1990s in penal de-escalation. The alarm around the soaring population resulted in a package of proposals aimed at reducing the numbers of prisoners to a manageable level. In a similar way, as Claudius Messner and Vincenzo Ruggiero illustrate, the judiciary in Germany were also involved in developing a policy of decarceration. The significance of the judiciary in these processes reflects the very different cultural expectations surrounding the appointment, role and removal of judges in these countries. Clearly this should not be idealized, but it does provide a sharp contrast with the obsessive concern for secrecy and hierarchy in countries like England and Wales. The chapters also illustrate the need for theoretical and political caution when analysing state institutions. In particular cultural contexts at particular historical and political moments, fissures within, and contradictions around, state power may prove to be decisive in subverting the ratchet of punishment. Exploiting these contradictions and linking them to wider counter-hegemonic and progressive social movements, difficult though that might be in the current political climate, may provide the basis for a way forward. The alternative scenario of building more prisons and extending the network of penal control will not bring peace or social justice to a Western European bloc that is deeply divided along the fault lines of social class, gender, race, sexuality and ability. More penal systems mean reproducing the same problems both within and without the walls of Western Europe's collective penitentiaries. As Barbara Hudson has pointed out:

> If it remains confined within its present parameters, penal discourse offers little hope of altering the differential impact of penal policy on rich and poor, black and white, conventional and unconventional. Just as penal policy can only have minimal impact on crime without broader social strategies of crime prevention, so it can have little impact on justice without broader policies to reduce inequalities and social divisions, and to increase social provision. (1993:179)

Learning this lesson and repudiating the current system's less than glorious history may be the most difficult thing of all for its defenders to comprehend and act on as a new millennium approaches.

References

Bhavnani K-K (1993), 'Towards a Multicultural Europe? Race, Nation and Identity in 1992 and Beyond' *Feminist Review* 45, August: 30–45

Björgo T and Witte R (eds) (1993), *Racist Violence in Europe* Basingstoke: Macmillan

Bottoms A (1983), 'Neglected Features of Contemporary Penal Systems' in D Garland and P Young (eds) *The Power to Punish* London: Heinemann

Box S (1983), *Power, Crime and Mystification* London: Tavistock

Brah A (1993), 'Re-Framing Europe: Engendered Racisms, Ethnicities and Nationalisms in Contemporary Western Europe' *Feminist Review* 45, August: 9–28

Bunyan T (1993), 'Trevi, Europol and the European State' in T Bunyan (ed) *Statewatching the New Europe* London: Statewatch

Cain M (ed) (1989), *Growing up Good: Policing the Behaviour of Girls in Europe* London: Sage

Carf (1993), 'Prisoners of Asylum' *Campaign Against Racism and Fascism* 13, March/April: 8–10

Carlen P (1988), *Women, Crime and Poverty* Milton Keynes: Open University Press

Cheney D (1993), *Into the Dark Tunnel* London: Prison Reform Trust

Christie N (1993), *Crime Control as Industry* London: Routledge

Clarke M (1993), 'EEC Fraud: A Suitable Case for Treatment' in F Pearce and M Woodiwiss (eds) *Global Crime Connections* Basingstoke: Macmillan

Clutterbuck R (1990), *Terrorism, Drugs and Crime in Europe after 1992* London: Routledge

De Sousa Santos B (1992), 'State, Law and Community in the World System: An Introduction' *Social and Legal Studies* 1, 2, June: 131–42

Dobash R (1994), Personal communication

Downes D (1988), *Contrasts in Tolerance: Post War Penal Policy in the Netherlands and England and Wales* Oxford: Oxford University Press

Feeley M and Simon J (1992), 'The New Penology: Notes on the Emerging Strategy of Corrections and its Implications' *Criminology* 30, 4: 449–74

Feeley M and Simon J (1994), 'Actuarial Justice: The Emerging New Criminal Law' in D Nelken (ed) *The Futures of Criminology* London: Sage

Fekete L (1993), 'Inside Racist Europe' in T Bunyan (ed) *Statewatching the New Europe* London: Statewatch

Gibson H (ed) (1993), *New Perspectives on the Welfare State in Europe* London: Routledge

Gill S (1992), 'The Emerging World Order and European Change' in R Miliband and J Saville (eds) *Socialist Register 1992* London: Merlin

Gordon P (1989), *Fortress Europe? The Meaning of 1992* London: The Runnymede Trust

Green P (1991), *Drug Couriers* London: Howard League for Penal Reform

Hall S, Clarke J, Critcher C, Jefferson T and Roberts B (1978), *Policing the Crisis* Basingstoke: Macmillan

Heidensohn F (1985), *Women and Crime* Basingstoke: Macmillan

Heidensohn F (1991), 'Introduction: Convergence, Diversity and Change' in F Heidensohn and M Farrell (eds) *Crime in Europe* London: Routledge

Heidensohn F and Farrell M (eds) (1991), *Crime in Europe* London: Routledge

Hillyard P (1994), Personal communication

Hudson B (1993), *Penal Policy and Social Justice* Basingstoke: Macmillan

Jones C (1993), 'Auditing Criminal Justice' *British Journal of Criminology* 33, 2, Spring: 187–202

Mayhew P (1994) 'Findings from the International Crime Survey' *Research Findings No. 8* Home Office Research and Statistics Department

Muncie J and Sparks R (eds) (1991) *Imprisonment: European Perspectives* Hemel Hempstead: Harvester Wheatsheaf

Neale K (1991), 'The European Prison Rules: Contextual Philosophical and Practical Aspects' in J Muncie and R Sparks (eds) *Imprisonment: European Perspectives* Hemel Hempstead: Harvester Wheatsheaf

Neale K (1992), 'The Demosthenes Programme: A Penological Challenge' *Prison Information Bulletin* 16, June: 3–4

Pease K (1994), 'Cross National Imprisonment Rates: Limitations of Method and Possible Conclusions' *British Journal of Criminology* 34, Special Issue: 116–30

Pease K and Hukkila K (eds) (1990), *Criminal Justice Systems in Europe and North America* Helsinki: HEUNI

Powell C (1994), 'Time for Another Immoral Panic? The Case of the Czechoslovak Gypsies' unpublished paper

Rentzmann W (1992), 'Present Situations in the Penological Field (Prison Sentences, Community Sanctions and Measures) in the Countries Participating in the 10th Conference of Directors of Prison Administrations and the Implementation of the European Prison Rules in the Member States of the Council of Europe' *Prison Information Bulletin* 17, December: 12–16

Ryan M and Ward T (1989), *Privatization and the Penal System* Milton Keynes: Open University Press

Sim J (1994), 'Reforming the Penal Wasteland? A Critical Review of the Woolf Report' in E Player and M Jenkins (eds) *Reform through Riot: Prisons after Woolf* London: Routledge

Smit D van Zyl and Dunkel F (eds) (1991), *Imprisonment Today and Tomorrow: International Perspectives on Prisoners' Rights and Prison Conditions* Deventer: Kluwer

South N and Weiss B (eds) (forthcoming), *Comparing Prison Systems* Langhorne: Gordon and Breach

Statewatch (1993), 'The Council of Interior and Justice Ministers: Brussels, 29–30 November' *Statewatch* 3, 6, November–December: 14–15

Statewatch (1994), 'Germany: 25 Deportees Died' *Statewatch* 4, 5, September–October, 1

Thomas P and Moerings M (eds) (1994), *Aids in Prison* Aldershot: Dartmouth

Tomasevski K (1992), *Prison Health* Helsinki: Institute for Crime Prevention and Control

Tomasevski K (1994), *Foreigners in Prison* Helsinki: Helsinki Institute for Crime Prevention and Control

Vagg J (1991), 'A Touch of Discipline: Accountability and Discipline in Prison Systems in Western Europe' in F Heidensohn and M Farrell (eds) *Crime in Europe* London: Routledge

Vagg J (1993), 'Context and Linkage: Reflections on Comparative Research and "Internationalism" in Criminology' *British Journal of Criminology* 33, 4, Autumn: 541–54

Vagg J (1994), *Prison Systems: A Comparative Study of Accountability in England, France, Germany and the Netherlands* Oxford: Oxford University Press

Whitfield D (ed) (1991), *The State of the Prisons 200 Years On* London: Routledge

Young W and Brown M (1993), 'Cross-National Comparisons of Imprisonment' in M Tonry (ed) *Crime and Justice: A Review of Research* Chicago: University of Chicago Press

2

The Dutch Prison System and Penal Policy in the 1990s: from Humanitarian Paternalism to Penal Business Management

René van Swaaningen and Gerard de Jonge

For a long time Dutch penal policy has been characterized as moderate and humane. In particular, the post-war politics of decarceration generated international interest and respect. Penal intervention was restricted by welfare, health-care and other agencies within the community, which were seen as preventive forms of social control. Custodial sanctions were relatively short. Prisoners were automatically released after two-thirds of their term, mostly independent of their behaviour during sentence and without parole hearings. The visitor would not find gloomy prison walls staffed with armed prison guards. Rather the prisons contained regimes which were built on strict timetables for work, recreation, education and other activities. This in turn created relatively quiet relations between staff and inmates and between inmates themselves. According to David Downes the central presence of these preventive and welfare measures provided a sharp contrast between the UK and the Netherlands in relation to the 'depth of imprisonment', a point we shall return to below (1988:163).

During the last decade or so many of the post-war welfare gains have been under severe pressure. Welfare provisions in the community have become more and more 'infected' by the rationale of repressive social control, for example, by treating people entitled to social security benefits primarily as potential scroungers and fiddlers. Custodial sanctions have become substantially longer, while it seems likely that the date on which prisoners are to be released will soon depend on their behaviour. In addition, small scale custodial units have been abandoned and replaced with large institutions in which the quality of the regimes is determined by punitive rather than welfare considerations. These changes are the product of a time in which the welfare state is declining as a whole, when managerial considerations and bureaucratic logic are driving away any serious discussion about more substantial and normative questions, and when conformity to some 'common standard' as closer European union approaches is continuously put forward as the rationale for introducing one repressive measure after the other. Dutch authorities appear to be afraid of the 'soft' image they might project in the eyes of their European neighbours, particularly with regard to their drug policies and the prison system. This fear means that they are unwilling to defend one of the more decent penal systems in the world. Until a decade ago progressive British scholars would look to the Netherlands as one example of a realistic reductionist penal agenda (Rutherford 1986). By 1994 it was predominantly Dutch officials who were looking to the UK for inspiration in terms of punitive penal policy.

Four White Papers, *Task and Future of the Dutch Prison System* (*Taak en Toekomst van het Nederlands Gevangeniswezen 1982*), *Society and Crime* (*Samenleving en Criminaliteit 1985*), *Law in Motion* (*Recht in Beweging 1990*), and *Diligent Detention* (*Werkzame Detentie 1994*), are indicative of a fundamental shift in judicial and penal orientation. From these White Papers a process of bifurcation in sanctioning has emerged, built on incapacitation for the 'real criminals', and community sanctions for those who are not yet considered to be unsusceptible to correction. In *Task and Future* the rehabilitation principle was toned down for the first time; *Society and Crime* pointed to the citizen's individual responsibility in respect of crime control; *Law in Motion* highlighted a normative reaffirmation of law and order; and *Diligent Detention* announced an overall 'retrenchment' of the prison system. This is the general political context in which we should interpret the following survey.

Some features of the Dutch prison system

Accountability

Formally speaking, the Public Prosecution Service (Openbaar Ministerie) is responsible for the execution of penal sentences (para. 553 Sv, Code of Criminal Procedure). However, its actual role is far more limited, dealing at a local level with collecting fines and, together with the probation service, in monitoring non-custodial sanctions. The management of the prison system is, however, centralized at the Ministry of Justice in The Hague, and while the Code of Criminal Procedure explicitly states that the court has to determine the place where a remand prisoner is to be detained (para. 78, sub. 4 Sv), the judiciary like the prosecution service has no real say in where prisoners are placed. This is the *de facto* responsibility of the Ministry of Justice operating its computerized cell-allotment system. At the Ministry it is the Directorate for the Care of Delinquents and Juvenile Institutions which is responsible for the administration of prisons. Ultimately it is the Minister of Justice who is politically accountable for penal institutions.

The institutions

At the level of the institution, prison governors are responsible for the daily administration of the regime. They receive instructions from the central administration in The Hague which in practice are applied with some personal discretion. Since the early 1990s a process of decentralization has developed in which prison governors, within the limits of the budget allotted to their institution, have been given autonomy to decide how the money is to be spent. By 1994 this gradual process had become formalized into an official policy which aims to transform the penal system into a government agency in which the influence of The Hague is limited to general administration, whereas more specific matters would be decided more autonomously by prison governors. Various authors have described this development as a form of back door privatization of the prison system, and indeed, in a philosophical and ideological sense, of the state itself. Every service except the actual control functions can be carried out by private enterprise, and the prisons will gradually be transformed into companies themselves, in the sense that they will have to produce a measurable 'output' and will be organized according to the bloodless norms and mathematical formulas of efficiency bureaux (Beyens et al. 1992:52–60; Kelk 1994)

The prison system numbers about one hundred different penal institutions, which are staffed by almost 8,000 people, of whom 62 per cent are warders. Quite often, two or more formally different institutions, each with its separate staff and governor, belong in a material sense to the same prison complex. The Amsterdam penitentiary Overamstel, for example, effectively consists of six different institutions run by six different governors, even though they share a common entrance. On 1 June 1994 the numbers were as shown in Table 2.1.

There has been almost a fourfold increase in prison capacity in less than twenty years. In 1975 the penal capacity was 2,356 and the rate of imprisonment was 17 per 100,000 of the population. In 1994 the capacity was 8,235 (Table 2.1) and the rate of imprisonment was 55 per 100,000: the Netherlands has a total population of 15.4 million inhabitants. Previously redundant prisons were closed, but now the Netherlands is in the middle of a large building

Table 2.1 *Prison capacity in the Netherlands, 1 June 1994*

Prison	Number	Capacity
Male remand centres	43	5,258
Male closed prisons	18	1,513
Male half-open and open prisons	23	995
Female remand centres	5	287
Female closed prisons	4	93
Female half-open and open prisons	3	38
Rest (disciplinary unit and penitentiary hospital)		51
Total		8,235

Source: *Differentiatieschema penitentiaire inrichtingen per 1 juni 1994*, circulaire van de Staatssecretaris van Justitie van 31 mei 1994, kenmerk 427286/94/DJ

programme. By the end of 1994 there will be 9,785 cells available, and by the end of 1995 the number will have climbed to 11,900. This will allow for a rate of imprisonment of 65 and 80 per 100,000 of the population respectively. Departmental sources doubt whether the expansion programme will be completed by the end of 1995. Based on mathematical extrapolations of current sentencing trends they predict a continuing demand for more cells up to and beyond the year 2000 (*NRC Handelsblad* 11 July 1994). It should also be noted that previous figures were based on the principle of one prisoner to a cell. This has now been abandoned and will allow more flexibility in the system. Furthermore, there are other places available for detaining prisoners which are not included in Table 2.1: 640 places in so-called 'emergency capacity', some 850 in various types of mental institution where people are placed who are certified to be (partially) not responsible for their acts by a criminal judge, 1,900 cells and so-called 'waiting-rooms' at police stations, and 120 places in a so-called 'border hostel' where refugees who are considered to have no chance of receiving asylum in the Netherlands await legal procedures leading to their expulsion. There are also separate prisons and boot-camps for juveniles not included in these figures.

The population
Throughout the 1980s the number of unconditional prison sentences averaged 16,000 a year. At the same time the average sentence length rose substantially: from 33 days in 1975 to 152 in 1992, nearly a fivefold increase. The number serving longer sentences has shown the greatest increase. The number serving a sentence of four

years or more increased ninefold from 1982 to 1992 (from 103 to 942), while those serving from one to four years increased by some 50 per cent (from 980 to 1,554). This increase in the length of prison sentences, together with a 40 per cent increase in the number remanded in custody, the increased length of the remand period, and the explosion in foreign remandees, is the major reason for the serious capacity problems facing the prison service.

The annual number of receptions to the prison system amounts to 37,910 persons (251 per 100,000 inhabitants). Only 40 per cent of these serve an actual prison sentence, 41 per cent are remanded in custody for a criminal offence, and 3 per cent are serving substitutory detention (for example, fine defaulters). The majority of the remainder are detained under the Foreigners Act. The so-called foreigners remand involves people who have not committed any crime, but who are remanded in custody because they have no legal status enabling them to remain in the Netherlands. Their number increased from 545 in 1986 to 4,611 in 1992, which is an eightfold increase in just six years. In 1994 the actual prison population exceeded formal capacity.

The principle of one prisoner to a cell was upheld until 1993, although over the years prison governors had been urged by the Ministry of Justice to fill cells up to 103 per cent, that is 3 per cent over capacity. This proposal caused turmoil among the prison staff, who feared that over-population would lead to a situation of increasing violence, health problems and hostile relations between staff and inmates. After an experimental phase, the resistance to cell sharing was finally broken by a Royal Decree of 8 July 1994. This change was mainly generated by the vociferous interventions made by the Public Prosecution Service about the shortage of prison capacity resulting in too many prisoners being released to await trial at home rather than in custody. A proposal to make conditional release possible after prisoners had served half of their sentence if accompanied by 'good behaviour' presented a means of reducing capacity problems. However, as some prison governors have correctly argued, this measure itself will probably lead to still longer sentences, because prosecutors and judges will be concerned with the actual time an individual is locked away and will construct their claims and sentences accordingly.

Characteristics of the prison population

What does the population of Dutch prisons look like?[1] We will mention the main categories. The largest category, some 50 per cent of all prisoners, are accused of or sentenced for an offence against property (of which 85 per cent concern theft); some 20 per cent for drugs offences listed in the Opium Act; 15 per cent for violent offences and crimes against life; and 5 per cent for sexual offences. More than half of all offences are estimated to be drug related, although in these cases the official charge is likely to be for theft. Regarding drug use, the rationale for penal intervention is largely based on the form and impact which particular forms of behaviour have on the offender's immediate environment or those in his or her orbit. In contrast, the harm done to the offender through his or her behaviour is primarily the domain of health-care agencies.

In 1993 the ethnic composition of Dutch prisons indicated a small majority of white Dutch prisoners (52 per cent). Of the remaining foreigners and Dutch nationals with a foreign ethnic background, 11 per cent were Surinamese, 8 per cent Moroccan, 6 per cent Turkish and 6 per cent Antillian. The rest was divided between 6 per cent from various European countries (of whom the biggest group, one-sixth, were Germans), and 11 per cent from non-European countries (of whom people from Africa, Latin America and the Middle East were the majority). Of the total number of people imprisoned for property offences, the various ethnic minorities were relatively under-represented (36 per cent); their share in violent crimes nearly equalled their general representation (46 per cent); and in Opium Law offences they were over-represented (69 per cent). We should stress that in the Netherlands the prison population is not registered in relation to race. Initially, individuals were registered in terms of their nationality. It was only in 1992 that the concept of ethnicity was included. Those people whose parents are not born in the Netherlands are defined as an ethnic minority. Together, these groups make up slightly less than 10 per cent of the Dutch population as a whole. A substantial number of the foreign prisoners have, however, never lived in the Netherlands (CBS *Gevangenisstatistiek* 1993:34, 40). In general there are no separate regimes for ethnic minorities in relation to food, working hours or spiritual assistance.

In terms of gender the vast majority of prisoners are male. In 1993 95.6 per cent of prisoners were male and 4.4 per cent female, but the percentage of female prisoners is increasing. The kinds of offence for which women are imprisoned are quite different from those of men. Women commit relatively few property offences which are accompanied by violence. Indeed they commit relatively few violent offences, but these are on the average more serious involving women who kill abusive partners. The most striking difference is however that 45 per cent of all women are convicted for an offence listed in the Opium Law – largely drug trafficking.

The ethnic composition of women in prison also shows some

differences compared with men. The percentage of Latin Americans and Germans is higher, but Turkish and Moroccans are virtually absent amongst female prisoners (CBS *Gevangenisstatistiek* 1993:27, 36, and 40). In contrast to the situation in penitentiary mental clinics (TBS), male and female prisoners are housed in separate regimes. Until recently women prisoners were disadvantaged because their regimes lacked variety and labour practices reinforced traditional role patterns; the laundry work of the prison system, for example, was done in a female prison. After the publication of the Green Paper *Women in Detention* in 1991, to which some women's groups contributed, different regimes were introduced, though the initial proposal for achieving a greater differentiation in regimes by transferring women to more open regimes with a population of both sexes was rejected because a large percentage of women in prison have a history of sexual violence committed against them and feared sexual intimidation in mixed regimes. Another important result of *Women in Detention* was an improvement in the level of education for women in prison, whose position in society was on average even more marginal than that of male convicts. Children can remain with their imprisoned mother until they are nine months old, but the 1991 Green Paper opened up the possibility that they could remain with the mother until their fourth year if there are no realistic possibilities of settling them in society. In these cases, the interest of the child prevails over the interest of the mother, and the opportunity of keeping children in detention with their mothers is rarely used (Ministerie van Justitie 1991).

The prison population, while traditionally young, gradually seems to be ageing: in 1993, 28 per cent of all prisoners was under 25 years old, whereas twenty years earlier almost half of the population was under that age. This is partially explained by demographic developments, but also by the introduction of non-custodial sanctions during this period which were particularly directed at younger offenders. The socio-economic position of prisoners is traditionally low, as is their level of education. A survey in the White Paper *Diligent Detention* published in 1994 showed that 46 per cent were living on social security benefits; 29 per cent had paid employment (generally unskilled); 15 per cent were their own boss (mostly in the catering industry); and 10 per cent had to live from other resources.

Overall the most striking feature of the Dutch penal system is that, in 1992, 10,493 prisoners were registered as drug addicts. In 1993 the figure was 8,781, of whom 5,533 were dependent on heroin. Sixty-five per cent of these prisoners were treated with methadone within prison. There are also special 'drug-free' units

(DVA) for those who want to avoid the confrontation with drugs inside prison. Inmates voluntarily subject themselves to a very strict system of urine and other tests which cannot be imposed in the normal regimes, because, without explicit permission, such infringements would be too serious a violation of people's constitutional rights. There were also 1,211 prisoners registered as alcoholics in 1993 who engaged in various educational and discussion programmes in the normal regimes. In the same year 17 people died in prison: 9 died of natural causes and 8 cases were reported as suicides – mostly by hanging (de Jonge 1994). Attempted suicides numbered 52. There was also a high number of self-mutilations (83), hunger strikes (16), swallowing of sharp objects (14), and arson (14). The percentage of suicides and self-mutilations is remarkably higher than outside: estimates vary from four to ten times higher.

It is also estimated that 10 per cent of the prison population cope with grave mental problems, while in total 36 per cent have personality disorders of some kind. The number of mentally disordered offenders is increasing owing to the lack of places in non-judicial psychiatric clinics and the decrease in ambulatory mental health care in the community. Special care units (IBA) are planned for various closed prisons to deal with these offenders. It should also be noted that there are no special regimes for sex offenders or potentially vulnerable groups – but all prisoners do have the right to apply for a transfer to another institution.

If prisoners are registered as having AIDS or being HIV positive this information is only available to medical staff: neither the disciplinary staff nor other prisoners are told. There is no obligatory testing for AIDS; other prisoners are not made aware of the medical condition of their fellow inmates; and preventive measures, such as condoms, should be available. Prisoners are transferred to the penitentiary hospital in Scheveningen when the illness becomes terminal, or are pardoned. In 1992 there were 42 prisoners with AIDS and 145 who were known to be HIV positive; the figures for 1993 were 44 and 86 respectively (Moerings 1994). Since there is no compulsory registration, these figures are not very accurate. AIDS campaigners mention a number, based on the high percentage of intravenous drug-users among prisoners, which is six times as high.

The regimes
The regimes in closed institutions are either communal, which means that detainees are only locked into their cells during the night and can move freely on the wing during the day when they are not engaged in specific activities; or limited communal, meaning

that they are only let out of their cells during working hours and for special activities like the visits of relatives, visits to the doctor, social worker or vicar, or for recreation and sports. They have to spend the rest of their time in their cell, which can amount to 21 or 22 hours a day.

Regimes in the half-open and open institutions are characterized by a lenient leave system: in half-open institutions a prisoner can spend a weekend at home every four weeks; in open institutions every weekend is spent at home. We should stress however that prisoners can only serve the last three to five months of their sentence in an open prison, whereas they can be placed in half-open prisons from the outset. In half-open prisons detainees generally work within the boundaries of the institution, whereas in the open prisons they are hired out to private companies, mostly in the neighbourhood of the institution. After an experimental phase, day detention centres were established in 1990 where prisoners can serve the last six weeks of their term. Here they receive training in various social skills, and spend the evenings at home. The process by which inmates gradually move to a more open regime is called the phasing of detention. This possibility is not open to everybody, but is dependent upon the inmate's behaviour. This is registered in a penitentiary dossier which is generated for all prisoners, and in which every member of staff, from warder to social worker, reports on an inmate's attitude. Basing his or her decision on this dossier, it is the prison governor who decides whether a prisoner can be transferred to a more lenient regime. The 1994 White Paper *Diligent Detention* contains new statistics about the levels of motivation of prisoners at work and on courses. Though it remains unclear as to the empirical data on which these statistics are based, motivation will become increasingly important as the measure used to determine the kind of regime to which prisoners are to be allocated.

At the 'deep end' of the prison system there are maximum security institutions which were introduced after a number of spectacular escapes which generated a moral panic in media and political circles. In 1991, a so-called carousel system of special security units with a very restricted regime (EBI) was introduced for prisoners who were labelled as extremely dangerous and liable to escape. This political decision had little to do with the actual number of escapes as the percentage of escapes fell from 3.8 per cent in 1984 to 0.7 per cent in 1992. There was a slight increase in 1993 but the downward trend was resumed in 1994, falling during the first six months to 0.25 per cent (MvJ Tweede Kwartaalbericht Gevangeniswezen 1994). The harsher regimes did however result in more violent escapes, and the fact that a high percentage of these escapes were indeed from the maximum security units made the Ministry decide in 1993 to concentrate this category of prisoner in one maximum security prison, Vught TEBI. The Council of Europe's anti-torture committee has argued that, 'despite the good material conditions, the overall quality of life of detainees left a great deal to be desired' (Council of Europe 1993:35). In a number of complaints to the penitentiary committees of surveillance and the civil courts alike, the legal status of the extra security regimes was contested because these were not regulated in the Prison Act. Case law however upheld the prevailing practices, when it was argued that: 'although the regime in an EBI is very strict, it remains within the limits of what the Prison Act defines as limited community' (District Court, The Hague 15 January 1993).

From resocialization to obedience

Since the introduction of the Principles Act of the Prison System in 1953 (BWG), all penitentiary regimes were oriented towards the resocialization of the offender. This key principle of detention implied both a paternalistic and a humanitarian orientation. In the post-war period, the qualitative standard of the prison system was seen to symbolize the level of civilization of society as a whole. In the 1970s, this ethical rationale was translated into the more neutral terms of social work and welfare, whose introduction into the prison system was thought to be crucial for the actual chances of successful rehabilitation. Although paragraph 26 of this Act still contains the resocialization principle, its effect is gradually waning. Since 1982, official policy has no longer been primarily oriented at the reintegration of the prisoner into society, but rather has been to limit, as it was called, the extra harm caused by detention (Kelk 1994; van Swaaningen and uit Beijerse 1993:137–9). This new realism has become the dominant view on rehabilitation in the 1994 White Paper, with the revealing title *Diligent Detention*. The official English title of this policy plan is *Effective Detention*, but this translation ignores the fact that the original title *Werkzame Detentie* is a pun, because the Dutch word *werkzaam* means both 'effective' and 'working', which also refers to the fact that the White Paper proposes to increase the number of working hours for prisoners from twenty to twenty-six hours a week.

A prison sentence serves primarily retributive purposes. Traditionally, the deprivation of liberty as such was interpreted as a sufficient embodiment of retribution. This implicit vision of retribution is, however, shifting to a more explicit focus, in which the retributive element is about making actual life within prison less 'comfortable'. The prisoner must again earn his or her own extras, and is henceforth supposed to live up to the specific demands of the prison regime, which will be the most disciplinary practised since the reforms of the post-war period. According to the 1994 White Paper, the execution of penalties will now be secure, decent and efficient. This implies a bias towards safety measures meant to limit escapes; a 'basic regime', that is just within the exigencies of international standards; and a strong focus on cutting back on costs. The consequence of any (attempt to) escape will be the loss of conditional release. Every new prisoner will start on the basic regime and can improve his or her conditions through complying with the rules. Costs are to be cut back through the introduction of 'maximum labour'. In line with Dutch penal history, new emphasis is put on prison labour. A diligent prison life serves two goals. First, it must discipline the prisoners (bad work will lead to bad conditions of detention). Second, it must relieve the financial problems of the institution. Prison governors will be expected to acquire financial orders and their prisons are expected to become little industries, competing with free enterprise businesses on the outside. However, the demand for the rather simple work performed in prisons is not particularly high, and the competition in this segment of the market is intense. In 1994 there was not even enough work to keep prisoners busy for twenty hours a week.

Prisoners' legal rights under the present and future Prison Acts

This new penal policy will also be supported by a new Prison Act. The current Principles Act of the Prison System is the product of the above mentioned post-war humanitarian thinking, which was advanced by the Utrecht School. These practical minded scholars laid the foundations for a relatively benign criminal justice policy, and had a particular influence on the way prisoners were to be treated; that is, as normal legal subjects, who should be helped to find their way back into society (de Haan 1990:64–81). The Prison Act (BWG) was the legal counterpart of the policy principles of civilized prison conditions and of resocialization. Together with the Prison Rules (GM) and a continuous flow of ministerial circulars, this Act regulated the powers and duties of the prison governor, and gave him or her directives about the management of the institution. It also granted some rights to prisoners, and since 1976 it has contained a complaints procedure to deal with conflicts about alleged violations of prisoners' rights (paras 51–8 BWG). The prisoner can complain about almost any act (or omission) by, or conducted on behalf of, the prison governor that has an impact on his or her personal situation. (It is not possible, however, to complain about rules or general directives as such.) The complaints are handled by an independent 'administrative' lay tribunal, the complaints committee (*beklagcommissie*), recruited from the external committee of surveillance (*commissie van toezicht*) which monitors every penal institution. Both the prisoner and the governor can appeal against unfavourable decisions to a central independent appeals committee (*beroepscommissie CRS*) in The Hague. Prisoners can also obtain free legal advice in order to prepare their cases.

The normative notion that prisoners should be enabled to exercise all of those constitutional rights which do not conflict with the deprivation of liberty has changed drastically since the economic recession of the early 1980s, which gave birth to a series of centre-right governments. These administrations responded with a more punitive orientation which also permeated the media and parliamentarians. With the massive expansion of prison capacity, the number of prisoners' complaints rose even more sharply – from 117 in 1977 to 3,046 in 1992 (CBS *Gevangenisstatistiek* 1992). Despite the fact that 80 per cent of these complaints either are not admitted as a justified complaint in law, or are declared to be unfounded, the commitment to legal guarantees was thought to have gone too far. During the 1980s the underlying rationale, that treating offenders as responsible legal subjects during detention was the only way to guarantee that they will behave likewise in society, was forgotten. Though critics claim that prisoners' litigation has gradually become a chain of formalities without any substantial meaning (Almelo et al. 1994), and the Minister's advisory Central Council for the Administration of Penal Law (*Centrale Raad voor de Strafrechtstoepassing*) is increasingly critical about the continuous expansion of legal boundaries by ministerial circulars, the authorities hold the opinion that prisoners have become too emancipated in their ability to mobilize the law, and that the easy access to the system of litigation needs to be curtailed. Present prison law is felt to offer insufficient possibilities for the exercise of the new penal policy, and limits the grip of the authorities over the inmates.

These views influenced the drafting of a new Penitentiary Principles Act (PBW), which will grant institutions a greater freedom of action towards detainees, introduce more duties for them, and curtail their legal rights. This draft also allows for a more detailed differentiation of prison regimes, and provides the legal basis (previously lacking) for maximum security prisons. In addition, it gives a formal basis to the new and more sober basic regime, which promises more liberties to the obedient prisoner and a 'zero regime' for those who are uncooperative. The draft also allows for the possibility of introducing special detention units (IBA) for the increasing number of people with personality disorders. It further-more allows the prison governor to order involuntary medical treatment whenever he or she judges this necessary for the avoidance of harm to the health of a specific prisoner or to his or her fellow inmates. Another important feature of the draft is that the complaints procedure will be restricted to explicit decisions of the governor.

Probation and non-custodial sanctions

Reclassering: the Dutch variety of probation
Probation services, which occupy a strategic role in the Dutch criminal justice system, were up to 1995 delivered by private organizations united in a federation. Probation officers traditionally saw themselves primarily as social workers, who worked, inde-pendently of the criminal justice system, on behalf of their clients. This situation has changed over the last decade. The Ministry of Justice has increased its influence over the national probation service by linking its funding directly to the services it grants to the criminal justice system. Because they are currently financially almost entirely dependent on the Ministry, the activities of probation officers are strongly concentrated on the production of social reports for the prosecution and the judiciary, and notably on monitoring non-custodial sanctions. The traditional focus on providing social work and aftercare has become of secondary importance, because the budget for this role has been cut drastically. Dato Steenhuis who, as the highest official in the Public Prosecution Service (OM), has the special task of co-ordinating the sanctioning policy, has claimed that the probation service is primarily a service for the prosecution. The organization of the service is already modelled on his favourite design as a production unit in the 'penal chain'. The frequent use of newspeak such as 'unit manager', 'case management', 'result oriented offer', 'input trajectory', 'process and product registration' and 'result measurement' is significant. The same kind of 'privatization' we described in respect of the prison system is also being carried through in the probation service. This development implied a further reorganization of the current feder-ation into an autonomous administrative body (*zelfstandig bestuurs orgaan*), which is entirely responsible for its own internal admin-istrative affairs, but will be managed by The Hague in terms of its general politics. (For contrasting views on these and other devel-opments in the probation service see Steenhuis 1994; Janse de Jonge 1993.)

Non-custodial sanctions

At virtually the same time as the expansion of the prison system began, various 'alternative sanctions', as they were initially called, were introduced. After the ethical phase of the 1950s, and the penal welfare phase of the 1970s, the chances of rehabilitation are now thought to increase if sanctions are executed in the community. Initially, these alternative sanctions were applied as a diversion from the penal process, and functioned as a condition either for dropping further prosecution, or for suspending a remand or prison sentence. The Dutch criminal justice system in which the public prosecutor has a pivotal role is well suited to encouraging 'extra-judicial' forms of diversion. However, operating community based alternatives in this way was undermined in the late 1980s by a number of developments, not least when they became formal penal sanctions which could only be ordered by judges. This was the fate of the community service order which, following a report in 1991 of the Advisory Committee on Alternative Sanctions (OCAS), became the new penalty of 'restriction of liberty'. As a punishment, 'restriction of liberty' means that firstly it should be 'useful' (for what and for whom remains unclear); secondly it should be executed in the community and be monitored by the probation service; and thirdly it should have a relation with, and knowledge of, the personality and personal circumstances of the offender, the seriousness of the offence and the circumstances under which it was committed (van Swaaningen and uit Beijerse 1993).

After the publication of the OCAS report, the development of non-custodial sanctions gained momentum. At the same time their primary goal changed from being an alternative to custody to one based on retribution and discipline. And, despite the fact that non-custodial sanctions are formally designed to replace custodial sentences of up to six months (para. 22b, Criminal Code), these short sentences are actually still widely applied. The large growth in the number of community service orders has only resulted in a very small decrease in the number of short prison sentences. This raises the question of whether non-custodial sanctions are a real alternative to imprisonment or only widen the net of penal control has become rather superfluous. They do widen the net, but since they are currently widely applied in penal practice this can no longer be an argument to reject them. Non-custodial sanctions should now be judged on their own merits. Measures which were initially presented as alternative sanctions are now called 'assignment penalties' (*taakstraffen*). This renaming is significant because giving the term 'assignment' priority over the word 'alternative' undermines the idea that a non-custodial sanction should offer an alternative to custody and, by calling this type of sanction a penalty instead, the punitive element is stressed. Yet these principal penalties are formally meant to replace custodial sanctions of up to six months. An assignment penalty consists of a task an offender has to fulfil under the supervision of the probation service. There are currently eighty-five different projects and courses which can function as such. And, whereas 15,683 unconditional prison sentences were imposed in 1993, the number of assignment penalties amounted to 12,754. (These figures need to be treated with some caution, as van der Laan 1993:89 mentions a figure of 11,000, while the Ministry of Justice has come up with even lower figures: these differences reflect the difficulty of counting sentences which are decentralized and which often operate in an informal way.) However, we must stress that financial sanctions – settlements with the prosecution (*transacties*) and actual fines – are by far the most frequently applied, but these are not seen as non-custodial sanctions. It should also be noted that by 1994 electronic monitoring, which in 1990 was rejected as an unrealistic and undesirable alternative to custody, was again being discussed with a view to introducing it by the end of the year (Ministerie van Justitie 1994:33).

It is not easy to obtain an overview of all of the eighty-five projects which have been designated as assignment penalties. There are still large regional differences, caused by the fact that the development of non-custodial sanctions is rooted in *ad hoc* initiatives of individual probation officers who have aimed to offer a practical means for the courts to divert a concrete case from the penal process, rather than being the product of a policy from the central justice administration. In 1994 assignment penalties could be classified as follows: educational courses; training schemes aimed at the improvement of the individual's chances on the labour market; community service, which is unpaid labour for the public; confrontation courses oriented towards providing an insight into the harm which is done to victims, for example, with respect to sex offences, or to the consequences of a criminal career; training schemes in social skills in order to compensate for personal shortcomings; intensive professional and social training schemes in a closed setting; mediation and victim compensation programmes; and therapeutic programmes on the management of certain behaviour, with regard to alcohol or drug abuse, problematic gambling or child abuse. These sanctions can be imposed independently, or in combination with other sanctions, including custodial ones. We have seen above that the social history of law-breaking women is quite different from that of men. Nonetheless, there are no programmes which are oriented at their specific problems. While is 1993 women made up 4.4 per cent of the prison population, their share in the assignment penalties was 10 per cent. Women convicted to these non-custodial sanctions are substantially older than their male counterparts. Some 30 per cent are between 30 and 40 years old. These are often single mothers who serve a community service order imposed for social security fraud. Male offenders on a community service order are largely convicted for vandalism or petty theft.

At this stage we would argue that there is little point in trying to make any comprehensive, once and for all judgement about the desirability of non-custodial sanctions. Some can be quite useful whereas others are based on narrow models of behaviourism. But beyond this, there is a strategic consideration which is important in respect of the political context we aim to outline below. In 1994 the development of assignment penalties was the only penal debate which was not yet primarily oriented towards repression, and which attracted a lot of public support (van der Laan 1993). Thus to argue against these sanctions, and for negative reforms in the sense of Mathiesen (1974), vacates the political space to those forces who want to increase the retributive elements in the assignments while at the same time alienating a relatively important lobby in the opposition against the further expansion of the prison system, namely, probation officers. It is important to retain their commitment to progressive penal reform by stimulating the few idealist forces still left in penal practice. Having implied that non-custodial sanctions should now be judged on their own merits, we remain concerned that their goal might well become primarily retributive, which will probably limit any rehabilitative potential. Their increasingly bureaucratic and 'output-oriented' implementation may well decrease any educational effects, which are most likely to follow from a personal approach and human contact. And their current control by the probation service and prosecution, without any enforceable legal guarantees, except the fact that these sanctions cannot be imposed without the consent of the offender, hardly offers any serious safeguard against abuses (uit Beijerse and van Swaaningen 1994).

We should acknowledge that the border between custodial and non-custodial sanctions is not absolute: a therapeutically oriented programme can come close to elements of a much more intensive and coercive programme, as for example in the case of a hospital order (TBS). This also applies, as we saw above, to prisoners at the end of their sentences who may perform virtually the same tasks as they would in a training scheme on social skills imposed as a penalty. And the multi-agency approach to crime prevention, which functions at a moment when the penal process has not yet started, may also consist of virtually the same sorts of courses and activities as the palette of community sanctions. A final point of consideration is that this 'shallow end' of the penal system may well have been a constitutive element in the process of worsening prison conditions. That is to say, probation officers tend to accept only those offenders into the programmes which function as an assignment penalty who are perceived as having a reasonable chance of success. Consequently, those offenders who are not admitted to non-custodial projects are concentrated in prison, and the process, which is euphemistically called the 'entrenchment' of the prison system, can more easily be presented and justified as an obvious reaction to a population which has simply become more difficult.

The logic of law and order

Throughout history alleged increases in crime have been the main argument for firm law and order campaigns. But there have also been periods when crime was increasing and punitive reactions were minimized. Those who wish to point this out are likely to be accused of playing down the crime problem. But this is manifestly untrue. It is perfectly clear to us, for example, that crime is a serious problem. Individual victims feel powerless and angry, and crime has disruptive effects on some of the most vulnerable groups in society. However, we doubt whether imprisonment is a 'serious' answer to these problems, just as we doubt whether a simple relationship between levels of various crimes and the intensity of penal control can actually be established.

Leaving aside the disputes over whether crime has increased in the last decade, it is clear that there has been a socio-cultural change in Dutch attitudes towards punishment. Particularly significant was an official announcement made in March 1994 at a congress on sanctioning organized by the research department of the Ministry of Justice: 'After the anti-authoritarianism and abolitionism of the 1960s and 70s, a turning-point in thinking about crime was reached by the beginning of the 1980s. Punishing is again "allowed", and the legitimation of penal sanctions is no longer solely sought in its re-socialising effect, but again in incapacitation and retribution as well' (text from congress brochure, *Straffen in de moderne samenleving* 1994). What therefore seems to have changed radically is the belief in punishment as the obvious, sound reaction to crime. The calculations of judges which had led them to eschew long prison sentences in the light of studies about the negative effects of imprisonment and the limited impact of penal measures on crime rates seem to be forgotten. Such rational calculations, which had also included an understanding that prisoners could not be expected to function in a fully independent way immediately after having spent long periods isolated from society, are rejected now, and the body of thought which inspired them has been discredited by making it a cliché. Punishment has gradually become once more an expression of a Durkheimian *conscience collective*, rather than an (ambiguous) means to control crime. In the popular press 'rising crime rates' are constantly presented as a consequence of 'soft' penal reactions, rather than as a by-product of social developments such as the anonymity in, and the bureaucratization of, society; the limited profit and efficiency orientations which have broken down informal mechanisms of social control; and the indifference produced by the lack of a clear vision of the future. In this context of managerial cynicism which permeates both society and the penal sphere, there is hostility towards advocates of social control policies with a human face, in which discourses of compassion and solidarity with the underdog, the collective responsibilities of society and a decent level of welfare still play a role – even when this approach has had a positive impact by encouraging low levels of violence and less polarized relations between different groups in society.

It has also been argued that because collective morality has fragmented, the criminal justice system can no longer be legitimized by appealing to collective values, but should instead embrace a so-called 'victimalized' morality legitimated by the services which it offers to victims of crime (Boutellier 1993). Support for this approach, even though it is a questionable interpretation of what has happened in the last decade, and one which fuels functionalist and individualist views of criminal justice, was reinforced by the unscrupulous exploitation of the 'fear of crime'. Victimization surveys which purported to show that the Netherlands was becoming one of the most criminal countries in Europe were important in facilitating a more punitive mentality. 'Getting tough on criminals' was presented as 'getting tough on crime'. In this way, the interests of victims have been played off against those of offenders, and indeed, against those of due process, whereas in reality victims experience little concrete benefits from the penal process, and 70 per cent of Dutch citizens surveyed in 1994 said that they *never* feel unsafe (see van Swaaningen et al. 1992 for a critique of Dijk et al. (1990) whose use of crime surveys helped to harden public sentiment against offenders in favour of victims).

The growing influence of policy considerations within the prosecution service has also played a leading role in the development of law and order responses to crime. This influence was originally quite progressive. To paraphrase August 't Hart, it was inspired by the enormous increase in the number of criminal cases, for which no adequate means to handle them were available (that is, the practical need to set priorities in a rational and uniform way); a necessity which was reinforced by the judicial crisis (at the end of the 1960s), which had to accommodate new modes of law enforcement and sanctioning to match what the public then felt to be a more appropriate reaction to new circumstances. (1994:117)

Such a political orientation gradually degenerated, however, into a professional style with the public prosecutor as a process manager without the magisterial role which the law attributes to him or her. The metaphor of the criminal justice system becomes that of a company which consists of several chains. Criminal procedure subsequently assumes the characteristics of a penal production process (Steenhuis 1986). We have seen examples of this managerial rationale throughout this chapter. This development can be interpreted as an ultimate consequence of the Weberian line of the rationalization of punishment, in which on the one hand bureaucratization has become 'a component of measured and impartial justice', yet on the other hand the 'professionalization of the punitive process . . . has reached a point where professionals have been able to redefine the social meaning of punishment' (Garland 1990:184). Consequently, the internal rationale of the system determines the social reality, rather than the social reality determining the responses of the system. This process of rationalization has furthermore resulted in a mode of thinking in which functionalist arguments have actually driven away normative considerations; rehabilitation was for example seen to have failed not because it was no longer a valid principle, but because it did not 'work'. An important consequence of this development has been that the managerial style which currently prevails in the administration of justice makes it much easier to push through a rather cynical policy of social defence, because it requires people, whether they are prosecutors, prison governors or probation officers, to respond as functionaries who 'just' act as a part of the system rather than as human beings who also have a personal commitment and responsibility to deliver justice.

By the end of the 1980s and into the 1990s two processes can be identified. On the one hand we find on a discursive level an increasing moralistic appeal to law and order, particularly evident in the impassioned speeches of the Catholic former Minister of Justice

Ernst Hirsch Ballin and Prime Minister Ruud Lubbers. On the other hand, actual policy developments are characterized by a form of planned justice, in parallel with the planned economy, in which principles of due process are gradually replaced by a management approach of an efficient procedural order and where even the quality of the rule of law is interpreted in terms of its organizational efficiency. With such an entirely functionalist discourse, we get close to what David Garland calls the limits of rationalization. In this context, the *splendor veritatis* of Hirsch Ballin and Lubbers is a welcome ideological addition to Steenhuis's management ideology. That is to say, while at the level of penal practice genuinely difficult moral choices are translated into simple technical and/or financial choices, at an ideological level the Durkheimian notion that punishment is first of all a 'passionate, vengeful reaction, motivated by outraged moral sentiments' is reaffirmed to the public at large. As Garland argues correctly: 'while legislators and judges make some claim to be expressing community feeling, and will adjust their penal reactions accordingly, the penal administration is not accountable in the same way' (1990:187–90). Thus a paradoxical situation emerges in which, at the concrete institutional level of the penal system, a bloodless managerial instrumentalism stimulates the very same normative bleakness, depersonalization and indifference which in the moralistic discourse on law and order are presented as important social causes of crime.

The main problem with current Dutch penal policy seems to be that it is based on factors without intrinsic limits. The fear of crime, the suffering of victims, are without a limit, and so may well be the symbolic display of power to compensate for these feelings. The dominance of political objectives in criminal justice leads to law enforcement without limits: we have already seen this in the authoritarian development of the *défense sociale* school. The managerial rationale of efficiency is without limits. If principles of due process are violated, or if more technical equipment is made available, more crimes will be 'processed'. And if the planning of the need for cell capacity is based on mathematical trend extrapolations with the consequent marginalization of alternative more liberal discourses then we will need more prison cells until eternity. As Gary Marx has noted: 'Too often technology driven reforms offer us answers, but fail to tell us what the questions are' (quoted on jacket of Ball et al. 1987). Does imprisonment deter? Does it have any effect on the conditions under which crimes are being committed? Is it beneficial for victims or does it at least result in less fear about crime? And where indeed would be the limit of instrumentalism? It has been the strongest point of the post-war

Dutch penal reformers that they actually did pose such functional and normative questions, and in comparison to the intellectual level of the debates and the genuine social commitment of those days, the complacent disdain and obtuse bookkeeper's logic of current policy-makers seems quite inappropriate.

Note

1   Figures on the Dutch prison population come mainly from a combination of *Gevangenisstatistiek* 1993 of the Central Bureau of Statistics and the *Beleidsinfo D&J Gevangenisstraffen en Voorlopige Hechtenis: ciifers en ontwikkelingen in de jaren '80* of the Ministerie van Justitie (MvJ) 1984.

References

Almelo L van, Borsboom A, Leijen G van, Velden R van der and Wiewel P (1994), *Crimineel Jaarboek 1994* Breda: Papieren Tijger–Coornhert Liga

Ball R A, Huff C and Lilly R (1987), *House Arrest and Correctional Policy* Newbury Park: Sage

Beijerse J uit and Swaaningen R van (1994), 'De zachte krachten zullen zeker winnen op 't eind; een op de praktijk gericht strafrechtshervormend perspectief op alternatieven voor detentie' in M J M Verpalen (ed) *Druk en Tegendruk: constructieve bijdragen aan de discussie over het cellentekort* Arnhem: Gouda Quint, pp. 23–50

Beyens K, Snacken S and Eliaerts Chr (1992), *Privatisering van Gevangenissen* Brussels: VUB Press

Boutellier J C J (1993), *Solidariteit en slachtofferschap: de morele betekenis van criminaliteit in een postmoderne cultuur* Nijmegen: Socialistiese Uitgeverij

Council of Europe (1993), *Report to the Dutch Government on the Visit to the Netherlands Carried Out by the European Committee for the Prevention of Torture and Inhuman or Degrading Treatment or Punishment from 30 August to 8 September 1992* Strasbourg: Council of Europe

Dijk J J M van, Mayhew P and Killias M (1990), *Experiences of Crime across the World: Key Findings of the 1989 International Crime Survey* Deventer: Kluwer

Downes D (1988), *Contrasts in Tolerance: Post-War Penal Policy in the Netherlands and England and Wales* Oxford: Clarendon

Garland D (1990), *Punishment and Modern Society: A Study in Social Theory* Oxford: Oxford University Press

Haan W J M de (1990), *The Politics of Redress: Crime, Punishment and Penal Abolition* London: Unwin Hyman

Hart A C 't (1994), *Openbaar Ministerie en rechtshandhaving: een verkenning* Arnhem: Gouda Quint

Janse de Jonge J A (1993), 'Om het behoud van de reclasseringsgedachte' in J A Janse de Jonge, L M Moerings and A van Vliet (eds) *Binnen de steen van dit bestaan: over rechtsbescherming en totale instituties* Arnhem: Gouda Quint

Jonge G de (1994), 'Deaths in Police Custody and in Prisons in Holland' in A Liebling and T Ward (eds) *Deaths in Custody: International Perspectives* London: Whiting & Birch

Kelk C (1994), 'Verzelfstandiging en management' in J Glastra van Loon, C Kelk, F A C M Denkers, F Kuitenbrouwer, ThA de Roos and C J M Schuyt (eds) *Strafrecht onder vuur: de bedreigde principes van de misdaadbestrijding* Amsterdam: Balans, pp. 43–64

Laan P H van der (1993), 'Het publiek en de taakstraf: een maatschappelijk draagvlak voor de taakstraf' *Justitiële Verkenningen* 19, 9: 89–110

Mathiesen T (1974) *The Politics of Abolition* London: Martin Robertson

Ministerie van Justitie (1991), *Vrouwen in detentie: rapport van de stuurgroep Herziening differentiatiestelsel gevangeniswezen* The Hague: MvJ/Directie Delinquentenzorg en Jeugdinrichtingen

Ministerie van Justitie (1994), *Werkzame detentie: beleidsnota voor het gevangeniswezen* Tweede Kamer 1993–4 (parliamentary paper no. 22.999)

Moerings M (1994), 'AIDS in Prisons in the Netherlands' in P Thomas and M Moerings (eds) *AIDS in Prisons* Aldershot: Dartmouth/Gower, pp. 56–73

Rutherford A (1986), *Prisons and the Process of Justice* Oxford: Oxford University Press

Steenhuis D W (1986), 'Coherence and Coordination in the Administration of Criminal Justice' in J J M van Dijk, Ch Haffmans, F Rüter, J Schutte and S Stolwijk (eds) *Criminal Law in Action: An Overview of Current Issues in Western Societies* Arnhem: Gouda Quint, pp. 229–45

Steenhuis D W (1994), 'Reclassering en Openbaar Ministerie: een dienstverleningsrelatie' *Justitiële Verkeningen* 20, 4: 21–7

Swaaningen R van and Beijerse J uit (1993), 'From Punishment to Diversion and Back Again: The Debate on Non-Custodial Sanctions and Penal Reform in the Netherlands' *The Howard Journal* 32, 2: 136–56

Swaaningen R van, Blad J R and Loon R van (1992), *A Decade of Criminological Research and Penal Policy in the Netherlands. The 1980s: The Era of Business-Management Ideology* Rotterdam: CISW-EUR

3

Flexibility and Intermittent Emergency in the Italian Penal System

Vincenzo Ruggiero

In the late months of 1993 the prison population in Italy was in excess of 50,000, an unprecedented figure for the institutions of the country (Dipartimento Amministrazione Penitenziaria 1994). Almost 60 per cent were on remand, 39.5 per cent were sentenced, and 0.5 per cent were held in penal institutions for mentally disturbed offenders (Ministero di Grazia e Giustizia 1993). This population figure is nearly double that recorded in 1990 and poses a problem for commentators and analysts. As Table 3.1 illustrates there was an increase from 26,424 in 1978 to a peak of 42,795 in 1984, and then a drop to 25,931 in 1990, the lowest figure in the history of the country. Understanding these changes requires more than a juridical or policy oriented account. It is the intention of this chapter to provide a more analytical account of this movement.

The changing social climate provides an inescapable backcloth for the explanation of these anomalistic figures. Who goes to prison? Why? What are the formal policies, the informal practices and/or the moods in the wider society which determine such capricious trends? Most importantly, is the recent upsurge a unique feature in the history of Italian penal institutions or is it an expression of a pre-existing pattern? Before attempting to tackle these issues a general overview of the penal system in Italy will be provided in order to set the framework for a subsequent critical analysis.

Imprisonment and crime trends

In Italy the rate of imprisonment per 100,000 of the population grew from 45 in 1990 to above 60 in 1993. Some commentators warn that, by 1995, the country may equal the notorious record of the United Kingdom (Pavarini 1994). As no prison building programme is in place, this means that overcrowding is destined to be one of the main features of the years to come, more so than ever

Table 3.1   *Prison population, 1978–1993*

Year	Total number of prisoners	Remand prisoners	Sentenced prisoners	Mentally disturbed prisoners
1978	26,424	18,159	6,452	1,813
1979	28,606	18,806	8,065	1,735
1980	31,765	20,851	9,191	1,723
1981	29,506	20,254	7,500	1,752
1982	35,043	24,004	9,294	1,745
1983	40,225	27,080	11,419	1,726
1984	42,795	27,342	13,592	1,861
1985	41,536	24,326	15,528	1,682
1986	33,609	20,099	11,906	1,604
1987	31,773	18,615	11,617	1,541
1988	31,382	16,386	13,557	1,442
1989	30,680	14,235	15,048	1,397
1990	25,931	13,779	10,938	1,214
1991	35,469	19,875	14,319	1,275
1992	47,316	25,343	20,567	1,406
1993	50,197	NA	NA	NA

Source: Dipartimento Amministrazione Penitenziaria 1994

in the past. Official guidelines suggest that the sentenced and remand population be separated. But the recurring periods of overcrowding nullify this principle, thus creating a chaotic situation where prison places are often shared by almost twice as many individuals as they are expected to contain. It is to be noted that these individuals represent a selected fraction, on average a third, of those who are found guilty of an offence. The remaining two-thirds are in fact either conditionally discharged or fined. The fine remains the most widely used sentence, and throughout the 1970s and 1980s constituted on average half of all sentences given (Dipartimento Amministrazione Penitenziaria 1994).

In 1993 the breakdown of the sentenced population with regard to the length of sentences was as follows. Among 118,116 found guilty, 14,911 were sentenced to up to 3 months imprisonment, 18,911 between 3 and 6 months, 13,554 between 6 and 12 months, 11,012 between 1 and 2 years, 6,185 between 2 and 5 years, 989 between 5 and 10 years, and 419 in excess of 10 years. No one was sentenced to life. One aspect emerges as immediately striking. This is that more than 80 per cent of the prison population is serving a sentence below 2 years. While the number of prisoners serving longer sentences remained almost unaltered over the years, it is this section of the population in custody which experienced the intermittent dramatic shifts I have referred to. Even between 1985 and 1990, when the number of homicides rose considerably, prisoners serving long-term sentences remained virtually constant. On the other hand, the bulk of the prison population upon which the changing social, legislative and judicial moods had a significant impact was formed by short-term prisoners.

Between 1982 and 1992 thefts, robberies and drug offences constituted more than 80 per cent of the offences for which prisoners were sentenced (Censis 1992). Data for 1992 show that property offences form more than 94 per cent of offences reported to the police. The relative increase of property crime and the parallel decrease of crimes against the person are part of a trend dating back to the last century (ISTAT 1992; Canosa 1991).

With a total of 1,433,548 offences reported to the police during the first four months of 1992, only 200,329 people were prosecuted. For the remaining offences either the police failed to collect enough evidence or judges found that evidence was insufficient to initiate prosecution. Leaving aside frauds and other offences which are defined by the Italian code as 'crimes against the public economy', thefts accounted for 80 per cent of property crimes against which penal action was initiated. Despite the non-violent nature of these offences, persons found guilty of thefts form the majority of the prison population in Italy.

An initial observation could be that the inconstant trend I referred to earlier is caused by the varying degree of harshness with which persons found guilty of theft are treated. The impact of illicit drug use and distribution, which in Italy are closely related to property crime, should also be borne in mind when examining these figures. This aspect will be discussed in more detail later, although it can be anticipated that drug related offences form a large part of crimes committed in Italy and, at the same time, drug offenders form the bulk of the prison population (Castellani and Di Lazzaro 1990; Pepino 1991; Lepri 1993).

Ethnic minorities

One of the most important changes which can be observed in the prisoners' composition concerns the growing presence of ethnic minorities. Between 1988 and 1992 their presence in Italian institutions almost doubled, from 3,150 to about 5,500, which constitutes more than 10 per cent of the overall prison population. Figures published in late 1992 indicate that this percentage is rapidly moving close to 20 per cent (Piroch et al. 1992). If we

Table 3.2   *Foreign prisoners, 1980–1990 (per cent)*

Year	Europe	Africa	Asia	Oceania	America[1]
1980	50.87	29.24	5.66	0.23	14.00
1981	48.32	32.85	6.55	0.26	11.98
1982	44.51	38.46	5.55	0.40	11.03
1983	43.41	40.51	6.50	0.28	9.28
1984	48.25	35.09	6.61	0.20	9.83
1985	45.81	39.66	6.27	0.32	7.91
1986	NA	NA	NA	NA	NA
1987	43.40	42.20	4.98	0.17	8.83
1988	40.37	47.54	3.88	0.13	7.65
1989	40.13	46.98	4.56	0.10	8.00
1990	28.94	59.82	3.48	0.04	7.40

[1] America includes both the United States and countries of South America. On average, 90 per cent of prisoners born in America are from South America.

Source: Ministero di Grazia e Giustizia 1993

consider that they form some 2 per cent of the general population, the rate of imprisonment of minorities is all the more striking.

Although there is an increasing tendency within public opinion to automatically associate 'immigrants' with drug offences, only 20 per cent of non-national prisoners were found guilty of such offences in 1992. The disadvantages suffered by this section of the prison population mirror the vulnerability of ethnic minorities in Italian society in general. Examples of these disadvantages will be provided when alternatives to custody are discussed. If the country of birth of ethnic minority prisoners is indicative of their social and economic condition, Table 3.2 shows how this type of prisoner is increasingly poor and vulnerable. Note for example how prisoners born in Africa grew from a third to more than half of non-national prisoners between 1980 and 1990.

Imprisonment and drug use

In 1992 prisoners identified as drug dependent formed more than 30 per cent of the overall prison population (Ceretti and Merzagora 1994). In the same year they were in excess of 50 per cent in the institutions of larger cities such as Rome, Milan, Naples and Turin. Only about 2 per cent received methadone in prison. About 8 per cent were officially declared HIV positive (Ruggiero and South 1995; Solivetti 1994). The impact of drug use and distribution on the penal system as a whole cannot be overstressed. Illicit drugs affected dramatically the features of the criminal economy and the social composition of those involved in it (Magliona and Sarzotti 1993; Ferazzi and Ronconi 1993). I shall return to these questions in the final section of this chapter.

Women in prison

Women prisoners formed 12–14 per cent of the overall prison population between the late 1970s and the early 1990s, with the incidence of drug related offences constantly increasing. In 1992 it was revealed that drug use and distribution accounted for about 60 per cent of the offences for which women were serving a custodial sentence. About 20 per cent were not born in Italy. The relationship between social marginalization and prison is much more evident for women than it is for men. Many women were caught in a vicious circle involving crime, prison, and back to marginalization and crime. The rate of recidivism for women was twice as high as that for men (Campelli et al. 1992). About 45 per cent of women prisoners were serving sentences up to three years. Among these 75 per cent were defined by prison administrators as drug addicts. These data seem to show that alternatives to custody are more difficult to obtain for women than they are for men. For example, all prisoners serving a sentence below three years may receive probation and community supervision orders. But the application of these alternatives to custody, as we will see, is discretionary. Habitual drug users, on the other hand, are entitled to receive treatment in therapeutic communities. Why these non-custodial measures are so often denied to women is open to debate. Perhaps deviant women, and in particular women drug offenders, are more stigmatized than their male counterparts? Or perhaps punishment in the community is inadvisable for women in that their marginalized condition hampers their rehabilitation? It is a fact that non-custodial punishment, as will be argued later, is preferably granted to those whose lifestyle and social condition is amenable to 'regular' behaviour. As the majority of women in prison are more economically disadvantaged than their male counterparts, and given their lack of support from family members, partners, friends and agencies, community sentences may be seen as less conducive to rehabilitation for them.

When we look at the characteristics of women prisoners in Italian institutions the very function of imprisonment could be put into question. We are facing a majority of offenders who serve relatively short periods of time in custody, and who after intermittent periods spent outside, return to prison. This routine, far from acting as a deterrent or a focus for rehabilitation, in fact exacerbates the marginalization of women and leads to more marginalization and crime. In this case prison functions as both a catalyst and the outcome of crime; it is in a sense part and parcel of offending and poverty, often regarded by women as a cyclical penalty or 'tax' they have to pay because of their social disadvantages (Faccioli 1992).

The phases of penal intervention

It is difficult to understand the dynamics of incarceration in Italy without addressing the different aspects or phases of which penal intervention is composed. First there is a legislative phase, which entails the statutory ruling of a minimum and a maximum penalty to be inflicted for any specific offence. Second there is a judicial phase, in which judges decide the 'quantity' of the penalty by graduating the sentence at a specific point between the statutory minimum and maximum. Finally, there is an executive phase, where prison administrations, jointly with judges supervising prison regimes, establish the 'quality' of punishment by applying a specifically identified and individualized regime. In practice, as we shall see, prison administrations go as far as recommending or sanctioning early release or home leave (Padovani 1990).

Because changes in the legislative aspects of punishment are more difficult and slow to carry out, decarceration or recarceration policies were often implemented within the domain of the judicial and executive phases. For example, in periods when lenient attitudes prevailed judges would apply the minimal penalty available for any specific offence. At the same time prison governors would play an important role in granting a number of benefits to sentenced prisoners, including non-custodial measures. It could be hypothesized that judges and prison administrations mirrored public sentiments and, through the varying degrees of harshness deployed, they ideally responded to the demand for punishment prevailing at a given moment (Wilkins 1991).

For decades there has been a large discrepancy between the severe sentences potentially applicable for any one offence and the actual sentences imposed by judges. The practice of 'softening' penal treatment is still regarded as legitimate also because penal legislation remains embedded in draconian principles drafted in the 1930s. 'To some extent, the very existence of a severe legislation lacking political legitimacy (since it was the offspring of fascism) has fostered the process of leniency in sentencing and enforcing legal punishment in the democratic era' (Pavarini 1994:50). This process of reforming the criminal justice system through judicial practice became evident and most fruitful in the mid 1980s, when institutions for young offenders were virtually emptied. This *de facto* abolition of custody for the under 18s was the result of judges, many of whom were women or politically progressive, applying minimal sentences sanctioned by law on the one hand, and utilizing the old positivist tool called 'pardon' on the other.

Another tool at the disposal of judges for the selection of offenders and the differentiation of their treatment is provided by the three-stage trial existing in the country. The three stages entail the first trial; an appeal stage which may be mobilized by either the defendant or the public prosecutor; and finally a third court hearing (carried out by the Court of Cassation) where the legal correctness of the previous trials is ascertained. When a pre-established maximum time elapses between the first trial and the appeal, and between this and the final verdict of the Court of Cassation, many charges are automatically dropped. There is also a pre-established maximum remand time which varies according to the type of offence. Therefore, while awaiting the final stage of the proceedings, and when the maximum time for their specific offence elapses, defendants must be released. There is reason to believe that judges deliberately delay the subsequent hearings when faced with what they consider minor offences, while speeding up trials involving offences which raise more public outcry. It is not known whether this strategy has been used to delete crimes committed by powerful people. However, the delay strategy is advantageous to all defendants. The timespan between being charged and being tried may 'cool down' the institutional reaction to offences while offenders may be able to prove, or claim, that their lifestyle has changed in the meantime.

The willingness of judges to use this space for manoeuvre may determine the extent to which the prison population rises or falls. Legislative power can also play a role through general amnesties for less serious offenders. These measures have usually been the result of both prisoners' pressure and the authorities' concerns about prison overcrowding and unrest. General amnesties empty turbulent institutions while easing the workload of prison officers.

Alternatives to custody

As in a number of European countries, the definition of alternatives to custody in Italy is very broad. They include a wide range of dispositions and measures which can be imposed at any moment of the criminal justice process. Vass (1990:1), when discussing alternatives to custody in Britain, also warns that there is no single definition of what they are, and that anything which involves crime prevention, and punishment or control *outside* custodial establishments can be legitimately defined as 'alternative'. His definition, which seems to apply to most European countries, reads as follows: 'Alternatives to custody are *those penalties which, following conviction and sentence, allow an offender to spend part or all of his or her sentence in the community and outside prison establishments*' (Vass 1990:2; emphasis in original). The author adds that even parole and remission of sentence, which epitomize attempts to reduce the prison population, fall within this category. I will adopt this definition, as it aptly describes the way in which alternatives to custody are understood in Italy.

Two types of alternatives to custody are in operation. The first type completely diverts offenders from the prison system, and their application is ruled by courts hearing specific cases. The second type relates to offenders who are already serving a sentence. These are formally ruled by judges who are in charge of prison supervision.

Alternatives in the judicial phase

Conditional discharge Conditional discharge is of the first type and the most widely utilized alternative to custody in Italy. Introduced in the country in 1904, this measure has always represented an effective way of reducing overcrowding, a problem which was recognized as early as the first half of the last century (Padovani 1990). The first condition for its application is that the offence dealt with does not bring a statutory sentence in excess of two years. This period of time is regarded by legislators as too short to allow for effective prison treatment but long enough, if spent in prison, to cause recidivism. Conditional discharge does not entail any type of community supervision. However, if those who are given conditional discharge reoffend, they may be given both a sentence for the fresh charge and a sentence for the old offence.

Another circumstance allowing for the application of conditional discharge is that the defendant has not been previously sentenced and is not deemed a 'habitual or professional' offender. Now, habituality and professionality are not easy to define as they are part of both the previous and the potential career of defendants. However, it is the task of judges to dispel the vagueness of these definitions and establish whether a defendant is likely to reoffend. This discretionary power offers yet another hint as to how the prison population in Italy can soar or shrink irrespective of the entity and nature of offences committed.

Alternatives to short sentences   A number of alternatives to custody can only replace short sentences of up to six months. These are semi-detention, which can replace sentences of up to six months; supervision order (*libertà controllata*), replacing sentences of up to three months; and fines (*pena pecuniaria*) up to one month. Semi-detention implies that the convict spends at least ten hours per day in the institution. In turn, the supervision order dictates that the person does not leave his or her residence town and that they contact a police station daily.

Negotiated alternatives   Other alternatives are applied in the judicial phase when defendants agree to 'negotiate' their sentence. This procedure goes beyond the guilty plea in Anglo-Saxon courts, as it literally leads to the common establishment of the length and nature of punishment. In these cases the sentence established by law is curtailed by the order of a third. With a similar procedure, a life sentence can be replaced by a 30 year sentence. It is to be noted that these reductions are related neither to specific offences nor to the presumed willingness of offenders to lead a law abiding life. They are simply the result of offenders accepting to 'negotiate', and serve the purpose of easing the courts' workload while shortening the duration of trials.

Probation and semi-liberty   A form of probation also belongs to the first type of alternatives, and is known as *affidamento in prova al servizio sociale*. It entails supervision by the local social services and can be given to defendants sentenced to a maximum of three months. The measure known as *semilibertà* also belongs to the former type, and is granted to offenders who are sentenced up to six months. It consists of day release allowed for work, education, or other rehabilitative activities outside the prison institution (Padovani 1990).

Alternatives in the executive phase
The second set of alternatives, as mentioned above, is applied when the executive phase of the penal process has already started. They can be granted to prisoners as forms of rehabilitative treatment which, according to the legislation in force, should 'tend to re-socialize offenders through contacts with the outside environment'. For a rehabilitative process to take place it is deemed necessary that external relationships include educational, recreational and cultural activities along with familial contacts. Among this set of alternatives is *liberazione anticipata*, which consists of a 45 day remission for every six months spent in custody. It is only given to inmates

who show willingness to participate in the process of their own re-education. This early release scheme operates in addition to other forms of early release which will be discussed below.

These types of alternatives can also be granted to offenders serving longer custodial sentences. In their case, a 'taste' of prison is deemed appropriate before alternative punishments are considered. These can only be granted after their behaviour in prison has been 'scientifically observed' for a period of at least a month. Alternatives such as 'house arrest' and 'leave awards' are of this type. House arrest can be given to those sentenced up to two years who fall within particular categories: for example, pregnant women, mothers of under 3s, individuals suffering from serious illnesses, or individuals of 65 years or over. Leave awards also can potentially be obtained for one or two week periods by all prisoners, and are meant to allow offenders some time with their family. The number of days granted to individual prisoners for leave awards must not exceed 45 days per year.

Conditional release is given to inmates who have shown good behaviour and are deemed reformed. It can be granted after the person has served at least 30 months. Lifers must have served 26 years, but they can also be granted *semilibertà* after serving a minimum 20 years.

The declining use of alternatives
Available data show that about 8,000 offenders were granted house arrest each year during the 1980s, whereas around 6,000 were given day release. More than 30,000 leave permissions were awarded in 1990. This figure does not suggest that 30,000 Italian prisoners enjoyed leave awards: rather, it implies that 10,000 'deserving' prisoners enjoyed three each in a year (ISTAT 1991). More recent data show that the number of offenders given *semilibertà* dropped from about 6,000 in 1986 to approximately 3,500 in 1992. Moreover, in 1986 about 60 per cent of prisoners' applications for this alternative punishment were successful, and by 1992 this figure had dropped to less than 30 percent. The degree of discouragement experienced by prisoners is indicated by the dramatic decline in applications for this alternative measure: from 9,745 in 1986 to less than 5,000 in 1992, and finally to about 1,500 in the late months of 1993. A similar trend can be observed for probation (*affidamento in prova*): from 3,417 granted in 1986 to about 2,000 in 1992. The most dramatic reduction regarded leave permissions: from 13,600 to 1,800 between 1986 and 1992 (Ministero di Grazia e Giustizia 1993).

Supplementary punishments

Along with discounts, detractions and alternatives, it is worth mentioning supplements to punishment which are available to Italian judges. Legislation dating back to the 1930s offers the possibility of adding a number of 'security measures' to the sentence inflicted on dangerous offenders. While the sentence itself is fixed, the duration of the security measure is indeterminate, its rationale being the positivist principle that offenders can be released only when their resocialization is completely accomplished. Among security measures are the requirement to reside in a certain town, away from the residence of accomplices, the obligation to report to a police station daily, and night curfew (Padovani 1990).

The role of prison administrations

This preliminary overview may render the dynamics of imprisonment in Italy more intelligible. Courts or prison administrations, in other words, seem capable of influencing the trend of the prison population at will. Prison administrations, for example, play a crucial role in determining whether conditional release, house arrest, leave awards, probation, *semilibertà* and all other alternatives to custody are given to offenders already serving a prison sentence. This prerogative was accentuated thanks to the Prison Reform Act 1981, which will be dealt with in the next section. Here, it may be useful to anticipate that with the new Act deliberations regarding the alternatives mentioned above are only theoretically and formally taken by judges who supervise prison institutions. In fact, these deliberations are heavily based on reports drafted by prison staff and governors who in the last analysis can reject or support prisoners applying for alternative treatment.

Reforming the system

The argument I have tried to develop so far contains a general point which can be summarized as follows. The model of penality that slowly established itself in Italy is one of flexibility. This is all the more surprising in a landscape dominated by a very stable and formally rigid legislative apparatus. The largely discretionary space in which courts operate, and the command of the judiciary over decision-making processes in the penal arena, have rendered this rigid apparatus extremely flexible. In Italy, it is often the case that legislators eventually adapt to innovation brought about by other powers or social groups, thus in a sense ratifying practices which are already in place. As we have seen, judges may present the legislative power with a *fait accompli*, namely with their own prerogative to differentiate between offenders and, in the last analysis, to trigger processes of decarceration and recarceration. The Prison Reform Act 1981 took this *fait accompli* into account, and even expanded those prerogatives. The Act and successive amendments, while emphasizing discretion in general, slowly removed it from the judiciary and increasingly granted it to prison administrations (Mosconi 1982; Di Lazzaro 1988). This trend, which was already present in the 1981 Act, was intensified and accelerated through amendments and periodical additions to the Act itself. Legislators seemed to respond in this way to the previous courts' practices, which at times had sanctioned *de facto* minimalist policies. Prison genuinely 'risked' becoming a last resort punishment. The amendments were therefore accompanied by legislation increasing minimum penalties for each offence, a circumstance which reduced the discretion of judges. Minimal custodial penalties became in many cases mandatory, a move that deprived judges of their diversionary power. Flexibility and discretion were increasingly transferred to prison governors and staff, who could now concentrate on and monitor the behaviour of individual prisoners. As I have already mentioned this discretionary power increasingly allowed prison administrations to determine the lengths of sentences and the use of alternatives. It should be noted that prison staff include not only prison officers, but also psychologists, physicians and social workers employed by the Ministry of the Interior, the ministry which is also responsible for the police force. In other words, the treatment of offenders, which should traditionally be presided over and supervised by the judiciary, partly became the preserve of staff directly dependent on the government, namely that section of the government which presides over issues of law and order.

The indeterminacy of pain

I will highlight the constitutional implications of this shift in another part of this chapter. What should be noted here is the degree of arbitrariness implied in the new legislation and the indeterminacy of both the quantity and quality of punishment suffered by prisoners. Punishment established by courts is now only virtual, and it does not tally with the pain effectively suffered by inmates (Mosconi and Pavarini 1994). This contradicts the principles drawn up by Beccaria, upon which the Italian penal system supposedly rests, and is also at odds with Weberian definitions of law as rational and predictable. Punishment therefore is no longer the precisely predetermined consequence of an offence, but rather it is the unpredictable response to the behaviour, lifestyle and individual characteristics of offenders. Based on the personal judgement of staff, there are wide discrepancies in the application of punishment in different areas of the country, to the point that criminal activities may soon be induced to operate in regions where prison regimes are more lenient. On the other hand, the indeterminacy of punishment translates into permanent insecurity for prisoners, and the complete absence of points of reference, both in a temporal sense and in terms of precise rules. This creates a situation where prisoners are subject to a never ending regime of self-control and fear that the time spent in jail depends on factors which are not rationally explicable or predictable, but are beyond their control.

Legal suffering and the absence of time

It is not surprising that, in the aftermath of the Prison Reform Act, studies concerning health in Italian institutions began to appear. The virtual doubling of the prison population between 1978 and 1993, it was argued, was not accompanied by a similar expansion of health services aimed at prisoners, whose demand for health could not be met (Commissione Sanità del Senato 1994; Zuffa 1994). Other studies identified flexibility and indeterminacy as two major causes of health debilitation for prisoners (Panizzari 1991; Curcio et al. 1991; Giordano 1990; Piperno 1989; Gallo and Ruggiero 1991; 1992). True, prison *per se* has always caused illnesses and diseases: even the most humane regime produces mental and physical deterioration (Clemmer 1940; Sykes 1958; Ministero di Grazia e Giustizia 1976; Gonin 1991). Moreover, it has already been suggested that environmental and communicative isolation determine two prevailing states of mind, related to aggressive behaviour on the one hand and depressive behaviour on the other (Gallo and Ruggiero 1991). But depression and aggressiveness, which are typical of any prison regime, may be compounded by what can be termed 'the absence of time', a crucial aspect exacerbated by the prison legislation in Italy. Where stable points of reference are difficult to find, a stress-inducing situation predominates. The prisoners know that their behaviour may affect the degree of punishment suffered and the rewards to be gained. Self-repression, in turn, goes hand in hand with the absence of an identifiable scenario. According to prison legislation, for example, each institution is supposed to establish an internal set of norms for the day-to-day life of the inmates. In fact very few institutions have a precise, written list of their internal regulations. The prison administration prefers their rules to be vague and opts for successive contingency orders. Instructions and orders are often contradictory, modifiable, and revocable in the space of minutes. This ever-changing scenario has proved to be a source of fatigue and, for those who control themselves the most, of psychological or psychosomatic diseases (Gallo and Ruggiero 1989).

It has been argued that punishment in Italy falls short of the traditional principle of exchange (Mosconi 1988). There is no longer a pure infliction of pain, exchanged with a passive party receiving that quantum of pain. Increasingly, the exchange seems instead to be of an active nature, in that it works in two directions and entails a production of symbolic behaviour also on the part of the recipient. The new prison legislation, in other words, implies a collusion which demands the participation of prisoners. This requires a high degree of self-control, and in many cases of self-humiliation. The quantity and indeed the quality of punishment depend on the behaviour displayed by prisoners, who feel constantly observed, monitored, even in their most intimate moments. Many are in fact obsessed by the idea of being spied upon, an obsession which is a logical consequence of the abuse, on the part of the administration, of the concept and phrase 'scientific behaviour observation'. The majority of prisoners experience long periods of depression as an inevitable result of self-constraint. Sudden bursts of aggressiveness may easily follow. Many have ulcers, an outcome of nervous distress, fatigue. Symbolically, ulcers can be likened to a process of 'autodigestion', autophagy, self-cannibalism, a solution offered to prisoners to disappear, thus avoiding those who 'scientifically' monitor their behaviour (Gonin 1991). But the extreme expression of the attempt to escape is self-mutilation, and finally suicide. After the new legislation was introduced, the number of escapes declined while incidents of self-injury and suicides increased dramatically. This was one of the outcomes of the greater discretionary power given to prison administrators in granting alternatives. In the 1994 annual report on the state of prisons, the Ministry for Justice showed that suicides in prison rose from 23 in 1990 to 61 in 1993 (*La Nazione* 26 July 1994). Even the loopholes, the 'openness' of prison reform, may well be yet another source of stress. Some prisoners, 'after being allowed a "peep" at the free society, turn down other short-leave permissions in order to avoid the trauma of having to return so soon behind locked doors' (Gallo and Ruggiero 1991:281). Does this partly explain the decline in the applications for non-custodial measures on the part of Italian prisoners?

The current debate

All of these developments are due to the increasing flexibility which, as a model of penality, has slowly established itself in Italy. Alternatives to custody are an important expression of this flexibility as they are individualized and applied with discretion. But why should one criticize non-custodial alternatives if they contribute to the reduction of prisoners' suffering? And why should one object to discretion and the individualization of punishment, if these lower the degree of harshness with which a number of prisoners are treated? In order to answer these questions the current debate among prison reformers should be sketched (Ruggiero 1991). This debate is centred on some specific aspects of the European and Italian juridical tradition. In Italy, flexibility and alternatives to custody are viewed with suspicion not only by abolitionist pressure groups, but also by moderate enlightened jurists. Let us see why.

It is felt that the central principle inspiring flexibility and alternatives to custody is connected with the necessity to manage the prison system and to defuse its internal tensions. As Pavarini (1988) has pointed out, only those alternatives to custody which result in the reduction of the penal system as a whole deserve to be recognized as alternatives. Furthermore, as he has noted: 'Nor does the potential availability of *legal* alternatives to custody boost what is really needed: decriminalization and depenalization' (1988:50).

As we have seen, according to current legislation, alternatives can only be granted to prisoners who demonstrate a willingness to participate in the rehabilitation process. A series of rewards and punishments are included within the main form of punishment administered. Alternatives to custody, in other words, and for that matter flexibility, hinge on custody as they owe their very existence to the necessity of keeping the management of prisons smooth, and prison disturbances at bay. It is important to reiterate that the only authority which is in a position to modulate the intensity of punishment, that is to say to grant awards and inflict supplementary punishments, is in the last analysis the prison administration. As we have seen, all decisions regarding day release, permission to leave, and other non-custodial benefits, although formally sanctioned by the judiciary, are primarily taken by prison governors.

In this context, the first constitutional dilemma with regard to Italian penal law emerges. The supervision of the prison regime, and all decisions regarding the prisoners' treatment, should be the prerogative of the judiciary. The interference of the prison administration in these matters can be regarded as illegitimate. In sum, the way in which alternatives are put into practice violate the constitutional division of powers. Furthermore, in the Italian context, flexibility has made punishment indeterminate and its intensity discretionary. This is at odds with the Enlightenment legacy cherished by many Italian jurists, according to which a predetermined menu of sanctions must be in place in response to specific offences. Law must be rational, predictable and determinate. Flexibility and discretion are therefore unconstitutional, and *sensu stricto* so is the way in which alternatives to custody are delivered.

Alternatives to custody also have negative repercussions on the offenders to whom they are denied. By virtue of the co-operation required of the inmates, these are led into narrow individualism, as benefits and rewards of the prison reform are selective and strictly granted *ad personam*. This causes a loss of collective bargaining power among the prison population as a whole, with the result that living conditions inside the institutions deteriorate. Furthermore, the inmates who are denied alternative punishments are likely to be regarded as undeserving, and therefore unworthy of any effort to improve their condition in custody. Flexibility and alternatives to custody, in sum, in acting as a sort of 'performance related pay or reward', may make custody worse. They may create unequal relationships and act as a divisive means in an oppressive, psychologically taxing and competitive environment.

The philosophy of flexibility, which is narrowly linked to the philosophy of custody itself, falls short of fundamental notions of justice inscribed in the constitution. I have already mentioned that according to Italian law, punishment must be informed by a series of principles which correspond to a written set of constitutional guarantees. Punishment is a pre-established penalty in response to an offence. The type and the limits of this penalty must be decided by the judicial authority within the sphere of individual rights (human guarantees), and in forms established by a written procedural code. In this respect, three principles should be borne in mind. The first has a most simple formulation: punishment is the judicial consequence of an offence, and the latter is the precondition *sine qua non* of punishment: *nulla poena sine crimine*. This indicates that punishment is not an antecedent but a consequent in relation to an offence, and therefore it does not incorporate any preventive element (Ferrajoli 1989). The second principle regards the strict legality of punishment. *Nulla poena sine lege* is the notion conveyed by Article 1 of the Italian Penal Code, whereby nobody can undergo forms of punishment which are not established by law.

Therefore, punishment must have exact and discernible limits, and must be definite in its form and intensity. Certainty and equality are also included in this principle. The third principle is summarized by the formula *nulla poena sine judicio*: punishment must be concretely determined by the jurisdiction, which is also charged with the task of supervising the agencies appointed for its implementation.

The above principles constitute the backcloth against which the debate concerning the penal system takes place in Italy. Critics point out that alternatives are inconsistent with the notions of 'certainty' and 'equality' in that they are built on something which is not discernible and scientifically measurable: the behaviour of prisoners and their dangerousness. Moreover, when alternatives are denied on the grounds of prisoners' behaviour, punishment becomes a tool allegedly aimed at pre-empting future offences rather than responding to them (Ferrajoli 1989). For example, alternatives to custody are denied to allegedly dangerous prisoners. In these cases, it is expected that the prisoners themselves provide evidence that they are not likely to reoffend. If they fail to do so, they are denied the benefit of non-custodial measures. In other words, they are punished with custody *before* they commit a crime. In this way, prison becomes an antecedent rather than, as said earlier, a consequent to crime.

The second principle is also disregarded when alternatives to custody are denied on the basis of the offenders' attitude or personality. For example, consider the case of prisoners who do not show a willingness to participate in the rehabilitative process. In such cases, it is the degree of conformity displayed by offenders which determines the amount of pain they suffer, rather than the severity of their law breaking. But no general law of the state dictates that punishment be geared to the degree of conformity shown by offenders. Alternatives to custody, therefore, also fall short of the principle which claims *nulla poena sine lege*.

The third principle is shattered by the practical way in which alternatives are implemented. When alternative, non-custodial, forms of punishment are granted, these result from favourable, or extolling, reports sent to appointed magistrates by prison governors. So-called scientific behaviour observation is in fact carried out by untrained prison personnel, and their role ends up outweighing the role of the judiciary. This has serious implications. A climate is created whereby individual officers or governors are deemed responsible for the amount of punishment suffered by prisoners. Owing to their pivotal role, prison staff are then put under extreme pressure, and are often exposed to bribes, or even to retaliation.

A brief look at the way in which alternatives are granted may also add to the argument. Research findings show that day release and permission to leave are usually awarded to prisoners with a 'regular' lifestyle. Those who are married, for example, have a higher chance than singles, for they are deemed to be more reliable. They are favoured by virtue of their conformist routine and because it is assumed that they bear responsibility for their dependants (Agazzi et al. 1991). Conversely, young single people find it harder to obtain non-custodial treatment in that their conduct is judged irregular and unpredictable. The consequence is that young first-time offenders may be treated worse than consummate recidivists.

Measures such as day release for work are obviously granted to those who 'invent' a job for themselves outside. Many prisoners find a convenient employer as a result of their network of relatives and friends. Others are helped in this task by agencies and voluntary organizations. But the more marginalized prisoners, for example those belonging to ethnic minorities, are devoid of social networks and, because they are often illegal immigrants, they are also 'invisible' to or uninformed about voluntary organizations and charitable agencies (Bouchard 1993; Mosconi and Pavarini 1994). Therefore, alternatives operate in a two-tier fashion, whereby socially disadvantaged prisoners see their disadvantages perpetuated by the very prison reform which was originally intended to favour them (Olgiati 1991).

This and other discriminatory elements which are incorporated in penal flexibility and discretionary alternatives to custody are the target of the Italian reform movement. Reformists argue that punishment displays a variable content: it is indeterminate, it is based not on legally assessed facts but on discretion (Eusebi 1991). And discretion approaches paternalism or even arbitrariness, especially in a situation where the relationship between citizens and authorities is informed by suspicion, and where therefore, unlike in other traditions, patronising attitudes are unacceptable.

Conclusion

It should be clear by now that changes in the Italian prison population cannot be accounted for by changes in the number of the overall offences committed. A piece of legislation may alone determine dramatic shifts. Similar results may be caused by an erratic demand for punishment. Tolerance and intolerance of legislators, judges and the public may in turn be influenced by the type of offences which are particularly stigmatized at certain periods of time and the social characteristics of those who commit them. Italy seems to offer a clear example of how the prison system needs a succession of alarms and alarming offenders, in other words, of *emergencies*, in order to survive. Without these emergencies, the penal system as a whole would lose part of its symbolic function. These emergencies can be identified with groups of offenders who are the target of specific pieces of legislation or specific judicial and executive policies. For these groups the demand for punishment becomes high at particular historical moments, a circumstance which influences agencies and policies, and which perhaps is simultaneously influenced by them in a typical self-validating prophecy. In Italy, armed robbers, terrorists, drug users and dealers, mafia members, and finally politicians have acted as successive emergencies. I will deal with each separately.

Throughout the 1960s a sense of insecurity was prevalently fostered by armed robbers, who were particularly active in the industrial cities of the north of the country. It was in these regions that inequalities in wealth were most visible, the industrial boom of those years having brought, along with unprecedented wealth, extensive inequality and social injustice (Notarnicola 1975; 1979). Prison became a symbolic monument aimed at tempering public insecurity on the streets. This was not due to the fact that the public itself was the target of armed robbers, who would instead mainly target banks or large businesses. However, the panic fostered by armed robbers resulted in the increased use of custody for offenders other than armed robbers. Table 3.3 shows that between 1961 and 1967, when the social panic regarding armed robberies reached its peak, the overall number of prison sentences dropped significantly. Armed robbery carried a sentence of ten years or more, whereas armed robberies causing the death of a victim carried a life sentence. As we can see, these types of sentences remained stable or declined during the period under investigation, while sentences between one and two years increased. In other words, those who bore the brunt of that specific social panic were minor property offenders.

When in the mid 1970s political prisoners belonging to extra-parliamentary groups of the left started filling Italian prisons, they found a system incapable of differentiating between offenders. It comes as no surprise that disturbances, which were rife in Italian institutions, became explosive after the arrival of highly politicized prisoners. This was the most intense period for prison struggles in Italy; it involved groups active both inside and beyond the prison walls, and included the organization of mass escapes. The number of left political activists held in prison peaked at around 4,000 in the early 1980s (Curcio 1993; Moretti 1994). This figure only partly

Table 3.3   *Prison sentences, 1961–1967*

Year	1–2 year sentence	10 years or more	Life sentence	Total prison sentence	Fine
1961	7,726	342	29	85,352	34,907
1962	7,424	308	24	80,727	33,534
1963	8,176	294	22	61,003	14,364
1964	7,608	378	23	68,264	27,611
1965	7,392	324	21	71,487	30,709
1966	8,848	298	21	66,749	20,993
1967	12,179	334	11	71,129	23,194

Source: Ministero di Grazia e Giustizia 1993

Table 3.4   *Prison sentences, 1978–1983*

Year	3–6 months	1–2 years	2–5 years	5–10 years	10 years or more	Fine
1978	13,055	6,940	3,445	504	246	50,975
1979	16,051	7,987	3,262	553	236	52,671
1980	16,879	9,114	3,787	647	338	68,187
1981	16,558	9,172	3,812	705	334	69,170
1982	17,377	11,824	5,070	881	448	54,859
1983	18,261	10,428	5,595	828	464	61,150

Source: Ministero di Grazia e Giustizia 1993

accounts for the increase in the prison population observed in those years. The period between 1978 and 1983 coincides with the core of so-called 'years of lead', when political armed struggle was wide-spread. In this period the number of prison sentences leapt from 52,048 to 66,515 (this figure does not correspond with the number of prisoners because, as explained above, a number of those sentenced to custody remained on bail while awaiting the three stages of their trial to be completed). Again, the social panic surrounding terrorism raised the rate of imprisonment for others. Table 3.4 indicates that between 1978 and 1983 all sentences increased, including fines.

During the following phase (1980–90), which partly overlaps with the previous one, the emergency was associated with illicit drug use and distribution. I have already mentioned the high percentage of inmates officially defined as drug addicts (about 30 per cent as a national average). It was estimated that 80 per cent of the prison population had committed offences in one way or another related to illicit drugs (De Gennaro 1990; Santino and La

Fiura 1993). These include, on the one hand, drug use itself, small dealing, and property crime to finance use; and on the other hand, larger distribution, trafficking, money laundering, and a number of violent offences committed at the top of the drug economy (Falcone 1991). In the late 1980s drugs also took on a symbolic role in Italian institutions in that the relationship each individual prisoner had with them ultimately determined their status both in prison and, when released, outside. Drugs caused some prisoners to become desperate and ill while others became rich and powerful. Ambitious prisoners who wanted to improve their position in the criminal hierarchy would resort to the drug business as soon as they were released, and with this in mind they would actively seek to establish the right contacts in prison (Ruggiero 1992; Ruggiero and South 1995). Drugs were so central in the prison system that many officers complained about their workload and claimed that they should be helped by outside medical staff. The new prisoners did not merely require restraint but were in need of specialist help which officers could not provide. Such prisoners, some officers argued, needed nurses, social workers and psychologists, a circumstance which diminished their role as custodians or guards. The fact that many drug offenders were devoid of previously acquired criminal skills, and were mainly extraneous to a precisely identifiable criminal subculture, made them all the more enigmatic and difficult for the officers to handle.

The social panic caused by illicit drugs was apparently focused on big traffickers and distributors, a circumstance which legitimized the use of harsh sentences and strict prison regimes. However, given the limited success of the authorities in apprehending these individuals, the renewed increase in custodial sentences was felt most heavily by small dealers and users (Prina 1993; Manna 1993).

The great 'internment' of drug offenders went hand in hand with the fight against the mafia, which was ideally the main target of institutional intervention. This symbolically powerful enemy, and in particular the social panic associated with mafia killings, contributed to the generalized increase in penalties for other less powerful actors. In this respect the statistics on homicide are illuminating. Between 1986 and 1992 homicides including attempted murder rose from 2,000 to more than 3,300 (Ministero di Grazia e Giustizia 1993). At the same time long prison sentences declined: from 465 to 419 for sentences more than 10 years, and from 3 to 0 life sentences. As already mentioned, the most dramatic increase was observed for sentences between 1 and 2 years (from 6,991 to 11,012), that is to say an increase affecting other than offenders charged with murder, let alone with mafia killings.

In the early 1990s, the role of a new emergency was performed by corrupt politicians. The widespread awareness and disgust about political and administrative corruption acted as a mandate offered to the judiciary to restore or boost the centrality and inevitability of imprisonment (Ruggiero 1994). Massimo Pavarini (1994:58) has argued that: 'The magistrates conducting investigations into political corruption have become the latest public idols, great moralizers because they are great judges. A television programme announcing a long interview with some of the judges engaged in investigations into corrupt dealing had audience ratings which exceeded the number of viewers who watched the Madonna concert.' Even the police, traditionally and with some reason viewed with both fear and disrespect, suddenly experienced great popularity. But the consensus gained by institutional agencies in the fight against the new emergency was translating into more punishment for all offenders. It is true, as Pavarini suggested, that for every mafia member sent to gaol, a hundred drug users were incarcerated; and for every corrupt politician punished, a hundred black immigrants were interned. However, this dynamic was not as new as the author seemed to imply. Corrupt politicians and mafia members were very old actors on the Italian scene. What was new was their *emergency status*, that is their being expressions of social alarm located in a chain of previous alarms. It was now their turn to allow the prison system to regain its centrality.

I have tried to describe an intermittent process within which emergencies are vital for the very existence of prisons in Italy. Optimistically, one could argue that the very existence of this process is due to the inherent weaknesses of prisons, their very function being cyclically thrown into doubt. For this reason incarceration as a way of dealing with crime may need an incessant ideological nourishment in the form of new phenomena and individuals who are given the task of re-establishing its necessity. That this process is intermittent was illustrated by other developments in the mid 1990s. The alarm about the soaring prison population affected and mobilized even legislators and cabinet ministers. The customary fear of overcrowding led to a new emergency package which was aimed to remove some 10,000 prisoners. House arrest could now be granted to all of those sentenced to up to 3 years (previously 2 years), semi-detention to those sentenced to up to 1 year (previously 6 months). Fines replaced custody for sentences up to 6 months (previously 3 months). Illegal immigrants sentenced to up to 3 years could receive the alternative penalty of deportation (Corbi 1993). In the mid 1990s Italy may well return to being one of the European countries with the lowest rates of imprisonment . . . pending novel unpredictable emergencies.

References

Agazzi A, Golfetto G and Peron G (1991), 'Discrezionalità nella riforma penitenziaria' *Dei Delitti e delle Pene* I, 2: 153–84

Bouchard M (1993), 'I minori stranieri' *Dei Delitti e delle Pene* 3, 3: 71–88

Campelli E, Faccioli F, Giordano V and Pitch T (1992), *Donne in carcere. Ricerca sulla detenzione femminile in Italia* Milano: Feltrinelli

Canosa R (1991), *Storia della criminalità in Italia 1845–1945* Torino: Einaudi

Castellani R and Di Lazzaro A (1990), *Indagine nazionale sui soggetti tossicodipendenti e affetti da virus HIV detenuti negli istituti penitenziari* Roma: Direzione Generale degli Istituti di Prevenzione e Pena

Censis (1992), *Contro e dentro. Criminalità, Istituzioni, Società* (Centro Studi Investimenti Sociali) Milano: Franco Angeli

Ceretti A and Merzagora I (1994), 'AIDS in Prisons in Italy' in P Thomas and M Moerings (eds) *AIDS in Prison* Aldershot: Dartmouth

Clemmer D (1940), *The Prison Community* New York: Rinehart

Commissione Sanità del Senato (1994), *Indagine sulla situazione sanitaria delle carceri* Roma: Camera del Senato

Corbi M (1993), 'Nuove carceri, più detenuti a casa' *La Stampa* 13 August

Curcio R (1993), *A viso aperto* Milano: Mondadori

Curcio R, Valentino N and Petrelli S (1991), *Nel bosco di bistorco* Roma: Sensibili alle Foglie

De Gennaro G (1990), *La guerra della droga* Milano: Mondadori

Di Lazzaro A (1988), 'Le misure alternative alla detenzione prima e dopo la Gozzini' *Inchiesta* XVIII, 79–80: 27–39

Dipartimento Amministrazione Penitenziaria (1994), *Eurises. Rapporto Italia* Roma: Poligrafico dello Stato

Eusebi L (1991), *La pena 'in crisi'. Il recente dibattito sulla funzione della pena* Brescia: Morcelliana

Faccioli F (1992), 'Le donne in carcere: la composizione sociale, i reati, le pene' in E Campelli, F Faccioli, V Giordano and T Pitch (eds) *Donne in carcere* Milano: Feltrinelli

Falcone G (1991), *Cose di cosa nostra* Milano: Mondadori

Ferazzi S and Ronconi S (1993), 'Il virus in carcere tra allarme e negazione' *Dei Delitti e delle Pene* 3, 3: 133–48

Ferrajoli L (1989), *Diritto e ragione. Teoria del garantismo penale* Roma–Bari: Laterza

Gallo E and Ruggiero V (1989), *Il carcere immateriale* Torino–Milano: Sonda

Gallo E and Ruggiero V (1991), 'The Immaterial Prison: Custody as a Factory for the Manufacture of Handicaps' *The International Journal of the Sociology of Law* 19, 3: 273–91

Gallo E and Ruggiero V (1992), 'Medicina penitenziaria e malattie da carcere' *Dei Delitti e delle Pene* II, 2: 173–8

Giordano V (ed) (1990), *Luoghi del tempo* Roma: Officina Edizioni

Gonin D (1991), *La santé incarcérée. Médecine et conditions de vie en détention* Paris: L'Archipel

ISTAT (1991), *Statistiche Giudiziarie* (Istituto Nazionale di Statistica) Roma: Poligrafico dello Stato

ISTAT (1992), *Bollettino mensile di statistica* (Istituto Nazionale di Statistica) 67, 12, Roma: Poligrafico dello Stato

Lepri G (1993), 'La struttura del mercato dell'eroina: valutazione degli effetti delle politiche repressive' in S Zamagni (ed) *Mercati illegali e mafie. L'economia del crimine organizzato* Bologna: Il Mulino

Magliona B and Sarzotti C (1993), 'Carcere e AIDS: le ragioni di un rapporto difficile' *Dei Delitti e delle Pene* 3, 3: 99–132

Manna A (1993), 'Gli effetti del referendum abrogativo sulla legislazione in materia di stupefacenti' *Dei Delitti e delle Pene* III, 2: 41–56

Ministero di Grazia e Giustizia (1976), *Deterioramento mentale da detenzione* Roma: Poligrafico dello Stato

Ministero di Grazia e Giustizia (1993), *Libro bianco. I dati essenziali del sistema penitenziario italiano in cifre* Roma: Dipartimento dell'Amministrazione Penitenziaria

Moretti M (1994), *Brigate Rosse: una storia italiana* Milano: Anabasi

Mosconi G (1982), *L'altro carcere* Padova: CLEUP

Mosconi G (1988), 'La trasformazione della pena nello spazio della cultura diffusa' *Inchiesta* XVIII, 79–80: 1–12

Mosconi G and Pavarini M (eds) (1994), *Flessibilità della pena in fase esecutiva e potere discrezionale* Roma: Centro Studi e Iniziative per la Riforma dello Stato

Notarnicola S (1975), *L'evasione impossibile* Milano: Feltrinelli

Notarnicola S (1979), *Con quest'anima inquieta* Torino: Senza Galere

Olgiati (1991), 'La criminalità dei minori extracomunitari' *Sociologia del Diritto* XVIII, 1: 143–64

Padovani T (1990), *Diritto penale* Milano: Giuffré

Panizzari G (ed) (1991), *Pratica non psichiatrica, antiproibizionismo, antisegregazione, antirazzismo* Roma: Lega per L'Ambiente

Pavarini M (1988), 'Misure alternative al carcere e decarcerizzazione: un rapporto problematico' *Inchiesta* XVIII, 79–80: 49–53

Pavarini M (1994), 'The New Penology and Politics in Crisis: The Italian Case' *British Journal of Criminology* 34, Special Issue: 49–61

Pepino L (1991), *Droga e legge. Tossicodipendenza, prevenzione e repressione* Milano: Franco Angeli

Piperno A (1989), 'La prisonizzazione: teoria e ricerca' in F Ferracuti (ed) *Carcere e trattamento* Milano: Giuffré

Piroch W, Miekle M R, d'Ottavi A M and Luchini D (1992), *Detenuti stranieri in Italia* Milano: Franco Angeli

Prina F (1993), 'Dalla repressione alla riduzione del danno' *Dei Delitti e delle Pene* 3, 2: 7–40

Ruggiero V (1991), 'Decarcerizzazione e ricarcerizzazione' *Dei Delitti e delle Pene* Nuova Serie, I, 1: 127–42

Ruggiero V (1992), *La roba. Economie e culture dell'eroina* Parma: Pratiche Editrice

Ruggiero V (1994), 'Corruption in Italy: An Attempt to Identify the Victims' *The Howard Journal of Criminal Justice* 33, 4: 319–37

Ruggiero V and South N (1995), *Eurodrugs: Drug Use, Markets and Trafficking in Europe* London: University College London Press

Santino U and La Fiura G (1993), *Dietro la droga* Torino: Gruppo Abele

Solivetti L (1994), 'Drug Diffusion and Social Change: The Illusion about a Formal Social Control' *The Howard Journal of Criminal Justice* 33, 1: 41–61

Sykes G (1958), *The Society of Captives* Princeton: Princeton University Press

Vass A (1990), *Alternatives to Prison: Punishment, Custody and the Community* London: Sage

Wilkins L (1991), *Punishment, Crime and Market Forces* Aldershot: Dartmouth

Zuffa G (1994), 'Medicina penitenziaria: Ippocrate o ipocrita?' *Narcomafie* II, 2: 4–7

4

The Penal System in France: from Correctionalism to Managerialism

Ermanno Gallo

French penal history can (and has) been divided into broad epochs (O'Brien 1982). However, such epochs are rarely watertight and practices which exist in one epoch are often carried forward into the next. For example, the introduction of the 1871 Penal Code after the Revolution protected the prisoner's body by a number of rights. The prison of the Enlightenment, from which the modern prison system derives, designated custody as the core of punishment, and discarded violence as a barbaric heritage of the past. Taking people's freedom was deemed a sufficient form of penalty. The era of suffering seemed to have come to an end. However, owing to structural and architectural deficiencies on the one hand, and the customary compromise between utopian projects and realistic need on the other, the Republican prison was unable to abandon its previous afflictive philosophy. For example, the death penalty, although rendered more humane by the painless and fast operating guillotine, was destined to remain in place until 1981. Furthermore, custody was accompanied by supplementary penalties such as forced labour, solitary confinement and the chain (Léauté 1968).

Alongside continuity, there also exists the problem of contradiction. For example, French penal history has been divided throughout its various epochs between a secular, 'neutral' model born with the Enlightenment, and a religious, confessional model aimed at the redemption of offenders. The prison system has never come to terms with this, its own double nature (Perrot 1980). How can redemption and utilitarianism be reconciled? How can the productive exploitation of offenders inside the prison (and formerly in penal colonies) co-exist with moral purification? Similar though not always strictly identical continuities and contradictions can be observed in the sketch of penal policy in the current century to which we now turn. This brief history will be followed by an overview of the operation of the French penal system as it currently exists before the chapter turns to a more interpretative account of current trends.

Hiding the punished

The most important innovation introduced before World War II was the abolition of transportation and the *bagne pénale* (Petit 1991). In 1938 the use of the penal colony in Guiana was abolished. Punishment was soon to be exclusively located in urban settings, in purpose-built institutions called *maisons de force*. According to Foucault (1977:10) it was the disappearance of public executions, a century earlier, which 'mark[ed] . . . the decline of the spectacle; but it also mark[ed] a slackening of the hold on the body'. However, it could be argued that it was only with the end of transportation that the punished and the paraphernalia of punishment became hidden from public view definitively. 'It is surprising that Foucault said almost nothing on the *bagnes pénales* and their suppression' (Léonard 1980:12). Chains, shackles, balls and shaved heads were finally hidden: in this way prisons seemed to protect prisoners from the anger of the outside society. In reality, they protected themselves and their practices from public scrutiny. Prison administrations became the exclusive guardians of the prisoners' body, which was definitively hidden behind the opacity of the institution.

The moral prison

While the prison estate in France continued to deteriorate and neo-classicists sustained a high profile in public debates, securing some notable victories including the introduction of capital punishment for certain forms of armed robbery, the penal system during the Fourth Republic (1946–56) reaffirmed its commitment to the transformation of prisoners through punishment. This rested on two main notions: moral correction and social rehabilitation (Faugeron 1991). The classification of prisoners was based upon their progression along the rehabilitative continuum. Treatment was structured on a model of 'systematic progression', whereby prisoners went through different stages from strict seclusion to increasingly open regimes, until a pre-release stage, and finally freedom. The model inspiring this type of progression was not so much the hospital as the convent. Prison did not provide a superficial body therapy, but rather favoured a process leading to interior healing. Treatment hinged on work, which was intended to bring redemption. Prison therefore performed a moral role, a role which was not relinquished even in the face of recidivists. No prisoner was regarded as irredeemable, and the possibility of social rehabilitation was seen as realistic even for the most consummate offenders. Legal reforms reflecting this optimism led to more support for early release or suspended sentences, and an enhanced supervisory role for external judges over prison regimes (Wright 1983).

The moral prison was deemed particularly suitable for women, because 'they benefit more from isolation and work more effectively in silence and solitude' (Pierre 1991:274). Therefore, the first stages of prison treatment, based on strict seclusion, were regarded as ideal for the treatment of women, whose 'stronger religious sentiments help them endure the loneliness of the cell'. On the other hand, the successive stages of treatment, which entailed increasingly open regimes, were seen as more volatile for women, because 'the communities of women pose more problems than those of men' (Pierre 1991:274–5).

Despite the critique one could level at the moral prison, important changes in the very philosophy of punishment were encouraged. The moral prison, at least, adopted a sense of mission, with many institutions resembling schools, and teachers, instructors and 'moral' tutors making an entry onto the scene (Lesage de la Haye 1992). This assertion of therapy provided the context within which morality through labour could be enforced. However, the contradiction inherent in the moral prison was the impossibility of reconciling the necessities of production with the systematic progression of inmates. In other words, prison, with its differentiated disciplinary stages, was too volatile an institution to guarantee the stability required by industry (Petit 1990). The rigidity of work and the mobility of prisoners through the stages of treatment were mutually exclusive. The experimental thrust of the moral prison was destined to fade away, in that its morality depended too rigidly on work. But the experiment, it has to be said, ran into difficulties with the onset of the Algerian War in the late 1950s and early 1960s, when the number of prisoners increased dramatically.

Prisons like hotels

While traits of rehabilitation – as we shall see – remained in place during the 1960s, the dominant penal theme, fostered by fears of public insecurity around the Algerian War and a series of sensational escapes, became security. De Gaulle is said to have snapped: 'In this country people get out of prison like they would of a hotel.' The obsession with security produced the identification of a new category of prisoners, namely *détenus particulierment signalés*. The regime imposed on these particularly difficult prisoners provided the blueprint for what were eventually to become high security prison institutions (*quartiers de haute sécurité*). It must be added that the classification of prisoners, based on their dangerousness or their likelihood to escape, was undertaken not by the judiciary or even the prison administration, but by the police. Traditionally, and constitutionally, the preserve of the Ministry of Justice, prison treatment therefore became one among other 'law and order' issues during the decade. The definition of dangerousness was applied to professional criminals or those prisoners who challenged the prison regime. The type of graded treatment prevalent in the 1960s, though formally still available, turned into differentiated treatment, whereby prisoners were classified on the grounds of their attitude towards the institution (Gallo and Ruggiero 1983).

Despite these elements of counter-reformation, the prison system still maintained its reformist traditions. Indeed, reform came to be identified with sheer innovation, usually of a technological type. The 'reform' *par excellence* was physically epitomized by a new prison building, whose architecture and functioning were deemed revolutionary. This was the prison at Fleury-Mérogis, completed in 1974, a new 'monster penitentiary' which, like La Santé in an earlier epoch, became the symbol of modernization. Containing 4,500 ventilated and modern cells and electronic surveillance systems, this immense technological prison was officially intended to replace the decaying institutions of the Parisian region. But the official intention proved optimistic or deliberately misleading: prisons fear empty spaces. As soon as it was completed, Fleury-Mérogis was already overcrowded, and as a consequence prisoners were incessantly diverted to the old Fresnes and La Santé, which therefore proved irreplaceable. Modernization also implied the recruitment of qualified, skilled personnel, whose efficiency was expected to ideally mirror the managerial spirit of the new institution. It was during this period that the 'managerial prison' began to emerge, although it was only during the 1990s that this form of punishment finally came to fruition.

On the other hand, it was during the 1970s that groups of doctors and psychologists started discussing the health of prisoners and began to claim their autonomy from prison administrations. Teachers and social workers also engaged with this 'movement of independence': modernization, in other words, caused the explosion of new contradictions. Disturbances occurred throughout the 1970s, and the need for links with the outside world, which these disturbances implicitly invoked, was met with widespread support.

Michel Foucault and Vidal-Naquet contributed to the creation of the Groupe d'Information sur la Prison (GIP), which was followed by the Groupe Multi-Professionnel des Prisons (GMP) and other organizations campaigning for the rights of prisoners.

In 1974, the prison system as a whole and the philosophy which inspired it seemed on the verge of collapse. Many institutions were destroyed in an outbreak of disturbances between July and August. In two months the police were mobilized 80 times to suppress as many disturbances. President Giscard d'Estaing agreed to meet a group of prisoners from Lyon, one of the most turbulent institutions, and this meeting marked a temporary truce. The French authorities pledged that new prison regulations would be introduced to conform to the standards suggested by the Council of Europe.

The second half of the 1970s was characterized by a new period of reform. More alternatives to custody were introduced, and wider supervisory powers were given to the judiciary on issues such as prison treatment and rehabilitation. Family visits became more open, and a general climate of 'permissiveness' was felt both inside the institutions and with regard to contacts with the outside (Gonin 1991). Pressure groups slogans such as 'prison and society: the same fight' emphasized the common links between the struggle for penal reform and societal change.

Sécurité et liberté

By 1980 this radical rhetoric was paralleled (and contested) by the consequences of recommendations contained in the report of the Peyrefitte Commission. Translated under the slogan *sécurité et liberté*, the report facilitated the introduction of a series of measures intended to reduce prisoners' rights, restrict the use of alternatives to custody and curtail the powers of supervising magistrates to intervene on behalf of prisoners. Furthermore, the population in custody, which grew substantially, experienced a new model of imprisonment which was defined as *la prison de l'insécurité* (Pauchet 1982). This definition conveyed the notion that it was less an increase in crime than a growing feeling of insecurity which determined the growth of the prison population (Gallo and Ruggiero 1984). This was confirmed by closer analysis of the social composition of those serving prison sentences. In particular, there was a growth in the percentage of foreign prisoners without work permits. This group had previously been tolerated. However, in the light of the new legislation they were regarded as a source of insecurity owing to their potential criminality, or because of their presence in the labour market where they were seen as competing for jobs with the indigenous population.

The resistible ascent of prevention

The legislation known as *sécurité et liberté* was partly repealed soon after François Mitterrand was elected president of the French Republic in 1981. Under a new Minister of Justice, capital punishment was abolished, the prison population was reduced from 42,000 to 30,000 within three months, and alternatives to custody were encouraged and redefined including the introduction of a new day fine system (Wright 1983). Also high on the agenda was the concept of 'prevention'. In 1983, amid a process of decentralization, local authorities and communities were entrusted with issues of prevention and resocialization. Judges presiding over the treatment of prisoners (*juges d'application des peines*, JAP) were required to seek advice from local probation boards, voluntary organizations, and representatives of the community. This permanent joint exercise was expected to devise preventive policies aimed both at recidivists and at individuals at risk in general. Prevention, in other words, came to be seen as a collective issue requiring the concern and commitment of all.

The new policies, promoted by the Socialist government, heralded an important shift from the past. In the 1960s, prevention policies were established at the national level, and little consideration was given to the local contexts in which they were eventually implemented. It comes as no surprise that they proved ineffective: their vagueness and lack of focus caused enormous difficulties for locally based agencies, let alone those on the receiving end of these policies. In those years, prevention sounded like a statement of principle, an idealistic proposition to which all 'open minded' officials felt they had to pay lip service. Preventive policies were therefore devoid of precise reference to the communities in which they were expected to operate. Instead, with the new government, specific practices were identified and roles apportioned within the local communities and their municipal or district representatives. Within these local contexts, an initial phase of consultation was expected to deliver a 'security diagnosis'. This preliminary joint exercise had the purpose of assessing the needs and problems of specific areas (de Liège 1988). The local consultative structures were then asked to propose policies and discuss them with national representatives. This consultation resulted in 'contracts' binding central government politically and financially. The local police were also required to participate or even guide the different stages of this exercise. The majority of the disadvantaged areas and districts within France signed such 'contracts' between 1984 and 1993.

Some of these projects could be regarded as part of the general welfare provision. 'On closer inspection, the French projects tend to be close to "secondary" crime prevention, that is focused on groups or situations that are pre-delinquent' (de Liège 1991:131). However, an important underlying principle was that local communities 'if strong and healthy, are ... able to bring into their fold those marginal groups and individuals who hitherto have been excluded from the mainstream of French society' (King 1991:92). The marginal groups addressed by intervention were disaffected youth, immigrants and the unemployed (Bonnemaison 1983; Dubet 1987; Delatte and Dolé 1987).

Under the new regulations, probation boards were required to work in the field of both individual and general prevention. This may have had an effect on the official crime rate. The Socialist Party claimed that in some local areas, in particular larger cities, the new preventive policies had produced a 20 per cent decline in recorded offences between 1983 and 1986 (Parti Socialiste Français 1986; Bonnemaison 1991). Other studies suggest that the decline observed was 2.78 per cent in 1985, 8.02 per cent in 1986, 3.68 in 1987, and 1.21 in 1988 (de Liège 1991). At the same time the number of those for whom probation officers were responsible increased by 10 per cent, while the number of ex-prisoners with special needs for whom they were also responsible increased by almost 20 per cent.

In 1986, however, after the political right won a majority at the national election, the prevention programmes so tentatively set into motion were strongly reduced. Security again became the key concept inspiring penal policies. Amendments to the penal code led to heavier statutory sentences, while new regulations reduced both the room for manoeuvre for 'lenient' judges and the impact of agencies involved in non-custodial initiatives. Under Chalandon, the Minister for Justice, there was a constant increase in the prison population which was highlighted by a number of international organizations. In overt defiance of the recommendations of these organizations, Chalandon did not attempt to reduce the use of pre-trial detention, nor did he expand the scope of non-custodial alternatives. Instead, he relied on the most ambitious and, in his view, pragmatic programme to fight crime: the building of new prisons and the expansion of their total capacity to 70,000 places. This programme was aimed at decongesting the unmanageable urban institutions. But the main thrust behind the programme was the idea of making the management of prisons as independent as possible. Prisons had to become self-sufficient microcosms, capable of reproducing themselves by virtue of their own internal work and administrative efficiency (ARAPEJ 1994). Like other productive organizations, they were expected to develop a corporate spirit, with prisoners contributing to productivity and management. It is within this philosophy that the process of privatization took place. This more recent development in the penal system will be described later in this chapter. The following section deals with the French penal system as it was in the early 1990s.

An anatomy of the penal system

The French Penal Code distinguishes between three main types of offence. This distinction is based on the seriousness of the offence, the way in which it is punished, and the corresponding agency responsible for punishment. Minor offences are dealt with by the police and receive 'police penalties'. More serious crimes are punished with 'correctional penalties', which are built on the official philosophy of rehabilitation. When receiving these types of penalties, offenders are still deemed 'corrigible'. Finally, particularly serious offences are punished with what the Penal Code defines as 'afflictive and infamous punishment'. This somewhat medieval definition alludes to the notion that some offenders are 'incorrigible' and must be dealt with purely by retribution. This tripartition corresponds to the division between petty, medium and serious criminality which is normally referred to in both judicial and lay jargon (Camillieri and Lazerges 1992).

Severity also determines which of the existing tribunals and courts will be designated to deal with offences. Some courts have the specific task of encouraging 'reconciliation' between parties. Police tribunals are entitled to impose fines and also prison sentences up to one month (two months for recidivists) (Pinsseau 1985). These tribunals mainly deal with traffic offences. In 1987 97,620 such offences (that is 20.3 per cent of all reported offences) were dealt with by police tribunals (Camillieri and Lazerges 1992). In general, at the police tribunal courts, 'fines are the rule and short-term imprisonment the exception' (Pease and Hukkila 1990).

Other courts only deal with summary trials, whereas 'correctional courts' deal with offences bringing a prison sentence of more than two months or a fine of more than 6,000 Ffrancs. The courts of appeal re-examine cases already dealt with by correctional courts, while *chambres d'accusation* rule on issues such as extradition, amnesty, and rehabilitation of offenders. The Court of Cassation can suspend the validity of decisions taken by the other courts and tribunals, although it cannot overrule them. Its role consists of ensuring that court proceedings adhere to the existing legislation. Finally, the Supreme Court plays a unifying and legitimizing role with respect to the current legislation, as it can quash decisions taken by other courts and demand that new proceedings be initiated.

This is a simplified version of the labyrinth through which defendants may be forced to travel. This labyrinth can only be avoided, and alternative punishments invoked, if the offences dealt with carry a prison sentence of less than a year. But before even entering the labyrinth, suspects may be stopped and held by the police for up to 48 hours, or for 10 days when it is alleged that 'crimes against the state' have been committed. Along with the police, investigative judges can also request that suspects be held in police custody pending a preliminary investigation. Police cells, it should be noted, do not fall under the supervision of the prison administration, and usually abuses committed in them go undetected. Police practices were heavily criticized by an Amnesty International report issued in 1994. The report selected 11 cases in the previous 18 months to illustrate a claim of reckless and illegal use of force. Amnesty said the victims were often juveniles and many were of non-European origin.

The state of French prisons

The French Prison Department became part of the Ministry of Justice in 1911. It consists of a central office located in Paris and a number of decentralized units in the different provinces (Léauté 1968). The Prison Department is one of the five sections which compose the Ministry of Justice, and is accountable to the head of this ministry: the Guardeseaux. The Department deals with remand and convicted adult prisoners, offenders who are given a suspended sentence and probationers. The treatment of young offenders is determined by another section of the Ministry of Justice, and is known as the Office d'Education Surveillée. Within the Prison Department there is an Inspectorate which is responsible for the administrative and technical services provided to all penal institutions. Until the mid 1980s the Inspectorate also used to provide health care in prison, but at that time such provision became part of the prerogatives of the Health Inspectorate, an organ of the Ministry of Health.

There are three types of prison institution: *maisons centrales, maisons d'arrêt et de correction,* and *centres pour rélégués.* The responsibility for running all these institutions lies with individual governors, who are advised by control commissions chaired by local prefects or vice-prefects. The first type of institution holds prisoners sentenced to more than a year. According to the standing legislation, their regime should be inspired by the Auburn model, which implies individual night confinement. But not all the *maisons centrales* are endowed with single cells, and those which are may resort to double occupation due to overcrowding. The second type of institution holds both remand prisoners and prisoners sentenced to up to a year. The third type functions as an institution for the observation of prisoners' conduct. These institutions hold sentenced prisoners whose behaviour is monitored with a view to releasing them before their sentence expires.

Throughout the 1960s and the 1970s, overcrowding was a constant feature of the French prison system. This was particularly acute in the Paris region, with the prison of Fresnes holding two and a half times as many individuals as the maximum officially stated number of places, and La Santé more than three times that number. In the same period, almost 40 per cent of the prisons were devoid of any form of heating, and 50 per cent of proper sanitation in individual cells. More than 60 per cent of the prisoners did not undertake any activity, with between 30 per cent and 40 per cent engaging in what were described as 'immoral acts' (Delteil 1986; Favard 1990).

The prison population increased into the 1980s. By the end of the decade it had reached almost 50,000. In the early months of 1993 there were 50,352 prisoners (Administration Pénitentiaire 1993) and by January 1994 the population had grown to 52,550 (Observatoire International des Prisons 1994). This meant that one person in 1,000 was incarcerated, although as we note below the rate of incarceration was not spread evenly throughout the French population. This increase reinforced the problem of overcrowding. In 1993 the average 'occupation rate' of prison cells was 113 per cent, but in Lyon the rate was 212 per cent, and in Cayenne (Guiana) it was a record 441 per cent (Observatoire International des Prisons 1994).

Sentencing

The increase in the prison population is largely the result of longer sentences imposed. Throughout the 1980s, despite the preventive rather than retributive philosophy officially put forward by the Socialist government, life sentences increased by 19 per cent, sentences of more than 10 years increased by 50 per cent, and sentences between 5 and 10 years increased by 120 per cent. Moreover, sentences between 3 and 5 years grew by 70 per cent, and those between 1 and 5 years by 45 per cent (Tournier 1992a). At the same time, as in other countries, a process of bifurcation took place whereby the number of offenders serving a custodial sentence for less serious crimes dropped by 40 per cent. It should be borne in mind that custodial sentences below 3 months form about 60 per cent of annual custodial sentences, but account for only 12 per cent of the daily average prison population. This suggests that the increase in the prison population in general is caused by a larger number of long sentences inflicted. The average length of prison sentences grew from 5.1 months in the mid 1980s to 7.3 months in 1994 (Administration Pénitentiaire 1994).

The following are the most relevant data concerning offences committed by sentenced prisoners. In January 1994 theft was the cause of imprisonment for 30.3 per cent of prisoners, followed by drug offences (21.3 per cent), sexual offences (11.7 per cent), murder (10.3 per cent), violation of the immigration law (5.6 per cent), violence against the person (4.9 per cent) and fraud (2.5 per cent) (Administration Pénitentiaire 1994).

The changes in sentencing are also reflected in changes in the composition of the prison population, and it is to this development that we now wish to turn.

Composition of the prison population

Information regarding the social origin of prisoners can be gathered from official data indicating the prisoners' levels of education. In January 1994 12.6 per cent of prisoners were illiterate, 58.4 per cent held a primary school certificate, and 29 per cent held a secondary school certificate (Administration Pénitentiaire 1994).

Women in prison
In 1960, out of a total of 26,794 prisoners, there were 1,034 women prisoners. In 1994, out of 52,550, women accounted for 2,204. The proportion remained therefore virtually unchanged, with around 4 per cent of the prison population being female (Observatoire International des Prisons 1994). Prison treatment for women varies according to the institution, with regimes being more severely differentiated than for men. Serious women offenders experience extremely harsh treatment, their serious offending being perhaps regarded as more monstrous than that of their male counterparts. Women, in other words, are only expected to commit offences such as shoplifting and prostitution. Those who engage in other activities are held in institutions such as Fleury-Mérogis. Here, when allowed

out of their cells, they exercise in yards as big as their cells. These yards resemble metal cages, with thick grilles positioned as security ceilings. The cells themselves have varnished windows which stop light filtering through.

In France, 200 pregnant women are imprisoned each year, and children born behind bars are allowed to remain with their mothers for a maximum of 18 months. Work for women prisoners is rarely available, and when it is it consists of menial tasks such as washing and scrubbing. The ideology behind this is that women's rehabilitation is achieved not through integration in the labour market, but through the imposition of housework.

In 1994 about 11 per cent of women prisoners had AIDS, a circumstance which indicated their prevailing patterns of offending: drug use and prostitution (Observatoire International des Prisons 1994). The percentage referred to the total prison population (including both men and women) was around 5 per cent (Seyler 1993; Magliona and Sarzotti 1993). Many prostitutes are brought to France by international organizations involved in a type of contemporary slave trade (Camillieri and Lazerges 1992). However, changes in the composition of women prisoners may be under way, as the number of female immigrants and refugees is increasing. In March 1992, for example, the percentage of imprisoned foreign women (more than 27 per cent) was close to that of men (31 per cent) (Tournier 1992a).

Foreigners and sans-papiers

The most significant shift in the composition of prisoners regards the percentage of non-French born: 31 per cent of the total prison population in 1993 as compared to 18 per cent in 1975 (Administration Pénitentiaire 1994). This phenomenal increase is due less to the prevalence of conventional offenders among foreigners than to the stricter regulations introduced in France as regards work permits and permits to stay (Wieviorka 1994). These administrative offenders, also called *sans-papiers*, constitute almost 30 per cent of non-national prisoners. Others are charged with drug offences, either as users or as small dealers. In June 1993, increased powers were accorded to law enforcement agencies for carrying out identity checks (de Brie 1993). According to Tomasevski (1994:41) these changes in legislation encouraged 'targeting people with "foreign physiognomy", the multiplication of grounds for expelling foreigners', and limited their possibility of appealing against expulsion orders. 'A large number of foreigners already residing in France thus find themselves in the position of having become offenders, subject to detention pending expulsion' (1994:41).

In May 1992 a number of Kurdish asylum seekers started a hunger strike to protest against the rejection of their applications for asylum (*Migration News* 1992). They 'were placed in detention, and it was reported that the government decided to arrest and detain such hunger strikers in the future' (Tomasevski 1994:24). There are 13 institutions holding individuals awaiting deportation orders. In 1994, without counting those detained in police cells, 12,180 non-nationals were held in such institutions. The treatment of these prisoners was recently made public. In Toulouse and Lille, they are not allowed out of their cells at all. Similar inhuman treatment was denounced in Lyon, Bordeaux, Marseille, Nantes and Sète. In the cellars of the Palais de Justice in Paris, an appalling dungeon was discovered: 13 foreigners awaiting deportation were packed into 10 square metres (*Rebelles* 7–14 January 1994). A final episode exemplifies the situation for foreign nationals. In January 1994, an illegal immigrant from Gabon, who was detained in Bois d'Arcy, was found dead of starvation in his cell. His weight was 30 kilograms, because being a vegetarian he refused the prison food. The local social services had been informed, and a doctor called, but no institution took responsibility for the prisoner's welfare (*Rebelles* 14–21 March 1994).

Remand prisoners

In 1994 data published by the Observatoire International des Prisons (1994) put France in fourth place with respect to the rate of imprisonment, but in first place with respect to the percentage of remand prisoners. Since the early 1970s this percentage has increased constantly, although the number of arrests and prosecutions has remained virtually unchanged. The 'fight against drug abuse' and, as we have seen above, the stricter control of immigrants, political refugees and other 'irregulars' seem to have caused this increase (Tournier 1992b). These vulnerable prisoners are detained either because they are homeless or because in the eyes of the prosecutors they are likely to go into hiding. Therefore being remanded in custody replaces bail and other non-custodial alternatives. In sum, these vulnerable subjects are not punished for their acts but for their social status and vulnerability (Bonnemaison 1991; Cassese 1994).

Prisoners on licence and in hostels

The following are measures which can only be granted to prisoners who have gone through the different stages of the judicial proceedings, and for whom no appeal is therefore pending. 'Permission to leave' or licences for brief periods of time are usually given to 'deserving' prisoners, who are thus given the opportunity to keep their family contacts. In 1992, the number of licences given amounted to 33,564, a drop of about 5 per cent on 1991. The number of prisoners who were given a licence was 14,225. The number of prisoners on licence who failed to return to prison was 238, that is 0.7 per cent. 'Semi-liberty' also dropped by about 2 per cent between 1991 and 1992, when 5,891 benefited from this measure. Semi-liberty consists of day release for work (in 77 per cent of cases), education (19 per cent), and for other reasons including financial support for the family (Administration Pénitentiaire 1993).

Placement a l'extérieur gives convicted offenders the option of being held in hostels or other institutions other than prisons. In 1992, 2,968 enjoyed this alternative to custody, although almost half of them eventually returned to prison because their placement was deemed inadequate. This alternative is only given to individuals sentenced to less than 6 months.

Alternatives to custody

In 1975 the notion of *peines de substitution* was introduced. Further legislation passed in 1983 potentially expanded the possibility of delivering alternative punishments such as fines, probation orders and mediation schemes. However, if we examine the prevalence of imprisonment in relation to other punishments available, this type of punishment has maintained a central role over the last 150 years. In other words, with the absolute decline in the number of people processed through the criminal justice system, imprisonment also declined in absolute terms, but the relative use of this form of punishment remained stable (Faugeron and Houchon 1985; Jouys 1990; Cantat 1991; Faugeron 1992). Critics suggest that alternatives to custody (including suspended sentences and probation) did not replace custody but rather replaced the fine as a mechanism of punishment for those unable to pay (Cantat 1992). It was also noted that all *peines de substitution* are only rarely utilized as penalties in their own right, but rather are inflicted as supplements to other penalties. In other words, they do not initiate a process of decarceration. But let us briefly describe the alternatives to custody available in France.

Work of general interest (*travail d'intérêt général*, TIG) consists of a non-custodial alternative which could be likened to a form of community service. Established in 1983, this measure allows the offender to carry out between 40 and 240 hours of work. It can apply as the only punishment for those who have not been sentenced to more than 4 months during the previous 5 years, but can also apply as a supplementary measure to a custodial sentence. In 1987, the application of the TIG was extended to most traffic offences to replace sentences up to 6 months (Dezalay 1988; Cantat 1991). An example of TIG regards a case in 1994 where a painter who was found guilty of drinking and driving was ordered to produce a painting to be used in the campaign against such behaviour. In January 1993 (the tenth anniversary of the introduction of this alternative), there were 12,996 individuals serving a TIG order, a 15.2 per cent increase on the preceding year (Administration Pénitentiaire 1994).

Although the French authorities are very proud of this alternative provision, two points should be reiterated. First, offenders who are granted TIG are mainly car offenders who would never have been punished before. Second, the TIG has replaced other non-custodial provisions such as minor fines. In this sense, one might say that the TIG is an alternative to already existing alternatives.

Another alternative punishment is the 'day fine' and consists of varying instalments up to 360 days. The rate of this fine cannot exceed 2,000 Ffrancs per day and is calculated on the basis of the daily earnings of offenders. Failure to pay results in imprisonment for a period which is half the duration of the day fine received. This alternative punishment can be combined with suspended sentences and with probation.

Conditional discharge can be granted to offenders who display 'social readjustment' (Administration Pénitentiaire 1993). The decision regarding conditional discharge must be ratified by the Ministry of Justice or the judge supervising the prison regime of the specific institution in which the offender is held. In 1992, among those sentenced to less than 3 years, 34,373 prisoners were granted conditional discharge (Administration Pénitentiaire 1993). About 10 per cent of them experienced a period of probation, with permission to leave prison during the day, before being given this non-custodial alternative. The condition for others was to undertake vocational courses or medical therapy. The composition of prisoners given conditional discharge was as follows: 42 per cent had committed property offences, 17 per cent violent offences and 19 per cent drug offences, and 4 per cent had been convicted of murder or serious violence against the person. Again in 1992, among the prisoners serving sentences longer than 3 years only about 900 were given conditional discharge, a decline of about 10 per cent on the previous year. Almost 50 per cent of these prisoners had been convicted of murder, 24 per cent of theft or immoral earnings, and approximately 10 per cent of rape.

It must be added that conditional discharge is usually granted when prisoners have served more than half their sentence. Moreover, when this non-custodial measure is given to those sentenced to more than 3 years, it implies obligations such as undertaking psychiatric treatment, compensating the victim, observing a night curfew, and a prohibition on attending certain places or meeting with certain people, usually associates in the commission of previous offences. As already mentioned, decisions regarding the application of conditional discharge are made by judges (*juges d'application des peines*) who preside over the treatment of prisoners. In this task, they are assisted by 'boards' formed by probation officers and social workers who are allocated individual cases and are required to assess the suitability of prisoners for this alternative punishment. For example, the members of these boards are required to describe the environment in which those released will be living, their family situation, and their occupational condition.

In the application of all alternatives to custody, the role of probation boards is central. These boards are appointed by local judges and are formed nationally by 2,312 people. In 1993, they had to deal with 94,933 cases. This situation was denounced by probation officers and social workers both in terms of the heavy workload involved and more generally in relation to rising unemployment which made it impossible for offenders and ex-offenders to compete with 'clean' people on the labour market. In other words, social workers and probation officers expressed their doubts as to the very viability of their mandate: that of helping ex-offenders start a real process of resocialization. On the other hand, their denunciation also targeted employers, who were said to be unwilling to give those with a criminal record a chance (*Le Monde* 27 November 1993).

Victim support

The old Napoleonic Code stipulated the creation of a monetary reserve fund to be constituted with the work and wages of prisoners. This fund was intended to serve as a non-specified compensation fund. However, it was only in 1982 that a fraction of this fund was actually used for the support of crime victims (Akermann and Dulong 1984). In 1986, compensation was extended to rape victims and victims of other violent offences. Victims of fraud or terrorism can also apply for compensation. In addition, there are local *maisons de justice* which offer support and counselling to victims and help them through the compensation procedure. These 'houses of justice' are also expected to counsel and support offenders on bail, and in a sense are places where the ideal encounter between offenders and victims could take place. However, their role as places of mediation has never been fully developed (AIV 1986; Bonafé-Schmitt et al. 1986).

Within the victim support movement, forms of mediation are also advocated. Experiments conducted in the Paris region in 1984 showed that mediation had been successful for a high proportion of cases in which it had been attempted (46 out of 55). The cases dealt with involved property offences, vandalism, and minor violent offences (Trioux 1985). However, these experiments were not continued both because of the state's unwillingness to fund them and for the official rejection of 'the concept of reaffirming people's power to manage their own conflicts' (Bonafé-Schmitt 1989).

Towards the managerial prison

Our earlier sketch of post-war penal history is a testimony to our starting point that penal change is subject to elements of continuity and contradiction. But what of the future? To be sure, prison labour and prison security will continue to have a high profile, but perhaps the technological and the managerial private prisons of the future will prove even more aseptic and dehumanizing than those of the past.

The 'Programme 13,000', launched by Minister of Justice Chalandon in 1986, initially envisaged the creation of 25,000 cells in new high-tech, 'riot proof' private institutions. This ambitious programme, which aimed at the privatization of 50 per cent of total prison capacity, was fiercely resisted by grass-roots organizations as well as the Socialist Party. As a result, the number of new prison cells entrusted to private companies was reduced to 15,000 (Parti Socialiste Français 1986). According to data provided by the Prison Administration in 1993, 14 of the original 25 institutions included in 'Programme 13,000' were running at full capacity. In the early months of 1994 the number of private institutions had risen to 17, accommodating over 10,000 prisoners (Administration Pénitentiaire 1994). Also, these establishments should, strictly speaking, be defined as 'mixed' or 'semi-private' as the government was forced to retain responsibility for their overall management and guarding functions while contracting out other functions to the same private companies which had built the prisons. These functions include education and labour for prisoners, the provision of meals, and the provision and maintenance of the technology for internal and external surveillance (ARAPEJ 1994; Gallo 1994). One of the largest private companies operating in French prisons is Siges, a subsidiary of Sodexo, which provides services at five establishments. The chief executive officer of this company has indicated that his task was 'to make a significant impact on the global corrections market at a time when every criminal justice system is seeking fiscally sound, technically innovative ways to solve their corrections problems' (Nathan 1994:17).

This new model of imprisonment was regarded as the ideal response to chronic overcrowding in French institutions, and as we have already mentioned, was initially intended to expand the number of cell places available to 70,000. But apart from these quantitative aspects, privatization can be interpreted as an experiment in the treatment of offenders which intensifies (or refines) some already familiar elements. That is to say, on the one hand the new private prisons through high-tech devices postulate the complete manageability of prisoners and their increased participation in the functioning of the institution, almost as robot prisoners or cybernetic prisoners, biological appendages to the machinery which controls them. On the other hand, the goal underlying private prisons is that all institutions should acquire complete economic self-sufficiency. Both things are the result of the state's unwillingness to spend public money to improve the prison system and the rehabilitative treatment of offenders. In these prisons the idea of rehabilitation is marginalized, or if it has any meaning at all, it is likely to apply to those white collar criminals, including corrupt politicians, who need to be taught the acceptable limits of their deviance. But what are the implications of this prison model which denies *a priori* the existence of a community of prisoners and their rights?

Bluntly put, prisoners must be fed, housed, impersonally controlled and, where possible, made productive through work. Prisoners have to serve a number of days, months and years, and the management's task is to ensure that they do not escape or sabotage the functioning of the institution. The 'security' component of 'Programme 13,000' is embedded in a sinister institutional utopia: the self-reproduction of prison. Internal work and productivity are designed to make the prison self-sufficient. Prisoners have the opportunity to spend the little money earned (that is what is left after statutory deductions) in the internal shops run by the same company which manages the institution. The cycle of exploitation is then complete. On the other hand, the 'self-sufficiency' of these institutions requires that all links with the outside world be severed. For this reason productivity and high security are aspects of the same regime. Any objective examination of the 'security' question simply reinforces this point. For example, in March 1994 the pressure group Os Cangaceiros produced a pamphlet on 'Programme 13,000'. The pamphlet, whose title translates as '13,000 Bollocks', argued that the tremendous display of info-tech devices, which are officially there in order to prevent prisoners from absconding, in fact do not serve this purpose. Even before the privatization programme was conceived, the escape rate in France was 0.8 per cent, that is 40 prisoners out of 48,000. Rather, the tools of the managerial prisons (automatic gates, magnetic passes, internal videos, anti-helicopter cables running above the open areas) are there to prevent disturbances and mutiny. Within private prisons, 'security' and control are intensified, a characteristic which makes them appealing to the state in the first place. Increasingly, security becomes tantamount to internal repression: special treatment for rebels, confinement cells, and other punishments within punishment. How could the managerial prison survive otherwise? Like other private firms, these institutions can only be run smoothly if industrial disputes are foiled.

It must be said, however, that as soon as the managerial prisons began operating they experienced a number of disturbances and demonstrations. These were triggered by the dire quality of food, the obsessive electronic control, confinement cells, the high prices of goods sold in internal shops, and the complete isolation from the outside world. In February 1994 the private prison of Salon, in the south of France, was wrecked by prisoners in revolt. As regards security, this seemed to be more symbolic than real. In May 1994, after 'visiting' a number of building sites where other private prisons were being built, Os Cangaceiros claimed to have tampered with the cement found there: by pouring a kilogram of sugar for every tonne of cement, they said, the cement will be of no use or, even better, the walls will lose most of their solidity. Perhaps the managerial prison is not as invulnerable as it seems.

Conclusion

As I have argued in the first part of this chapter, the prison of the Enlightenment was unable to abandon the afflictive philosophy inherited from the *ancien régime*. Custody, which was designated as the core of punishment, was destined to be accompanied by supplementary penalties including forced labour and solitary confinement. Moreover, the death penalty was in place until 1981, when it was finally abolished under the presidency of François Mitterrand. In other words, the barbaric heritage of the past was never fully abandoned. Alongside this contradiction, the French prison system has never come to terms with another aspect of its double nature. This is the co-existence of a secular, utilitarian and 'neutral' model of punishment on the one hand, and a religious model aimed at the redemption of offenders on the other.

The semi-privatization of French prison institutions epitomizes a somewhat natural evolution of these contradictions. The new private prisons are inspired by the utilitarian principle of making prisoners productive through work, and at the same time they are based on religious principles of the redemption of offenders through confinement. The utilitarian aspect of these prisons is apparent in the economic benefit they bring to the private companies which are granted building and maintenance contracts. Here, one could talk of the 'industry of imprisonment' which, like other industries, is required to effect market research, statistical projections of offending populations and demographic studies related to marginalization and crime. The aspect of redemption is fulfilled through the increasing isolation of prisoners which is achieved by the growing use of high technologies. This double nature of the French prison system constitutes the unresolved contradiction which, despite countless efforts by enlightened reformers throughout the last two centuries, makes this system a machine of destruction.

References

Administration Pénitentiaire (1993), *Rapport Annuel 1992* Paris: La Documentation Française

Administration Pénitentiaire (1994), *Rapport Annuel 1993* Paris: La Documentation Française

AIV (1986), *Rapport d'activité 1986* Grenoble: Aide Information aux Victimes

Akermann W and Dulong R (1984), *L'aide aux victimes: premières initiatives, premières évaluations* Paris: Maison des Sciences de l'Homme

ARAPEJ (1994), *Bulletin Prison-Justice* 69 Paris: Association Réflection Action Prison et Justice

Bonafé-Schmitt J P (1989), 'Alternatives to the Judicial Model' in M Wright and B Galaway (eds) *Mediation and Criminal Justice: Victims, Offenders and Community* London: Sage

Bonafé-Schmitt J P, Gerard C, Picon D and Porcher P (1986), *Les justices du quotidien: le modes formels et informels de réglement des petits litiges* Lyon: Université de Lyon

Bonnemaison G (ed) (1983), *Face à la délinquance: prévention, répression, solidarité* Paris: La Documentation Française

Bonnemaison G (1991), 'Répression et prévention' *Apres-demain* 339: 13–14

Camillieri G and Lazerges C (1992), *Atlas de la criminalité en France* Paris: La Documentation Française

Cantat M (1991), 'Les peines de substitution' *Apres-demain* 339: 23–31

Cantat M (1992), 'Peines de substitution. Quel bilan?' in C Faugeron (ed) *Les politiques pénales* Paris: La Documentation Française

Cassese A (1994), *Umano-Disumano. Commissariati e prigioni nell'Europa di oggi* Roma-Bari: Laterza

de Brie C (1993), 'En France et en Europe, ces lois qui créent des clandestins' *Le Monde Diplomatique* July

Delatte J and Dolé P (1987), *La récomposition du champ sociale et des pratiques de prévention* Paris: Ministère de la Justice

de Liège M-P (1988), 'The Fight against Crime and Fear: A New Initiative in France' in T Hope and M Shaw (eds) *Communities and Crime Reduction* London: HMSO, pp. 254-9

de Liège M-P (1991), 'Social Development and the Prevention of Crime in France: A Challenge for Local Parties and Central Government' in F Heidensohn and M Farrell (eds) *Crime in Europe* London: Routledge

Delteil G (1986), *Prisons, dossiers brulants* Paris: Le Carrousel

Dezalay Y (1988), 'La justice negociée comme renégociation de la division du travail; l'exemple français' *Annales de Vaucresson* 29, 2: 159-64

Dubet F (1987), *La galère* Paris: Fayard

Faugeron C (1991), 'Les prisons de la V Republique' in J-G Petit (ed) *Histoire des galères, bagnes et prisons* Toulouse: Bibliotèque Historique Privat

Faugeron C (ed) (1992), *Les politiques pénales. Problèmes politiques et sociaux* Paris: La Documentation Française

Faugeron C and Houchon G (1985), 'Prisons et pénalité' *Année Sociologique* 35: 143-5

Favard J (1990), 'Justice pour les victimes' *Projet* 222: 76-9

Foucault M (1977), *Discipline and Punish: The Birth of the Prison* London: Allen Lane

Gallo E (1994), 'Carcere privato. La reclusione quotata in borsa' *Narcomafie* II, 8: 11-13

Gallo E and Ruggiero V (1983), *Il carcere in Europa* Verona: Bertani

Gallo E and Ruggiero V (1984), 'L'assetto carcerario in Francia. Dagli elementi ereditari della deportazione al carcere dell'insicurezza sociale' *Critica del Diritto* X, 32: 47-62

Gonin D (1991), *La santé incarcérée* Paris: L'Archipel

Jouys B (1990), 'Une peine hors les murs' *Projet* 222: 68-75

King M (1991), 'The Political Construction of Crime Prevention: A Contrast between the French and British Experience' in K Stenson and D Cowell (eds) *The Politics of Crime Control* London: Sage

Léauté J (1968), *Les prisons* Paris: PUF

Léonard J (1980), 'L'historien et le philosophe. Debat avec Michel Foucault' in M Perrot (ed) *L'impossible prison* Paris: Seuil

Lesage de la Haye J (1992), *La guillotine du sexe* Paris: Monde Libertaire

Magliona B and Sarzotti C (1993), 'Carcere e AIDS: le ragioni di un rapporto difficile' *Dei Delitti e delle Pene* III, 3: 101-32

Migration News (1992), 'Authorities Decide to Be Firm with Rejected Asylum-Seekers' June, 111

Nathan S (1994), 'Private Prison Contracts' *Prison Reform* 28: 15-18

O'Brien P (1982), *The Promise of Punishment: Prisons in Nineteenth-Century France* Princeton: Princeton University Press

Observatoire International des Prisons (1994), *Rapport 1994* Lyon: OIP

Parti Socialiste Français (1986), *Les murs d'argent. Manifeste contre la privatisation des prisons* Paris: Parti Socialiste

Pauchet C (1982), *Les prisons de l'insécurité* Paris: Les Editions Ouvrières

Pease K and Hukkila K (eds) (1990), *Criminal Justice Systems in Europe and North America* Helsinki: Institute for Crime Prevention and Control, United Nations

Perrot M (1980), *L'impossible prison* Paris: Seuil

Petit J-G (1990), *Ces peines obscures. La prison pénale en France* Paris: Fayard

Petit J-G (ed) (1991), *Histoire des galères, bagnes et prisons* Toulouse: Bibliotèque Historique Privat

Pierre M (1991), 'La prison repubblicaine' in J-G Petit (ed) *Histoire des galères, bagnes et prisons* Toulouse: Bibliotèque Historique Privat

Pinsseau H (1985), *L'organisation judiciaire de la France. Notes et études documentaires* Paris: La Documentation Française

Seyler M (1993), 'La prison française et le SIDA' *L'Esprit* 195: 148–53

Tomasevski K (1994), *Foreigners in Prison* Helsinki: European Institute for Crime Prevention and Control

Tournier P (1992a), 'Les transformations du sentiment d'insécurité' in C Faugeron (ed) *Les politiques pénales. Problèmes politiques et sociaux* Paris: La Documentation Française

Tournier P (1992b), *Les étrangers en prison* Paris: Centre de Recherche Sociologique sur le Droit et les Institutions Pénales

Trioux M (1985), *La médiation pénale* Paris: Ministère de Justice

Wieviorka M (ed) (1994), *Racisme et xénophobie en Europe* Paris: La Découverte

Wright G (1983), *Between the Guillotine and Liberty: Two Centuries of the Crime Problem in France* New York/Oxford: Oxford University Press

5

The Penal System in England and Wales: Round Up the Usual Suspects

Mick Ryan and Joe Sim

Since the early 1970s the penal system in England and Wales has frequently been described as being 'in crisis'. Various interpretations have been suggested to account for the crisis. These interpretations have come out of very different sociological and political traditions and have ranged from what Cavadino and Dignan (1992) have labelled as the orthodox account of Evans (1980), the radical analysis of Fitzgerald and Sim (1982), the mainstream interpretation of Bottoms (1980), the liberal account of Lord Justice Woolf (1991) and the radical pluralism of Cavadino and Dignan themselves. During the early 1970s the potential of the system, and of the prison in particular, to reform offenders generated a specific crisis of confidence. As one study after another revealed high rates of recidivism new pressure groups like Radical Alternatives to Prison (RAP), and even long-established groups like the Howard League, began to argue that the use of imprisonment should be restricted and more constructive, community based alternatives developed instead (Ryan 1978). Under the influence of Scandinavian and Dutch theorists some English and Welsh groups even went so far as to advocate prison abolition (Mathiesen 1974).

While there were key differences between the various pressure groups involved, there were also important areas of agreement, especially the view that the alternatives suggested were arguably less destructive, physically, psychologically and socially, than imprisonment, and it was believed that they would at least help to salvage the existing penal enterprise as a going concern, albeit with a changing emphasis.

Prison officers not surprisingly saw the crisis mainly in terms of deteriorating pay and conditions. The Prison Officers Association (POA) which represents all main grade staff actively encouraged disputes which contributed to the government setting up the May enquiry in November 1978. For their part, prisoners not only voiced discontent at their marginalization in a series of disturbances, the worst of which was at Hull prison in 1976, but also in the form of Preservation of the Rights of Prisoners (PROP) who began their own assault on the mechanisms of reform, particularly the use of executive discretion in areas like parole. Reinforced by support from prisoners' rights movements in Scandinavia and the USA, this voice helped forge a coalition against reform in England and Wales in favour of a penal policy driven more by the idea of justice or just deserts, some elements of which slowly gained favour even in official circles as the 1980s progressed (Ryan 1983:6–9).

The drift from the *rhetoric* of reform to justice in England and Wales was never, as this suggests, swift or total. Nor for that matter was it wholly coherent (Hudson 1993:17). It was also not without its ironies. For example, the demolition of reform, the radical lobby's insistence that criminals were rational actors, men and women whose actions did not have to be pathologized, coincided with the rise of the new right with its emphasis on individual moral responsibility and punishment pure and simple. With very few exceptions, neo-classical approaches to crime, and to punishment in particular, were very much the order of the day, an ideological drift which was further reinforced by the emergence of what came to be labelled 'left realism' (Young 1986).

Official signification of this came in the government's 1990 White Paper *Crime, Justice and Protecting the Public* (Home Office 1990). The White Paper plainly stated that criminals should get their 'just deserts' and that the severity of any sentence should be 'directly related to the seriousness of the offence' (para. 1.6). Furthermore, the White Paper stressed that magistrates and judges should not knowingly translate a relatively minor offence into a serious one simply because the offender had been convicted previously, even for similar or related offences. In other words, they should concentrate on the case before them and not on the offender's antecedents.

While stressing the government's determination to deal harshly with what it defined as serious crime – e.g. armed robbery and rape – the White Paper also pointed out that most crimes were not violent and that for people who commit them punishment in the community was the preferred option. This was not just because keeping offenders out of prison would make some form of restitution/compensation for the victims more likely, which should be the courts' first consideration, but also because no one any longer believed that prisons were an 'effective means of reform for most offenders'. Indeed, a prison sentence could be an 'expensive way of making bad people worse' (para. 2.7). However, in looking towards community alternatives, it was important that in many cases they should be seen to 'intrude on normal freedom' (para. 4.3). Curfew orders combined with electronic tagging were to be legislated for as one possibility (para. 4.24), and combining probation supervision with an element of community service another (para. 4.16). In order to reduce the large number of those imprisoned for fine default, a new system of unit fines geared to the offender's ability to pay was also promised.

Given its punitive stance on the practice of alternatives to custody and the fact that the changes it proposed to parole left executive discretion mainly in place, the White Paper was not seen to be either liberal or consistent with justice. On the other hand, in stressing that prison should only be used for punishing the most serious offenders and by insisting that, except where public safety might be at issue, judges and magistrates should only punish the offender for the offence for which he or she was before the court, the Criminal Justice Act 1991 which embodied the White Paper's proposals was thought by liberal opinion to have reductionist potential. And indeed, the early evidence was promising as in the first year of its operation there was a significant decrease in the proportionate use of immediate custody and a significant drop in the overall prison population, by 4,600 to 40,000. Regrettably this was not sustained. From the beginning of 1993 there had been a huge increase in the prison population. By February 1994 it had reached just under 48,000 and we were reliably informed that there was yet 'another crisis waiting in the wings' (Prison Reform Trust 1993a). This warning was repeated as the year progressed (Cavadino 1994), but went unheeded. By October 1994 the number of prisoners hovered around 50,000.

The evolution of penal policy which we have sketched did not take place in a vacuum. How governments respond to crime, and what they believe should be done with those who break the law, and who the police and Crown Prosecution Service decide should be processed through the criminal justice system, cannot be divorced from wider political, social and economic concerns. By this we do not mean that there are, for example, necessary causal connections between crime and unemployment (Box 1983). However, it is our contention that shifting penal paradigms do reflect wider social forces which are structured as much – if not more – by the interaction of political, economic and social forces, including the media, than by expert testimony or any objective assessment of what available evidence there is. Thus, the anxieties which accompanied an increase in recorded crime in the 1970s and 1980s in England and Wales cannot be separated from the widespread political, economic and social dislocation of these years and the construction of what has been labelled the 'authoritarian consensus', of which tough law and order policies were an integral part (Hall et al. 1978; Scraton 1987; Sim 1987).

While it is not our intention to rehearse, or more to the point, refine and develop these well known arguments here, we will return to the wider context they embrace as it is only by situating current penal policy in this way that we can explain why key elements of the Criminal Justice Act 1991, such as the instruction to magistrates and judges to guard against translating repeated minor offences into serious ones and the introduction of the unit fine, have been so quickly reversed; why the prison population is expanding; and why other new proposals threaten to destabilize the penal system still further. In the meantime we turn to the topography of the penal system in England and Wales, beginning with a look at the range of penal sanctions which are currently available to the courts.

Sentencing dispositions

In England and Wales by no means all of those who are known to have committed offences in any given year come before the courts. The Crown Prosecution Service, for example, may decide that the public interest would not be served by prosecuting this or that offence, while many who admit their offences, particularly if they are first offenders or juveniles, are simply cautioned by the police and no further penal sanction is taken against them. The number of cautions in 1993 was 311,000. However, most known offenders, even those who admit to their guilt, have to go before the courts, and in 1993 1.43 million offenders were duly processed at various levels and then sentenced, 7 per cent less than in 1992 when allowance is made for improved recording procedures (Home Office 1994a: para. 7.5).

Table 5.1 shows the penal sanctions which are available to the courts in England and Wales to impose on those offenders who come before them. A good deal of care needs to be used in interpreting this table as it refers to all known offenders, including corporate offenders. Also, no distinction is made between male and female offenders, nor do the aggregates always distinguish between young offenders and those over 21 years of age who are the main focus of this chapter. Additionally, it obviously cannot reflect all the changes brought about by the Criminal Justice Act 1991 and the Criminal Justice Act 1993. Notwithstanding these difficulties, and with the promise to both refine and update the material where we can, Table 5.1 represents the latest, authoritative information available to us at the time of writing, and it does at least tell us

Table 5.1 *Offenders sentenced for all offences by type of sentence or order in England and Wales, 1989–1993 (thousands)*

Type of sentence or order	1989	1990	1991	1992	1993
Absolute discharge	19.5	20.4	21.5	23.8	25.9
Conditional discharge	85.4	94.5	102.0	109.8	111.6
Fine	1,227.8	1,192.7	1,166.6	1,183.8	1,091.5
Probation order	44.2	47.7	47.5	43.9	43.8
Supervision order[1]	6.7	6.7	6.3	5.9	7.3
Community service order	33.9	38.6	42.5	44.1	48.0
Attendance sentence order[2]	7.7	7.9	8.2	7.2	6.8
Care order[1]	0.3	0.4	0.3	–	–
Combination order	–	–	–	1.3	8.9
Young offender institution	19.1	16.2	16.9	15.1	15.2
Imprisonment					
Fully suspended	29.8	27.4	28.1	22.0	3.8
Partly suspended	2.2	1.5	1.1	0.6	–
Unsuspended	42.8	39.8	43.2	42.3	43.2
Otherwise dealt with	14.6	20.0	19.6	20.1	19.1
All sentences or orders	1,534.1	1,513.9	1,503.9	1,519.9	1,425.0
Of which:					
Immediate custody	64.1	57.6	61.2	58.0	58.4
Community sentences[3]	92.5	100.9	104.5	102.4	114.8

[1] Supervision and care orders involved children under 17 years.

[2] Attendance centre orders involve young people up to 21 years.

[3] Probation orders, supervision orders, community service orders, attendance centre orders and combination orders.

Source: adapted from Home Office 1994a:Table 7a

something important about the broad sweep of sentencing in England and Wales in recent years.

To begin with it is clear from Table 5.1 that the *fine* is the most popular and widely used penalty. In 1993, for example, it was used for 77 per cent of all offenders. Not surprisingly the proportionate use of the fine decreases in indictable or more serious cases, but even here it is still widely used. In 1993, for instance, it was imposed for 38 per cent of all males over 21 sentenced for indictable offences and on 31 per cent of all females over 21 sentenced for indictable offences (Home Office 1994a:Tables 7.6 and 7.13). *Absolute and conditional discharges* are also widely used for all offenders, and taken together in 1993 they were imposed on 18 per cent of all males over 21 sentenced for indictable offences and on 34 per cent of all females over 21 sentenced for indictable offences (Home Office 1994a:Table 7.13). These sentences are used when courts take the view that, even where guilt has been established, no punishment is required. However, in the case of a conditional discharge, if the offender breaks the law within the time specified by the court he or she is liable to be sentenced for the original offence.

Community service, combination and probation orders are also popular sentences for all offenders. In fact, these community punishments in one form or another were given to 23 per cent of all male offenders over 21 sentenced for an indictable offence in 1993, and to 24 per cent of all females in the same category (Home Office 1994a:Table 7.13). Probation orders may have conditions attached to them requiring the offender to attend a probation centre for training or even to live in specified accommodation. Whatever the requirements the offender must keep in touch with his/her probation officer who is technically at least still an officer of the court who is required (increasingly) to report on his/her progress. Over 80 per cent of probation orders are satisfactorily completed. Community service is a more recent sentence originally – but no longer – designated specifically as an alternative to imprisonment. Offenders can be required to spend between 40 and 240 hours on community service work in any given year. In 1993 community service orders showed a 9 per cent increase over the previous year (Home Office 1994a:Table 7.6). Probation officers normally place offenders on these programmes which are sometimes run by volunteers. Under the provisions of the Criminal Justice Act 1991 a new and tougher *combined order* was introduced which combines probation super-vision with community service. In 1993, the first full year in which it was available, 8,900 of these new orders were issued, and this arguably helps to explain why the number of probation orders issued has registered a slight decline (Home Office 1994a:Table 7a).

What Table 5.1 also suggests is that while as a *proportion* of all sentenced offenders the number of those sentenced to *imprisonment* of one sort or another is modest, the actual numbers involved are considerable. For example, those sentenced males over 21 receiving immediate prison sentences for indictable offences have averaged between 32,000 and 33,000 in the years 1991–3. For sentenced females over 21 the average for the same period was between 1800 and 1900 (Home Office 1994a:Table 7.12). These figures serve to remind us that in England and Wales the number of women offenders is small compared with the number of male offenders. Abolishing the *partly suspended* sentence where an offender spent some of his/her sentence in prison with the rest suspended, and in advising only the very exceptional use of the *fully suspended* sentence, both of which were done under the Criminal Justice Act 1991, led to a sharp drop in the use of fully suspended sentences in

Crown Courts where the most serious cases are tried. They declined from 16 per cent in 1991 to 2–3 per cent in 1993 (Home Office 1994a:Table 7b).

From our discussion so far it is clear that the courts in England and Wales have a wide variety of penalties available, the number and type determined by Parliament in a piecemeal fashion. New penalties, or adjustments to existing ones, are simply embodied in separate Acts of Parliament as and when required. There is also no rigid tariff scale, which is thought by some to be necessary for a fully blown justice model. Instead, the Acts simply specify minimum and maximum penalties. Of course, these can be changed. For example, the Criminal Justice Act 1991 to which we have been referring reduced the maximum sentence for non-domestic burglary from 14 to 10 years and for theft from 10 to 7 years respectively. Within the minimum and maximum penalties decreed by Parliament, individual courts can use their own discretion. This leads to a degree of disparity between different courts. In order to secure greater consistency the higher judiciary has increasingly issued guidelines to the lower courts on sentencing levels and, in controversial areas, delivered clear judgements setting out what it thinks the appropriate tariff should be. For example, in 1986, and partly in response to the activities of the pressure group Women Against Rape, it judged (*R.v.Billam*) that the sentences being passed in rape cases were not reflecting the seriousness of the offence. Penalties for this offence were expected to increase. However, it remains a matter of contention if such an increase has occurred.

It is important to intervene here to point out that the judiciary is separately administered in the UK through the Lord Chancellor who is appointed by the government of the day. Lord Chancellors in their turn are responsible for appointing magistrates and judges, a process which is subject to little or no democratic scrutiny or balance. There is thus no all-embracing Ministry of Justice to oversee the work of police, judiciary and prisons. Nor for that matter is there an all-embracing penal code setting out the principles on which the penal system should operate and/or incorporating changes as and when they are made to existing (or new) offences and their attendant penalties.

Finally, what should also be clear from our discussion is that many sentenced offenders – indeed, the vast majority of offenders – walk away from the courts in any given year and are not subject to any form of penal supervision. This is not to suggest that most of these offenders go unpunished. Far from it. For many offenders paying a fine can be an onerous task: many are later brought back before the courts and imprisoned for non-payment. There were 22,754 such cases in 1993 (NAPO 1994). Furthermore, many offenders who eventually receive a fine or a non-custodial sentence will have spent weeks or months on *remand in custody*. This is a common fate, with the proportion of remand prisoners held in the prison system increasing year by year so that it nearly doubled in twenty years to reach 22 per cent in 1992 (Central Statistical Office 1994:161).

But what of the rest, those tens and thousands under some form of community supervision and the 40,000 plus sentenced prisoners? Which agencies are responsible for their supervision? How are they structured and to whom are they answerable? It is to these questions we now turn.

Agencies

Perhaps the most important point to make about the structure of the English and Welsh penal system in the 1990s is that it is potentially on the threshold of major changes. These changes will chiefly affect the prison system which, as we saw in the previous section, receives large numbers of sentenced and unsentenced prisoners each year from the courts.

The prison system in England and Wales was nationalized in 1877. At a single stroke all local and regional prisons were swept into central administrative control and, through the Prison Commission, made answerable to a minister in Parliament. All aspects of prison life, from prisoners' diets to their earnings, were subject to detailed administrative control from the centre by those civil servants who comprised the Prison Commission. (Salary scales and conditions of service were eventually unified and negotiated at the centre.) This process of centralization was fully consolidated in 1963 when the Prison Commission was finally absorbed into the machinery of central government as a department of the Home Office (Ryan 1983). This highly centralized, unified system is now in the process of being dismantled in two ways.

First, the present Conservative administration is determined to reduce what it sees as 'big government' and is hiving off the administration of a whole range of what have previously been thought of as government functions to quasi-autonomous agencies. The prison service was given what is called 'agency status' in 1993. What this means is that except for agreeing a corporate plan with a minister at the Home Office, and reporting to him or her on serious matters of public interest, the new director of the prisons' agency is supposedly to be left to run the prison service as he or she pleases, subject only to the financial constraints of the Treasury which votes the prison service its funding on an annual basis in Parliament (Home Office 1993a). Unlike its predecessor, the Prison Commission, the new prison agency is being encouraged to assert its independence, and in particular, to decentralize its operations by giving more power to local prison governors under a system of performance related contracts (Home Office 1993b). However, while agency status does indeed relieve the burden on central government for the day-to-day administration of services such as prisons, it can be argued that the government's political control over their activities, by virtue of tightly drawn contracts, is strengthened, an argument we will return to below. (The first director of the new agency took up his post in January 1993. He had previously been the chair of a satellite television company and had apparently no previous experience of prison policies or issues.)

Second, the present government also wants the agency to press ahead with privatizing the delivery of services such as health and education in state run prisons and to extend the number of private prisons so that by 1998 10 per cent of all prisons will be in private hands (*Hansard* 18 November 1993). (The necessary legal changes to make private prisons possible were incorporated into the Criminal Justice Act 1991.) In October 1994 there were four private prisons in England and Wales. The Wolds is a remand prison, Blakenhurst and Strangeways hold both remand and sentenced prisoners, while the newest private prison at Doncaster is expected to hold mostly young offenders. The government has only so far contracted with the private sector to manage prisons; it has retained the ownership of these prisons and also paid for their building and/ or refurbishment. However, it was announced in 1993 that the Home Office was planning to invite the private sector to finance, build and manage six new prisons and the planning process for the first of these is already under way. Concern over the operational efficiency of all private prisons has been expressed, though most notably in respect of Doncaster where staffing levels are said to be dangerously low (*The Guardian* 17 August 1994).

Taken together, these changes are clearly intended to transform the structure and operation of the prison system in England and Wales. A once unified, hierarchical service is slowly being replaced by two more decentralized systems, each offering different conditions of service for their employees and each under contract to provide different prison regimes and levels of service. The fact that both state and private prisons are answerable to the new prison agency for their performance related contracts cannot disguise the fact that two separate systems are now emerging. This development has been opposed by the Prison Officers' Association on the grounds that it will worsen their members' conditions of employment and, in the longer term, lead to job losses. However, the union's attempt to take strike action around this issue was effectively ruled out by a court judgement in November 1993 which granted an injunction against prison officers (Ryan 1994).

Immigrant detention centres

These centres were first sanctioned by a Labour government after it had moved to restrict immigration from the black Commonwealth in the 1960s. Paradoxically, perhaps, they have been run by the private sector right from the start. There are holding centres at Heathrow, Gatwick, Manchester and Stansted airports and longer-stay facilities at Harmondsworth, Hasler and Campsfield. During the 1980s a group of Tamil refugees were housed on a decommissioned ferry, the *Earl William*, before it finally broke its mooring and ran aground. The leading private operator in this field is Group 4, the company which currently runs the Wolds remand prison.

While most illegal immigrants and asylum seekers are held in these specially designated centres, it is important to point out that for a number of reasons many are also held in the mainstream prison system, including local prisons. Conditions in some of these local prisons are poor, especially in London, and fears for the safety of these vulnerable prisoners has been voiced by such groups as INQUEST. Tensions have also built up around the newest detention centre at Campsfield in Oxfordshire where a hunger strike by twenty-six detainees in March 1994 was followed by an uprising in June which the local police had to be called in to put down.

The ultimate responsibility for these centres rests with the Home Office which lists as one of its main priorities a determination to play its part in 'strengthening the external frontiers of the EC' and in restricting the numbers 'coming to live permanently or to work in the UK' (Home Office 1993c:5, 49).

Probation and aftercare service

We noted earlier that the number of offenders being supervised in the community under various forms of court order has grown considerably in recent years. The responsibility for this supervision rests largely with the probation service which is also responsible for the 'throughcare' of certain categories of offenders while still in prison and the 'aftercare' of many others who are released on licence in one form or another. (About 40 per cent of the service's time is involved in supervising offenders in the community and 32 per cent in throughcare and aftercare (Audit Commission 1989).)

The control of the service is nominally shared between central government, in the form of the Home Office, and local government, with probation officers being employed by one of the 55 local probation committees which are dominated by local magistrates, a minority of co-opted locally elected politicians and a few selected specialists. These local committees have a degree of autonomy, but the influence of the Home Office in determining probation objectives has grown in recent years. This is because the Home Office now funds up to 80 per cent of most aspects of probation work, largely controls the training of probation officers and in 1984 negotiated a Statement of National Objectives and Priorities with the service in an attempt to bring it more into line with central government priorities, as well as to secure greater consistency between different probation areas. Central government has also sought to persuade the probation service that it should see itself more as a service drawing up an initial programme of needs and/or activities for offenders and then arranging for these to be met by other agencies. It has been suggested that the service should be prepared to buy in such services under contract, from either the voluntary or the private sector (Audit Commission 1989).

Fearing that this could lead to fewer jobs for its members, especially in aftercare and in the running of bail hostels and probation centres, the National Association of Probation Officers (NAPO) entered into an agreement with a number of voluntary agencies to prevent job substitution (Ryan and Ward 1990–1). The determination of the Home Office to bring the service more into line with central government priorities, the suggestion that it should modify its traditional role of 'advising, assisting and befriending' individual offenders and take on instead directing or overseeing more punitive forms of supervision, has made its relationship with NAPO – like its relationship with the POA – a difficult one in recent years. In contesting (and modifying) the government's original Statement of National Objectives and Priorities and keeping privatization at bay, NAPO has been arguably far more successful than the POA in resisting change.

Following this essentially historical and descriptive account we now develop a critical anatomy of the penal system. We shall do this by focusing on a number of important areas which, taken together, will provide not only an insight into the operationalization of power but also into the fact and nature of penality in England and Wales in the mid 1990s.

Costing the system

In 1979 it was noted that 'prisons are big business, spending millions of pounds and employing thousands of people' (Fitzgerald and Sim 1979:31). The intervening fifteen years have only under-lined this point, particularly with the emergence of multinational companies as buyers and sellers of penal 'services'. In 1979, £206,731,000 was spent on prisons in England and Wales. By the financial year 1993–4, the 130 penal institutions cost just over £1.5 billion to run, or 25.6 per cent of the law and order budget (Fitzgerald and Sim 1982:22; Home Office 1994b:6). The cost of keeping individual prisoners inside also rose dramatically during this period. In 1978–9 it cost £232 a week to confine an individual in a male, maximum security prison: by 1992–3 this had climbed to £816. The overall average weekly cost of prison in 1992–3 was £494 per prisoner (Fitzgerald and Sim 1982:33; NACRO 1994a:1).

The impetus for the major rise in expenditure came in the 1980s, the law and order decade. Between 1979–80 and 1985–6 it rose by 36 per cent in real terms and by 156 per cent in cash terms (Home Office 1986:34). It is important to note that throughout the 1980s there was also a major prison building and refurbishment pro-gramme taking place. Between 1980 and 1994 the government spent £1.2 billion, which provided 11,000 places in 21 new prisons and 7,500 in existing ones. The majority of expenditure on prisons, over 80 per cent, is devoted to staff costs. Once again, the number employed has risen substantially in the last three decades. Between April 1965 and March 1978 total staff employed increased by 88 per cent, from 11,759 to 22,146: the prison population increased by 38 per cent during the same period (Home Office 1979:113).

In contrast, expenditure on the probation service has come much lower on the funding ladder. The ideological drive towards supporting the prison has even over-ridden the prudent concern for savings which has dominated Conservative philosophy for the last two decades. As the National Association for the Care and Re-settlement of Offenders has consistently pointed out, community penalties are significantly less expensive than a prison sentence. Indeed 'the figures suggest that keeping an offender in prison for *three weeks* is more expensive than supervising him or her on community services for a year . . . even the most expensive com-munity penalties, such as probation hostels, are less than half the cost of prison' (NACRO 1994a:2, emphasis in the original).

At one level, the argument that alternatives to custody come low on the ladder of expenditure appears to be contradicted by the fact that expenditure on probation increased by 70 per cent in real terms between 1970 and 1980 and the number of probation officers increased by nearly 2,000 over the same period. By 1989, England and Wales had the largest probation service in Europe (NACRO cited in Cavadino and Dignan 1992:198). These figures, however, need to be contextualized within the pattern of expenditure on law and order in general. Seen in this context not only is expenditure low, but it can be subject to severe and debilitating cuts. In 1988–9 for example, only 5.5 per cent of the total law and order budget went on the probation service, in 1993–4 the figure was 6.3 per cent, and by 1996–7 it will be 6.4 per cent. This apparent and negligible rise, however, masks the fact that between 1994 and 1997 the 55 probation areas in England and Wales will be asked to make 'efficiency savings of 9 per cent' (Home Office 1994b:6–13). As we illustrate in the conclusion to this chapter this will not only have severe implications for the provision of alternatives, but reinforce the prevailing orthodoxy that prisons are *the* place for the punishment of offenders.

People in the penal system: social characteristics

The two great institutions of the criminal justice system in England and Wales – the court and penal systems – provide a stark and vivid contrast in terms of the background and characteristics of those involved. The judiciary is still overwhelmingly drawn from white, upper and middle class backgrounds with a preponderance of males in the higher echelons of the courts. In contrast those who appear in the courts as defendants and, more significantly for our purposes, those who are punished overwhelmingly come from the economically and politically marginalized and the racially disadvantaged. There is also the important issue of gender differentiation which we consider in a later section.

There has been an official reluctance in England and Wales to discuss the characteristics and backgrounds of those individuals caught up in the penal system. However, in 1991, the Office of Population Censuses and Surveys surveyed the prison population for the Home Office. This National Prison Survey (NPS) identified a number of key points in relation to the confined: the prison population was very different in structure from the general population with respect to age, sex, ethnic group and social class; prisoners were much younger than the general population; women made up 4 per cent of the prison population yet were 50 per cent of the general population; 41 per cent of male prisoners came from occupations defined as partly skilled or unskilled (social classes 4 and 5) as opposed to 18 per cent of the general population; and 15 per cent of males and 23 per cent of females described themselves as black or Asian compared with less than 5 per cent of the general population (Walmsley et al. 1992:8–10). Other research has also pointed to the last issue, which raises a series of key questions about crime, policing, criminalization and sentencing which are beyond the scope of this chapter.

However, there are three further dimensions in relation to the social characteristics of offenders which should be noted. First, the increasing number of foreign prisoners, particularly women, has become an important issue. As Deborah Cheney has pointed out, 'the number of foreign prisoners is under-recorded because of a confusion with ethnic monitoring.' The figure, however, has been calculated for some prisons. In January 1992, 30 per cent of prisoners in The Verne Prison were foreign nationals (Cheney 1993:3–5). Second, and allied to this, is the number of Irish prisoners whose position is rarely discussed. They not only come from one of the most economically disadvantaged groups in England and Wales but also 'are 20 per cent more likely to receive prison sentences than White Europeans'. The Irish also have the highest rate of admission to psychiatric institutions of any ethnic group in England and Wales (Murphy 1994:5). Finally, ethnic minority prisoners often experience regimes where their welfare, educational and medical needs remain unmet, where the worst prison jobs are assigned to them and where racism prevails, which more often than not goes unreported (Cheney 1993; Genders and Player 1989; Burnett and Farrell 1994). It should also be observed that the number of black people working in different areas of the criminal justice system is not only minimal (for example 70 of the 23,344 prison officers in post in August 1992 were black) but these officers also experience personal and institutional racism (Alfred 1992).

The NPS, which we discussed above, found a range of other characteristics associated with prisoners: early institutionalization as children; high rates of local authority care and mental illness; fractured personal relationships which had a particular impact on the children of women prisoners; homelessness which coupled with living in hostel and rented accommodation meant that few prisoners were owner occupiers compared with the general population; lack of educational qualifications (over 45 per cent of the prison population under 30 had no qualifications compared with under 20 per cent of the general population); and finally high levels of unemployment when compared with the general population. Again there were important gender differences. Women were much less likely to be in paid employment than men; 6 per cent of male prisoners and 12 per cent of female prisoners had never been in paid employment; 40 per cent of prisoners under 25 were unemployed compared with less than 15 per cent in the general population (Walmsley et al. 1992:8–21).

The relationship between poverty, sentencing and punishment which the NPS hinted at but never developed is an area which in the words of John Hughes, has been 'strangely neglected' (1991:9). Hughes himself has conducted a small scale study in Somerset and found that 70 per cent of those with an income below the poverty line received financial penalties from the courts and that more poor offenders received custodial sentences for less serious offences compared with those who were not poor. More recent research has pointed to the link between poverty, punishment and rates of imprisonment. In May 1994, the National Association of Probation Officers highlighted the increasing use being made of prisons as 'debtors' gaols'. In 1993 the numbers jailed for non-payment of fines rose by 17 per cent on the previous year. Since January 1990 the figure had risen by 36 per cent. Those jailed for non-payment of fines in 1993 accounted for over 25 per cent of prison admissions for the whole year:

> Of those sent down in 1993, 845 were jailed for using a TV without a licence and a further 504 for non-payment of the community charge. Of all the defaulters, the overwhelming majority were male. Figures from February 1994 showed that 95% were male and 5% female. However a large proportion, some 36%, of those jailed for TV licence evasion were women. In addition the number of females jailed for non-payment of TV licences rose from 136 in 1991 to 292 in 1993, a rise of 115% . . . Most of those jailed had large debts usually for essential items. (NAPO 1994:3–7)

Prosecution and imprisonment for vagrancy and begging also rose significantly during the 1980s reflecting the fact that the number of homeless people has trebled since 1979 and that by 1994 11 million people were living on or below income support levels (*The Observer* 22 May 1994). Between 1988 and 1990 (the last year for which figures were available) there was a rise of 150 per cent in the number of individuals prosecuted for begging and sleeping rough. These prosecutions were carried out under the Vagrancy Act which was passed in 1824 (*The Guardian* 30 May 1994).

The relationship between poverty and punishment is also reflected in those who receive non-custodial penalties. While we await the results of the Home Office's own detailed survey in this area, in May 1993 NAPO analysed the financial circumstances of 1,331 offenders. It found that the overwhelming majority of those on probation supervision were out of work, on benefit and in chronic debt, two-thirds were either long-term unemployed or too sick to work (this figure rose to over 80 per cent in the inner cities), eight out of ten were reliant on benefits as their only source of income, and a further 3 per cent had no income at all. Only 12 per cent were either fully waged or in training but the majority of this group were low paid (NAPO 1993).

It is also clear that those who are offenders and who are poor are themselves likely to be victims of crime and to be discriminated against by police and welfare agencies. As Peelo et al. have pointed out:

> The inability to protect oneself, family or property from crime in areas where crime is prevalent is one aspect of poverty whilst another is the economic deprivation wrought by 'minor' offences. While most people are distressed by offences committed against them, few suffer the economic crises these offender/victims could face when their giros went missing, their washing was stolen, or their rented televisions, videos, furniture or clothing disappeared. (1992:29)

Research published by the Home Office in July 1994 confirmed the relationship between unemployment and imprisonment. While arguing that the research should be treated with some caution, the researchers noted a number of important processes at work: in magistrates courts those unemployed at the time of their sentence were more likely to be given custodial sentences than those in employment and were more likely to be given probation; offenders in employment were more likely to be fined; in crown courts 53 per cent of unemployed offenders compared with 36 per cent of employed offenders were given custodial sentences; in these courts the unemployed were also more likely to be given probation and less likely to be fined or given a community service order. The research also noted that while the proportionate use of the fine fell during 1993 and was most marked amongst the unemployed, at the same time the average amount of fine levied *rose* for unemployed offenders, from £66 to £78 (Home Office 1994c:5–6).

Three final developments should be noted in relation to the background characteristics of people in the penal system. First, the number of Immigration Act detainees held in prisons and immigration detention centres tripled between July 1993 and July 1994. In April 1994 there were 920 detainees. The rise in the number detained has been paralleled by a huge rise in the percentage of people refused asylum (from 20 per cent to 80 per cent). As we noted earlier, not only has there been a wave of demonstrations, hunger strikes and escapes from these institutions, but also as detention centres are contracted out to private security firms these centres do not come under the formal scrutiny of HM Inspectorate of Prisons. This raises serious questions both about the treatment of detainees and about the accountability of the institutions in which they are detained (Pirouet 1994:10–11).

Second, the number of prisoners suffering from drug dependency increased from 19 per 1000 first receptions in 1987–8 to 24 per 1000 receptions in 1991–2. In numerical terms this meant an increase from 2,628 prisoners to 2,718 prisoners.

Third, official figures suggest that the number of HIV/AIDS prisoners may be increasing, although this is a notoriously difficult area to discuss because of the problems of reporting. At the end of March 1992 the aggregate number of HIV cases reported since monitoring began in 1985 was 374 (325 males and 49 females). By the same date 25 cases of AIDS had been reported since monitoring began, 24 males and 1 female (Her Majesty's Prison Service Health Care 1993:Appendix 1). By May 1994 there were 377 reported cases in the aggregate category but as the Prison Reform Trust has pointed out this is likely to be a gross underestimation. The actual figure is likely to be between four and ten times higher than the official figure (*The Guardian* 17 May 1994). The discrimination and stigmatization which these prisoners experience and the segregation which comes with this discrimination has also been raised as an important issue (Turnbull 1993). In a new development the Home Secretary has reinforced this discrimination by announcing a plan to randomly drug test 60,000 inmates a year; those who test positive could face another 28 days in prison, be confined to their cells and lose other privileges (*The Guardian* 20 October 1994).

Prison trends

Before discussing the number of offenders involved in the penal system it is important to stress that there are two quite distinct sets of statistics to be considered. First, there are the number of receptions into prison over the year. If this group is added to those given community sentences then it is possible to highlight the number of individuals punished with custodial and non-custodial sentences on a yearly basis. The second statistic (and most popular in terms of the media, official publications and politicians) comes from focusing on the average daily population (ADP) which gives a snapshot of the prison population only at particular points during the year. Both sets of statistics raise some important questions about the processes of punishment although it should also be noted that it is much easier to obtain ADP figures than the reception figures.

As with all official statistics we must be aware of their social construction. In the case of reception figures it is also important to heed the warning given by the Home Office that the process of double-counting individuals makes this statistic problematic. Nonetheless, this statistic does allow us to recognize that 'most custodial experiences are surprisingly transitory ... the overwhelming majority are in prison for a matter of days, weeks or months rather than years' (Morgan 1994:902–3). Table 5.2 highlights the number of receptions into prison service establishments in 1992 (the last year for which figures were available at the time of writing).

There were 57,551 remands in custody during 1992. Additionally, 26,676 individuals were received under an immediate sentence (a figure not included in the table), while nearly 23,000 were imprisoned for non-payment of fines or as non-criminal prisoners. Altogether, 107,162 persons were initially received into prison service establishments. This figure does not include community punishments such as probation and community service orders which, as Table 5.1 shows, amounted to 102,400. Overall then there were approximately 209,500 'contacts' with the penal system in 1992. Even with the qualifications noted above in relation to double-counting, this is still a substantial figure. The question of remand prisoners crystallizes many of the issues in relation to yearly receptions. Most have been charged with non-violent offences, a disproportionate number are from minority groups while 'around 60% ... are subsequently acquitted or receive non-custodial sentences' (NACRO 1993a:5). Many of these prisoners and other short-term prisoners will be held in prisons which are overcrowded, unhygienic and brutalizing. Given the rise in overcrowding which accelerated between March 1993 and March 1994 many will also be held at a distance from family and friends (NACRO 1994b).

The ADP, described above, provides a different but no less interesting picture. What is important about this figure is that it highlights the increasing percentage of prisoners who are serving longer sentences. This process has been propelled forward by what Tony Bottoms (1977) has described as 'bifurcation', that is distinguishing between dangerous and non-dangerous offenders and responding accordingly by incapacitating the former for longer periods while sentencing the latter to punishment in the community. Since the mid 1960s there has been a significant increase in: the number of prisoners serving very long sentences; life sentence prisoners; the proportion of sentences actually served in prison; and the length of the long-term sentence. Eleven per cent of prisoners in the mid 1960s were serving 4 years or more; by 1990 this figure had climbed to 46 per cent (Morgan 1994:903–6). A similar picture

Table 5.2 Receptions into prison service establishments and average population in custody, by sex and type of custody, England and Wales, 1992 (number of persons)

Type of custody	Receptions into prison service establishments			Average population		
	Males	Females	All males and females	Males	Females	All males and females
All persons in custody	–	–	–	44,240	1,577	45,817
Prisoners on remand	54,614	2,937	57,551	9,707	383	10,090
Untried criminal prisoners	47,501	2,368	49,869	7,805	271	8,076
Convicted unsentenced prisoners awaiting sentence or enquiry	20,051	1,199	21,250	1,902	112	2,014
Received under section 37 Mental Health Act 1983	–	–	–	103	8	111
Others	–	–	–	1,799	104	1,903
Prisoners under sentence	66,630	3,202	69,832	34,230	1,190	35,420
Young offenders	16,941	515	17,456	5,336	133	5,469
Detention in a young offender institution	12,691	339	13,030	5,169	125	5,294
Section 53 C&YP Act 1933 (excluding life)	107	5	112	105	5	110
Life (including HMP and custody for life)	32	–	32	62	3	65
In default of payment of a fine	4,111	171	4,282			
Adults	49,689	2,687	52,376	28,894	1,057	29,951
Immediate imprisonment (excluding life)	34,828	1,800	36,628	25,830	950	26,780
Life (including HMP and custody for life)	190	14	204	2,812	95	2,907
In default of payment of a fine	14,671	873	15,544	252	12	264
Non-criminal prisoners	2,968	141	3,109	303	5	308
Held under the Immigration Act 1971	1,221	51	1,272	224	3	227
Others	1,747	90	1,837	79	2	81

Source: adapted from Home Office 1994d

emerges with life sentence prisoners. In June 1991 there were 2,900 such prisoners; this was 73 per cent above the figure for June 1981 (Home Office 1993d:121).

The process of bifurcation was not a natural event but throughout the 1980s and 1990s was determined by a series of major changes in policy and practice which had a significant effect on the size of the prison population. There were eleven such changes during those years. These changes included the introduction of partly suspended sentences in 1982; the restriction on parole for particular groups of long-term prisoners in 1983; the reduction in the minimum qualifying period for parole in 1984; the introduction of half remission in 1987; and the passing of two Criminal Justice Acts in 1988 and 1991. The majority of these changes affected the population of short- and medium-term prisoners, reducing their number inside. As the Home Office has noted, 'between 1974 and 1992, the average annual increase was about 500 and 4,500 over a nine year period though the average annual increase would have been around 10,000 but for policy interventions' (1993e:4–7). The Home Office has pointed out that the adult male population 'has changed markedly' as a result of the increasing number of individuals being incarcerated for crimes of violence. For example, between 1984 and 1991 the number of men serving sentences for rape increased by 157 per cent. Altogether those serving sentences for violent offences accounted for 33 per cent of the total in 1984, 45 per cent in 1990 and 'had edged down to 43 per cent in 1991'. For adult sentenced women a similar picture emerges in terms of the increase in long-term prisoners. In June 1991, 49 per cent were serving sentences of over 3 years while 'the number serving over 5 years and less than life increased from 30 in June 1984 to over 200 in June 1990'. At the same time the average length of sentence for adult women received under sentence of immediate imprisonment excluding life doubled between 1981 and 1991 (Home Office 1993d:79–94).

Taken together the issues we have pointed to so far reinforce the argument made by Barbara Hudson, namely that the criminal justice system filters 'all sorts of individuals committing all sorts of harms'. The result of this process is the creation of a 'homogeneous population suffering a homogeneity of penalties' (1993:87). The question of gender and punishment, which we consider in more depth below, lends further support to this argument.

Gender and the penal system

Numerically the criminal justice system is dominated by men, both as offenders and as workers. In the case of the latter not only are women in the minority but they are concentrated at the lower end of the hierarchies in the police, courts, prison and probation services. At the end of 1991, for example, 8 (15 per cent) of the 55 chief probation officers were women; while in May 1992, 47 (3 per cent) of the 1,448 principal prison officers in post were women (NACRO 1992a).

In this section we want to highlight particular processes involving women and the penal system and to trace these processes through the remand, custody and post-custody experiences of women. As was argued in the introduction to this volume, these experiences themselves raise broader theoretical questions about the differentiation of punishment in terms of gender, questions which despite a strong and rigorous body of feminist literature still remain ignored in many sociological and official studies in the mid 1990s.

Women on remand

Between 1981 and 1991 the number of women held on remand nearly doubled (Prison Reform Trust 1993b). At the same time only one-quarter of women remandees received a custodial sentence. Women were therefore more likely than men to be remanded, particularly in order to allow the authorities to prepare medical reports on them (Player 1994). The average time women spent on remand also increased throughout the 1980s, from 26 days in 1979 to 44 days in 1989 (NACRO 1993b:5). For particular categories of women the situation was even more difficult. Women defendants charged with offences involving dishonesty or drugs were at a significantly greater risk of custody than men. Foreign women were confronted by the unwillingness of the courts 'to grant bail to foreign nationals or even for solicitors to pursue bail applications on their behalf' (Prison Reform Trust 1993b:4). The small number of remand prisons available for women (three in 1993) further compounded the female remandees' problems, particularly in terms of maintaining personal relationships in a situation where they could be held at some distance from their children and community.

The issue of remands raises a more general question about the availability of alternatives to custody for women. A number of recent studies (Barker 1993; Her Majesty's Inspectorate of Probation 1991) have pointed to the differential access that women offenders have to these alternatives. The report by the Probation Inspectorate published in 1991 noted the 'disproportionately small use of community service for female offenders'. In particular it pointed to the fact that community service has been seen 'as largely a male preserve . . . traditional attitudes about what is appropriate work for women may in the past have excluded them from being considered for community service' (cited in Barker 1993:9). A second reason for excluding women is related to their role as mothers. Community service will be specifically rejected in social enquiry reports on the grounds that the women had children to look after and would therefore be incapable of completing a community service order. As Mary Barker has noted: 'there is an obvious but tragic irony for these mothers in as far as motherhood has been seen as a bar to community penalties but has not stopped them from going to prison with the inevitable consequences for their children' (1993:10). Finally, more women than men are given probation orders. This may not necessarily reflect a more lenient view taken by the courts because, as HM Inspectorate of Probation has noted, among magistrates women are perceived as needing welfare intervention which 'is undoubtedly a factor in the large number of women on probation for minor transgressions and for their first offence' (cited in NACRO 1992b:2).

Sentenced women
The National Association for the Care and Resettlement of Offenders has noted that one in five offenders are women (this refers to offenders of all ages). Twenty-one per cent of the offenders found guilty or cautioned by the courts in 1990 were women. Altogether 226,600 women came into these categories which represented an increase of 32 per cent since 1980. This was largely due to a growth in the number of women found guilty of television licence evasion, from 22,800 in 1980 to 82,300 in 1990 (NACRO 1992b:1).

During the 1980s women experienced a greater increase in the proportionate use of custody and average sentence length than men (HM Inspectorate of Probation 1991:57). Furthermore while women were less likely to be convicted for a crime of violence they were 'proportionately more likely than men to have been received [into prison] for drug offences'. In June 1980 such offenders accounted for 6 per cent of all sentenced women; by June 1990 'the proportion had grown to 28 per cent' (Player 1994:204). Until the early 1990s the average daily population of women prisoners was between 1,500 and 1,600, or 3 to 4 per cent of the prison population. In December 1994, this figure had climbed to just over 1,900, a 17 per cent rise over the average for 1993. The number in custody awaiting trial rose by 21 per cent (*The Guardian* 5 December 1994).

Details about and the characteristics of women in prison are still relatively scarce in England and Wales. This is hardly surprising given the traditional invisibility of women in the criminal justice system, a situation compounded by the fact that the two major inquiries conducted in the last fifteen years – the May and Woolf inquiries – failed to provide any details of or discuss the position of women in prison despite the latter being heralded as the most important inquiry into British prisons for one hundred years. Within conventional social science, the position is hardly any better. Despite a range of critical studies in recent years around women in prison (Carlen 1983; Dobash et al. 1986; Green 1991; Eaton 1993), the 1,259 page, 25 chapter *Oxford Handbook of Criminology* published in 1994, which claimed to be 'one of the most ambitious enterprises ever attempted by British criminologists' (Maguire et al. 1994:1), contained very little detail on women in prison and no separate chapter on their situation.

Despite this official and academic myopia it is possible to construct a partial profile of women in prison through a combination of official reports and the critical studies mentioned above. In the case of the former, the National Prison Survey, which we discussed earlier, provided some empirical details about confined women. The survey noted that: female prisoners tended to be older than male prisoners; a higher proportion were in the short-sentence category of up to 18 months when compared with male prisoners; they were more likely than men to be either divorced or separated and to have dependent children; and they were less likely to have support from their partners in relation to child care arrangements. Additionally a much higher proportion of female prisoners (14 per cent as compared with 1 per cent for men) lived with dependent children and no other adult. The percentage with children in care consequently was much higher than for men (Dodd and Hunter 1992:10–16).

This survey failed to deal with the social class background of women prisoners, preferring solely to look at the occupation of male prisoners when compared with the composition of the male labour force of working age. The work done by critical sociologists, while not providing hard quantifiable data, has provided strong qualitative support for the argument that women prisoners come from the most economically and politically marginalized group in society, that is women at the bottom of the social hierarchy in England and Wales. Studies by Pat Carlen (1988) and Mary Eaton (1993) have pointed to the working class and racial backgrounds of women in prison whose lives have been structured by deeply embedded processes involving class, gender and criminalization which cut through the criminal justice system:

> Taken together these factors have ensured that a greater proportion of poorer (rather than richer) law-breakers are brought before the courts.

Once in court they are again disadvantaged by their poverty and powerlessness. Their inability to pay for adequate legal representation, plus their effective exclusion from judicial proceedings . . . enhance their chances of conviction. Inability to pay a monetary penalty, together with factors such as homelessness or a previous history of institutionalization, increase the likelihood of a custodial penalty. (Carlen 1988:6)

There are a number of other factors which differentiate the background of women from men: they are more likely to have been institutionalized at an earlier stage of their criminal careers (Carlen et al. 1985); they are likely to have had particular experiences of abuse and victimization quite distinct from male offenders (Peelo et al. 1992); they are more likely to have a drug dependency problem than men (NACRO 1992b). According to Mary Eaton many have few ties in the community, have no stable family base and are 'homeless or lacking secure accommodation' (1993:113). In addition the population is more likely to be drawn from particular racial backgrounds. As NACRO has noted, 'the number of black women in prison is disproportionately high.' While black people made up 5 per cent of the general population in June 1991, 29 per cent of women in prison were known to be black compared with 17 per cent in June 1985, the first year that records were kept. Approximately one-third of the women were drug couriers who were to be deported after serving their sentences (NACRO 1992b:3).

In prison, women's experiences are also different to those of men. In 1993 there were nine prisons which held convicted women, both young and old. As with women on remand, these women were more likely than men to be held at a distance from family and friends (Eaton 1993). The regimes are also different and have been characterized as being built on discipline, infantilization, feminization, medicalization and domestication (Carlen and Tchaikovsky 1985).

Women after prison

Finally, in this section we want to point to an area which still remains under-researched but which is nonetheless very important for developing a full, critical anatomy around gender and the penal system. This concerns the kind of support structures available to women when they leave prison. For example, as Eaton has noted, women leaving prison are particularly affected by lack of housing provision. As she notes, 'women who are poor are among those most affected by the unavailability of housing.' In addition, there has been 'little recognition of the specific employment needs of women, or even that employment is a major issue for women'

(1993:118–20). Finally there are the specific issues around welfare and general support such as those relating to employment benefit and regaining the custody of children. As Eaton concludes:

> For too long women have been penalized because of their small numbers within the criminal justice system. Provision, both within and beyond prison, has been aimed at the majority male population. Women have their own needs as women and as women prisoners and these must be acknowledged if they are to be given the space from which to move back into a society which has marginalized and excluded them. (1993:121–2)

The fact that a recently published four page paper by the Home Office (1994e) seeks to dismiss much of what we have argued here, but fails to deal with gender as an analytical category and ignores the work of most of the feminist academics we have cited in its meagre nine references, does not convince us.

Managing the unmanageable

What are the theoretical and political implications of this critical anatomy? In the last part of this chapter we want to raise a number of theoretical questions concerning the complex relationship between the penal system, state power and political economy. In particular we wish to focus on what Malcolm Feeley and Jonathan Simon have called 'the imperatives of the new penology, that is, managing a permanently dangerous population while maintaining the system at a minimum cost' (1992:463). In order to pursue this argument we shall initially highlight the most recent changes that have occurred in England and Wales in relation to the penal system as well as pointing to changes that were being proposed at the time of writing in late 1994 but which had not yet become law. A critical examination of these issues will allow us to raise a set of broader theoretical questions about the politics of the penal system in England and Wales in the mid 1990s.

In the early 1990s following the implementation of the Criminal Justice Act 1991 there was a fall both in the average daily population (to 41,561 in January 1993) and in the proportionate use of immediate custody for persons of all ages sentenced for indictable offences (from 15.7 per cent to 11.6 per cent) (Cavadino 1994:4). However, in February 1993 the prison population began to rise so that by February 1994 it stood at 47,906, an increase of 12 per cent on the previous year. Much of this growth was propelled by prisoners on remand: in January 1994 the remand population stood at 12,100. According to the Prison Reform Trust this was 'an all-time record'. Between January 1993 and January 1994, the number of women remand prisoners grew by 30 per cent alone (Prison Reform Trust 1994a:1–5). The proportionate use of custodial sentences also began to rise sharply during this period: from 42 per cent in January 1993 it had climbed to 54 per cent the following August (Cavadino 1994:5). By July 1994 the average daily population stood at 49,227, a rise of 9,000 over the previous eighteen months.

At the same time, Home Office research indicated that a number of changes in sentencing had occurred during 1993 partly as a result of the Criminal Justice Act 1993. In particular there was a rise in the immediate use of custody which was most apparent among offenders found guilty of property offences and those with between six and twenty previous convictions. In magistrates courts the proportionate use of custody rose to 7 per cent and in crown courts to 52 per cent, '4 and 12 points higher than the same quarter a year earlier' (Home Office 1994c:3). The research also pointed to a decline in the proportionate use of the fine and in community sentences. It should also be noted that these changes were occurring at a time when fewer cases were reaching the courts (*The Guardian* 22 July 1994).

Projected figures for the year 2001 have estimated that the prison population will be 56,600, an increase of 5,000 from previous projections. According to the Home Office, the new projection was based on the assumption that changes in sentencing introduced by the Criminal Justice Act 1993 'will result in an increased proportion of offenders receiving custodial sentences; and increases in sentence length. There may also be a small increase in the remand population as a result of the introduction of a prosecution right to appeal against bail' (Home Office 1994f:10–11).

These wider changes were mirrored in a series of other changes which were proposed towards the end of 1993, changes which affected both the nature of prison regimes and the role and function of alternatives to custody. In October, Michael Howard, the Home Secretary, announced a 27 point law and order package which, amongst other things, included imposing tougher restrictions on granting police bail, producing a review aimed at imposing harsher sentences in the community and doubling the maximum one year sentence in young offender institutions (*The Independent* 7 October 1993). The following month further measures were announced. These included: giving judges the power to bring defendants back to court by revoking their bail if new information about an offence was discovered; removing the traditional assumption in favour of bail for those charged with serious offences allegedly committed on bail; granting the police powers to attach conditions to bail without waiting for a court hearing; and finally allowing the police to arrest without warrant for breach of police bail (*The Guardian* 10 November 1993).

In May 1994, other alternatives to custody were confronted by a series of proposed changes built on the same disciplinary drive. Offenders sentenced to probation who flouted new rules around lateness and abusive language were to be returned to court to face the very real prospect of a custodial sentence. Other suggestions included the proposed introduction of uniforms for probation officers and the employment of increased numbers of former soldiers and police officers to generate a greater disciplinary ethos in the welfare culture of the service (*The Independent* 5 May 1994; *The Guardian* 27 June 1994). These proposals were themselves underpinned by a number of other suggested policy changes including reducing the use of police cautioning and reintroducing electronic tagging and curfew orders. The welfare role of probation was also under attack materially as well as ideologically. In 1994–5 the budget was to be cut by 3.5 per cent, while a further cut of 8 per cent was planned for 1995–6. Plans to build 40 new bail hostels were shelved while a number of the existing 112 hostels faced the possibility of closure, the consequences of which are now being felt (*The Guardian* 1 December 1993; 14 August 1994).

The prison service was also confronted by a number of changes. In December 1993, under proposals in the Criminal Justice and Public Order Bill, privatization was reinforced and extended; state prison governors were to be given powers to run private prisons in the event of an emergency; and following discussions with a Liverpool based shipping line the use of prison ships was to be legalized (*The Guardian* 18 December 1993).

Once inside, prisoners are to be placed in regimes which will emphasize austerity rather than rehabilitation, security rather than justice and privileges rather than rights. Austere regimes will include extending the maximum use of solitary confinement from 3 days to 14 days for adults (and to 7 days for young offenders); banning radios and smoking in punishment cells; and removing beds and bedding during the day leaving only a table and chairs. Privileges earned will also be taken away for misconduct (*The Guardian* 4 November 1993; 9 December 1993). The cutback in the greater use of home leave, the rejection of in-cell television and the postponement of an end to slopping out only reinforced the emphasis on disciplined austerity as the preferred response to dealing with offending behaviour.

Purposes and intentions

How are these changes, together with the figures and issues identified in this chapter, to be interpreted and understood?

Liberal commentators have maintained that the spiralling prison population is the result of a number of interconnected processes: first, the marginalization of the reforms proposed by Lord Justice Woolf in the wake of his inquiry into the furious 25 day demonstration by prisoners at Strangeways and other prisons in April 1990; second, the role of the media in calling for harsher responses to crime, particularly those involving juveniles; and third, the ideological and pragmatic interventions made by successive Home Secretaries Kenneth Clarke and Michael Howard who rejected the reforming parts of the Criminal Justice Act 1991 and the rhetoric of justice and reasserted the conservative view that the 'austere' prison and the 'disciplinary' community are *the* sites of punishment for the morally bankrupt, the plain evil and the ill-disciplined.

At one level there is some analytical support for this liberal perspective. The processes which this argument has identified clearly have had a powerful influence on the state of the penal system and the law and order debate in general. However, there are significant sociological and political problems with this analysis. Space does not permit us to fully discuss these problems here: they have been documented elsewhere (Sim 1993–4). Nonetheless we do want to argue that a key problem with this position is that it continually fails to confront the sociological fact that the historical, contemporary and future role of the penal system in England and Wales has been and is likely to remain its coercive capacity to manage and regulate those on society's economic and political margins who have simultaneously been positioned within a set of discourses which have denigrated, demonized and dehumanized them. In short, liberals have failed to consider the complex, dialectical relationship that exists between the material and symbolic role of the penal system, the shifting contours of state power and the maintenance of a social order deeply divided along the fault lines of social class, gender, race, sexuality and age (Sim 1994).

In taking this position we are not presenting an instrumental, a homogeneous or a conspiratorial view of state power, nor are we constructing an easy 'fit' between the state, punishment and the dynamics of a monetarist, patriarchal political economy. This relationship is clearly more complex and contingent than a reductionist position implies (Jessop 1990). At the same time, and contrary to the still sociologically ill-informed assertions of self-styled 'left realists' (Young 1994), we are not dismissing the impact that crime has on the lives of the powerless within a materially unequal society. But, as Dario Melossi has noted, the complex questions of criminality, criminalization and who is to be punished do not stand outside or above particular political moments, but rather are caught up in the complex balance of forces through which those who hold the reins of power are able to define and mobilize key themes and images:

> The changing sensibilities of society tend in fact to vary according to the sensibilities of its elites. Society's members learn to believe that the concerns and the enemies of the elites are their concerns, and their enemies. This is hardly the result of conspiracies. It is indeed part of, and not an irrelevant contribution to, what we refer to as 'hegemony'. (1993:274)

In England and Wales the relationship between the penal system, an emerging law and order state and the struggle for hegemony was an important theme in the sociology of the prison in the 1980s (Box 1983; Sim 1987; Hillyard and Percy-Smith 1988). This work, which built on the penetrating analyses developed by Nicos Poulantzas, Andrew Gamble and Stuart Hall concerning the ascendancy of the new right and the concomitant state and social authoritarianism that flowed from this ascendancy, pointed to the place of the penal system in the emergence of a more integrated and less informal system of justice. This system was increasingly responding to problems of crime and public disorder in a manner which was 'rational, professional and ultimately ruthless' (Sim 1987:205). Between 1979 and 1989 successive Conservative governments not only instigated and consolidated a massive prison building programme but also introduced a range of Acts, Orders and Bills which increased the power of the state to intervene in the lives of individual citizens and particular demonized groups. Between 1985 and 1989 alone there were 11 major pieces of legislation which centralized and increased state power, removed and restricted a range of civil liberties and welfare rights and criminalized the activities of groups such as trade unionists, political demonstrators and gay activists (Scraton et al. 1991:156–7). This ruthless process of intervention and criminalization was paralleled by an equally ruthless process of state disengagement from policing and regulating the activities of the economically powerful and politically influential. During the 1980s this disengagement was clearly seen in the investigation and (non-) prosecution of large scale fraud (Levi 1989) and in provision for health and safety at work (Scraton et al. 1991:158).

In the 1990s the drive towards social authoritarianism and the centralization of power has been maintained, though the groups towards whom this has been directed have been broadened. Increasingly this has been done on the back of strident calls for more law and order and the continual targeting of those groups seen as responsible for turning the nation into a moral and criminal wasteland. The measures discussed above which have tightened the penal screw still further have been supported by a range of other clauses in the Criminal Justice and Public Order Bill which was passing through the British Houses of Parliament in July 1994. These clauses were designed to criminalize the activities of groups such as peaceful protesters, travellers and squatters. Clauses 56 and 57 will make it a criminal offence for a squatter to remain in a building 24 hours after being served with an interim possession order. This order can be obtained at an *ex parte* court hearing in the absence of the defendant. Ignoring the order will carry a six month prison sentence and/or a £5,000 fine. The police will be able to proceed on a discretionary basis and arrest anyone whom they reasonably suspect of being guilty. Finally, clause 71 allows violent entry by owners of properties or anyone acting on their behalf. These clauses are reinforced by the public order sections of the Bill which will allow the police to control access to public space particularly in relation to mass gatherings, strikes and protest meetings. Clauses 52 and 53 will make obstructing a bulldozer on a peaceful protest a criminal offence punishable by three months in prison and/or a £2,500 fine. A similar punishment awaits those who fail to leave land and whom the police reasonably believe are *about* to commit aggravated trespass (*New Statesman* 29 April 1994).

In contrast to this draconian, interventionist legislation with the enormous potential for criminalization that comes with it, the Deregulation and Contracting Out Bill which was launched in January 1994 is designed to remove 450 pieces of legislation and regulations governing, amongst other things, employment protection and the powers of local authorities to enforce regulations covering hygiene and building and construction work. It will also give the government the power to make these changes and repeal primary legislation by ministerial order without any debate in the elected forum of the House of Commons. Health and safety legislation is also targeted in the Bill and, although plans for the sweeping deregulation of this legislation are unlikely to be forthcoming in the short term, the danger in the long term is that 'the government might eventually seek to water down statutory "codes of practice" which are seen to be almost as regulatory as the law itself' (*The Independent* 21 May 1994; *The Guardian* 20 January 1994).

David Farnham and Sylvia Horton have made the point that the emergence of the strong state has been tied not only to the deregulation of the economy and the articulation of the goal of popular capitalism but also to a series of reforms which have branded the discourses of efficiency, prudence, competition, individual responsibility and performance contracts onto the collective body of state, welfare and public service institutions in society (1993:19–24). At the same time, the emergence of quasi-autonomous agencies to which we referred earlier has intensified in the 1990s. By 1996 it is estimated that more than 7,700 public bodies will be controlled wholly or partly by government appointees who will be responsible for 'nearly £54 billion of taxpayers' money. Repeated attacks on local government by consecutive Conservative governments have shifted power away from democratically elected bodies to agencies filled by appointees either directly or indirectly put in place by Ministers' (Beavis and Nicholson 1993:18). According to the Prison Reform Trust, agency status for the prison service has in some ways only increased the political control to which the service is subjected. As the organization has pointed out, 'the process of target-setting backed up by key performance indicators allows Ministers to decide the priorities for every prison governor. By demanding a reduction in the overall cost per prisoner, for example, the Home Secretary is fuelling the push towards civilianization of prison officer posts and further contracting out' (1994b:3).

Space does not allow us to analyse the full implications of this development in relation to theories of the state in general or the penal system in particular. However it is important to note that the emergence and consolidation of these agencies does raise significant sociological and political questions about the shifting contours of state power, the relationship between the private and the public, the nature of democratic accountability and the impact of the decisions made by these agencies on those who are at the sharp end of the decision-making process. In terms of law and order 'agencies' it is extremely debatable if this development will mark a significant shift away from those groups who have been the traditional property of these agencies. The delivery may change but the targets for regulatory management are likely to remain the same. The anatomy and background of the 56,600 incarcerated in 2001 are unlikely to be very different from the anatomy and background of the current prison population which we discussed earlier.

Conclusion

This is the material and ideological context in which developments in the penal system in England and Wales in the mid 1990s should be understood. In the febrile law and order climate that dominates political and popular debate, these institutions, along with other micro sites of power such as the family, school and welfare, are regarded as the sites where discipline is to be reasserted and imposed onto the bodies and into the minds of those identified as responsible for the apparent disintegration in moral values, community life and respect for the law. The presence, behaviour and lifestyle of single parents (particularly women), young people, the homeless, scroungers, drug takers, illegal immigrants and the conventional criminal have been elided into one apocalyptic vision of chaos and breakdown, an unmanageable detritus out of control. As Dario Melossi has observed, this moral construction builds on a 'vocabulary of punitive motives' held by the powerful and has a direct influence on rates of imprisonment:

> While it may be that higher imprisonment rates are influenced by the unintended consequences of a set of micro decisions . . . it is also true that these micro decisions (not only by court personnel but also by police officers, lawmakers, moral entrepreneurs, etc.) are not made in a vacuum. They have to be accounted for, on both legal and moral grounds, within a hegemonic discourse, a discourse toward which those who administer the criminal and penal justice systems feel particularly responsible (whether or not they share the wisdom of the contingent political arrangements of those systems). The concept of a changing hegemonic 'vocabulary of punitive motives' may help us explain the *consistent* character of all these micro decisions avoiding at the same time the assumption of conspiratorial intentionality generally assigned to those who are entrusted with making these decisions. (1993:273–4 emphasis in the original)

Given this scenario the future looks bleak in England and Wales. The historical marginalization of rehabilitation and reintegration has become intensified within a penology which as we noted earlier is built on 'programmes [which] . . . can best be understood in terms of managing costs and controlling dangerous populations rather than social or personal transformation' (Feeley and Simon 1992:465).

In European terms the future may also be bleak if British penal policy becomes normalized within the police, judicial and penal complex of Fortress Europe. This policy may not experience the same hostility and opposition usually accorded to British views on a range of legislative areas, particularly if it is seen to be 'successful' in the regulatory incapacitation of the difficult, deviant and subversive. Ironically, therefore, the present government's often stated desire to be at the heart of Europe may be fulfilled by the one thing that the country remains good at – locking people up.

References

Alfred R (1992) *Black Workers in the Prison Service* London: Prison Reform Trust

Audit Commission (1989) *The Probation Service: Promoting Value for Money* London: HMSO

Barker M (1993) *Community Service and Women Offenders* London: Association of Chief Officers of Probation

Beavis S and Nicholson J (1993) 'Rise and Rise of the Quangocrats' *The Guardian* 19 November 1993

Bottoms A (1977) 'Reflections on the renaissance of dangerousness' *Howard Journal of Penology and Crime Prevention* 16, 2: 70–96

Bottoms A (1980) 'An introduction to the coming crisis' in A Bottoms and R Preston (eds) *The Coming Penal Crisis* Edinburgh: Scottish Academic Press

Box S (1983) *Power, Crime and Mystification* London: Tavistock

Burnett R and Farrell G (1994) *Reported and Unreported Racial Incidents* Oxford Institute of Criminology Occasional Paper 14

Carlen P (1983) *Women's Imprisonment* London: Routledge

Carlen P (1988) *Women, Crime and Poverty* Milton Keynes: Open University Press

Carlen P and Tchaikovsky C (1985) 'Women in Prison' in P Carlen, D Christina, J Hicks, J O'Dwyer and C Tchaikovsky *Criminal Women* Cambridge: Polity

Carlen P, Christina D, Hicks J, O'Dwyer J and Tchaikovsky C (1985) *Criminal Women* Cambridge: Polity

Cavadino P (1994) 'Recent Developments in England and Wales' unpublished paper

Cavadino M and Dignan J (1992) *The Penal System* London: Sage

Central Statistical Office (1994) *Social Trends* London: HMSO

Cheney D (1993) *Into the Dark Tunnel* London: Prison Reform Trust

Dobash R, Dobash R and Gutteridge S (1986) *The Imprisonment of Women* Oxford: Blackwell

Dodd T and Hunter P (1992) *The National Prison Survey 1991* London: HMSO

Eaton M (1993) *Women After Prison* Buckingham: Open University Press

Evans P (1980) *Prison Crisis* London: George Allen and Unwin

Farnham D and Horton S (1993) 'The political economy of public sector change' in D Farnham and S Horton (eds) *Managing the New Public Services* Basingstoke: Macmillan

Feeley M and Simon J (1992) 'The New Penology: Notes on the Emerging Strategy of Corrections and its Implications' *Criminology* 30, 4: 449–74

Fitzgerald M and Sim J (1979) *British Prisons* 1st edn, Oxford: Blackwell

Fitzgerald M and Sim J (1982) *British Prisons* 2nd edn, Oxford: Blackwell

Genders E and Player E (1989) *Race Relations in Prison* Oxford: Clarendon

Green P (1991) *Drug Couriers* London: Howard League for Penal Reform

Hall S, Critcher C, Jefferson T, Clarke J and Roberts B (1978) *Policing the Crisis* Basingstoke: Macmillan

Her Majesty's Inspectorate of Probation (1991) *Report on Women Offenders and Probation Service Provision* London: Home Office

Her Majesty's Prison Service Health Care (1993) *First Report of the Director of Health Care for Prisoners* London: Home Office

Hillyard P and Percy-Smith J (1988) *The Coercive State* London: Fontana

Home Office (1979) *Committee of Inquiry into the United Kingdom Prison Service* Report, Cmnd 7673, London: HMSO

Home Office (1986) *Criminal Justice: A Working Paper* London: Home Office

Home Office (1990) *Crime, Justice and Protecting the Public* London: HMSO

Home Office (1993a) *HM Prison Service, Framework Document* London

Home Office (1993b) *HM Prison Service, Corporate Plan* London

Home Office (1993c) *Home Office Annual Report* Cmnd 2208, London

Home Office (1993d) *Prison Statistics England and Wales 1991* Cmnd 2157, London: HMSO

Home Office (1993e) *Home Office Statistical Bulletin Issue 6/93* London: Government Statistical Office

Home Office (1994a) *Criminal Statistics, England and Wales 1993* Cmnd 2680, London: HMSO

Home Office (1994b) *Home Office Annual Report 1994* Cmnd 2508, London: Home Office

Home Office (1994c) 'Monitoring of the Criminal Justice Acts 1991 and 1993: Results From a Special Data Collection Exercise' *Home Office Statistical Bulletin* 20/94, July, London: Home Office

Home Office (1994d) *Prison Statistics England and Wales 1992* Cmnd 2581, London: HMSO

Home Office (1994e) *Does the Criminal Justice System Treat Men and Women Differently?* Home Office Research and Statistics Department, Research Findings No. 10, London: Home Office

Home Office (1994f) 'The Prison Population in 1993 and Long Term Projections to 2001' *Home Office Statistical Bulletin* 16/94, June, London: Home Office

Hudson B (1993) *Penal Policy and Social Justice* Basingstoke: Macmillan

Hughes J (1991) *Poverty and Offending in Somerset* Somerset: Somerset Probation Service

Jessop B (1990) *State Theory* London: Polity

Levi M (1989) 'Fraudulent Justice? Sentencing the Business Criminal' in P Carlen and D Cook (eds) *Paying for Crime* Milton Keynes: Open University Press

Maguire M, Morgan R and Reiner R (eds) (1994) *The Oxford Handbook of Criminology* Oxford: Clarendon

Mathiesen T (1974) *The Politics of Abolition* Oxford: Martin Robertson

Melossi D (1993) 'Gazette of Morality and Social Whip: Punishment, Hegemony and the Case of the USA, 1970–1992' *Social and Legal Studies* 2, 3, September: 259–79

Morgan R (1994) 'Imprisonment' in M Maguire, R Morgan and R Reiner (eds) *The Oxford Handbook of Criminology* Oxford: Clarendon

Murphy R (1994) 'The Invisible Minority: Irish Offenders and the English Criminal Justice System' *Probation Journal* March: 2–7

NACRO (1992a) *Statistics and Women Working in the Criminal Justice System* London: NACRO

NACRO (1992b) *Women and Criminal Justice: Some Facts and Figures* London: NACRO

NACRO (1993a) *Remands in Custody: Some Facts and Figures* London: NACRO

NACRO (1993b) *Women Leaving Prison* London: NACRO

NACRO (1994a) *The Cost of Penal Measures* NACRO Briefing, 23 July, London: NACRO

NACRO (1994b) *Prison Overcrowding: Recent Developments* London: NACRO

NAPO (1993) *Probation Caseload: Income and Employment. A Study of the Financial Circumstances of 1331 Offenders on Probation Supervision* London: NAPO

NAPO (1994) *Fines, Default and Debtors Gaol* London: NAPO

Peelo M, Stewart J, Stewart G and Prior A (1992) *A Sense of Justice: Offenders as Victims of Crime* London: Association of Chief Officers of Probation

Pirouet L (1994) 'Detention not Refuge' *Prison Report* 27, Summer: 10–11, London: Prison Reform Trust

Player E (1994) 'Women's Prisons after Woolf' in E Player and M Jenkins (eds) *Prisons after Woolf* London: Routledge

Prison Reform Trust (1993a) *Prison Overcrowding: A Crisis Waiting in the Wings* London: Prison Reform Trust

Prison Reform Trust (1993b) *Women Prisoners on Remand* London: Prison Reform Trust

Prison Reform Trust (1994a) *Whatever Happened to the Bail Act?* London: Prison Reform Trust

Prison Reform Trust (1994b) *Prison Report* 27, Summer, London: Prison Reform Trust

Ryan M (1978) *The Acceptable Pressure Group, Inequality in the Penal Lobby: A Case Study of Radical Alternatives to Prison and the Howard League* Farnborough: Teakfield

Ryan M (1983) *The Politics of Penal Reform* London: Longman

Ryan M (1994) 'Private Prisons in the United Kingdom: Radical Change and Opposition' in P Moyle (ed) *Privatization of Prisons and Police in Australia and New Zealand* Sydney: Pluto Press

Ryan M and Ward T (1990–1) 'Restructuring, resistance and privatization in the non-custodial sector' *Critical Social Policy* 30, Winter

Scraton P (ed) (1987) *Law Order and the Authoritarian State* Milton Keynes: Open University Press

Scraton P, Sim J and Skidmore P (1991) *Prisons under Protest* Buckingham: Open University Press

Sim J (1987) 'Working for the Clampdown: Prisons and Politics in England and Wales' in P Scraton (ed) *Law, Order and the Authoritarian State* Milton Keynes: Open University Press

Sim J (1993–4) 'Turning the Prison Screw' *Criminal Justice Matters* 14, Winter: 12

Sim J (1994) 'Reforming the Penal Wasteland?' in E Player and M Jenkins (eds) *Prisons after Woolf* London: Routledge

Turnbull P (1993) 'Drug Use, Drug Injecting and HIV in Prisons'. Paper presented at the *Physicians for Human Rights Conference* London, July

Walmsley R, Howard L and White S (1992) *The National Prison Survey 1991: Main Findings* Home Office Research Unit No. 128, London: HMSO

Woolf Lord Justice (1991) *Prison Disturbances 1990* Cmnd 1456, London: HMSO

Young J (1986) 'The Failure of Criminology: The Need for a Radical Realism' in R Matthews and J Young (eds) *Confronting Crime* London: Sage

Young J (1994) 'Incessant Chatter: Recent Paradigms in Criminology' in M Maguire, R Morgan and R Reiner (eds) *The Oxford Handbook of Criminology* Oxford: Clarendon

6

Germany: the Penal System between Past and Future

Claudius Messner and Vincenzo Ruggiero

In recent years the German criminal justice system, including the penal system, has received more than its fair share of attention. During the 1970s it was widely criticized for its severity in dealing with political dissent and the actual (and perceived) threat of armed struggle. The special legislation introduced in those years included longer remand periods and solitary confinement for those charged with political violence. It also entailed a widening of power for the police who could cordon off and raid entire urban areas, and hold suspects for days without pressing charges (Ferrajoli and Zolo 1977; Seelmann 1981). The effects of this legislation culminated in 1977, when three political prisoners were found dead in Stammheim prison, as a result of what the authorities unconvincingly described as a 'group suicide' (Silvi 1977). Paradoxically, by the late 1980s Germany's success in reducing the overall size of the prison population, as well as in improving the safeguards theoretically offered to those in custody, was praised. An analysis of this reduction will be attempted. More recently the pendulum has swung back again. The German prison population is rising, fuelled it seems by public anxiety in the aftermath of unification, but also by the perceived threats of immigration and drug related crime. In the following pages we will discuss whether these fears are justified. In the meantime we shall simply sketch out the sources, procedures and principles which underpin German criminal law.

Sources, procedures and principles

The Bundestag is the legislative authority of the states which form the Federal Republic of Germany. According to the constitution it is also the authority that presides over the criminal justice system and the administration of the penal system. In these fields, in other words, individual states are subject to federal authority.

The fundamental source of German criminal law is typically

made up of formal written statutes passed in the Bundestag, although in certain circumstances the findings of the Federal Constitutional Court also apply as law. Furthermore, and obviously perhaps, the judiciary also has a significant role in shaping the criminal law as statutes and constitutional rulings need to be interpreted and applied. Except for some minor respects, German criminal law applies to all states of the Republic equally, as do the Penal Code and the Code of Criminal Procedure. The latter establishes the way in which criminal proceedings are to be initiated and take place, and guides trials through their different stages. Another body of procedural legislation establishes which court in the judicial hierarchy is to hear a case, as well as the criteria for the appointment of lay judges and other court staff. Prison regimes and custodial treatment of offenders are established by the specific Law of Prison Administration.

The constitution has a guiding as well as a correcting function with respect to the criminal law, as it guarantees fundamental individual rights and establishes a number of principles that the criminal law itself is to follow in order for these rights to be guaranteed. However, it has to be stressed that the constitution does not indicate the principles or the philosophy upon which the penal law should be based. Except for the principles securing the abolition of capital punishment which are clearly stated, the constitution is confined to the vague enunciation of a number of formal principles regarding the 'legality' and humanity of punishment and the appropriate procedure for the delivery of sentences. Although these principles are important for the safeguarding of individual rights, there is no general constitutional statement included as to the meaning and objectives of the criminal and the penal law, and the 'reasonable' results that both are expected to achieve.

The Penal Code comprises two sections. The first is a general section containing guidelines for sentencers, and consists of general rules which are to be applied in the treatment of all offences. The principles of the constitution are enshrined in this general part. The second section of the Penal Code is also known as the special part, and includes a description of specific offences, their characteristics, and the range of penalties available for each of them. The specific legislation included in the second section of the Penal Code is underpinned by the general principles described in the first. The second section was historically regarded as more relevant by reformers, who centred their campaigns on it until the turn of the century. Since 1900, however, the general part of the Penal Code has undergone more substantial changes than the special part as campaigners – especially in the 1920s and 1960s – concentrated their efforts on the well-being of offenders, the development of alternatives to custody, and the improvement of prisoners' rights.

Criminal procedure

A number of principles underpin the procedural aspects of German criminal law. These provide details as to how investigation and sentencing are to take place, along with the roles of the institutional actors involved. As with those underlying punishment, these principles are inscribed within the notion of the rule of law.

There is, first of all, the principle of 'innocence before guilt is proven'. During the preliminary investigation the onus is on the prosecutor to gather evidence that an offence has been committed. The burden of proof, in other words, rests exclusively with the prosecution. Second, prosecutors are required to search for the truth, regardless of the defendants' claims or their desire to 'negotiate' their guilt. In this light, plea bargaining theoretically should be excluded, although forms of plea bargaining are in fact in operation. Third, defendants have a right to be heard. No decision may be taken by the courts unless those affected by the decision are given the opportunity to explain their views. Fourth, offences must be processed irrespective of the victim's will. There are exceptions to this general principle, as the investigation and prosecution of some very minor offences may only take place after the victim's explicit request. Moreover, some offences of a political nature (for example political violence) may only be brought to court when formal permission is granted by the government or parliament.

The prosecution is also governed by the principle of *legality*. This entails that a charge must be brought whenever there is sufficient grounds for suspecting a person. This principle is in a sense neutralized by its opposite, namely the principle of *opportunity*. According to this principle, prosecutors may drop charges with a view to relieving the workload of courts, thus applying a *de facto* decriminalization policy. Finally, prosecutors are not only required to conduct the pre-trial investigation, but also to formally bring the case before a judge. Without the formal presentation of a case in court, the case cannot be heard.

All of these principles apply to the procedural aspects of German criminal law and inform all stages included in it. These stages concern: investigation, intermediate proceedings, and main trial. First, prosecutors (with the co-operation of the police) investigate whether an offence has been committed. When evidence has been collected, prosecutors may decide either to drop the case or to bring it to court. Second, the court decides whether the case should undergo trial. This stage, which precedes the proper trial, is usually the longest in the whole process as details regarding charges and the circumstances in which the offences have allegedly been committed are still being investigated. When this stage is completed either the prosecution is initiated or the defendant is released.

The public prosecutor has the prerogative to both conduct the investigation and formally initiate the prosecution. Theoretically, the police should only act as an auxiliary force in these processes, but in reality they play a central role in them, with the public prosecutor merely providing legal supervision. When enough evidence is available, the prosecutor is required to bring the case before a court. As we have already seen, without this formal act, the case will not be heard. During the trial, public prosecutors act as representatives of the state.

Judges deliberate on cases and, according to the constitution, they are to be impartial and independent from the other bodies of the state. When defendants have grounds to challenge their impartiality and independence, judges may in theory be disqualified and replaced.

Because of the varying nature and seriousness of offences, courts which are allocated cases also differ. There are local courts (*Amtsgerichte*), district courts (*Ländgerichte*), and high courts (*Oberländesgerichte*). The second group are courts of appeal, which re-examine cases already dealt with by local courts. In turn, high courts only examine the legality and the appropriateness of the procedure adopted by the previous two courts. The Federal Supreme Court (Bundesgerichtshof) performs the same function, and returns verdicts as to the legality and formal correctness of trials. Finally, the Constitutional Court (Bundesverfassungsgericht) is the supreme German court, and its pronouncements may be solicited when defendants feel that their constitutional rights have been violated.

In the following section we deal with the outcome of criminal procedure, namely the processing and punishment of offenders.

The use of fines and imprisonment

The most widely used penalties in Germany are the fine and imprisonment. Both are to be proportional to the severity of the offence.

In 1991, the latest date for which official figures were available at the time of writing, the number of persons found guilty of an offence, including both adults and juveniles (between 14 and 17), was 622,390, of which 521,000 received a fine. Since the late 1980s, fines represent on average more than 80 per cent of all penalties, of which 6 per cent eventually become custodial sentences for fine defaulters (Statistische Bundesamt 1993). Data published since the late 1980s suggest that there has been no dramatic shift in the dominance of the fine as a punishment. Since 1975, fines have been no longer imposed as a lump sum, but determined as a per diem charge. The minimum daily rate is 2 Deutschmarks and the maximum is 10,000 Deutschmarks. The number of days for which fines are inflicted varies between 5 and 360. The daily fine rate is determined on the basis of both the nature and the severity of the offence and the monthly income of the offender. Fines extending to as long as 180 days may be suspended subject to a probation period of between one and three years. However, courts do not make much use of this suspension (in 1990 they only did so in 184 cases), as those suitable for probation are already given this punishment without being given a fine (Statistische Bundesamt 1993).

Fines usually replace prison sentences up to three months. Despite this potential abolition of short custodial sentences, and owing to the increase in the number of fine defaulters, prisoners serving up to nine months still form about a third of the German prison population. Among these, prisoners released after serving a third or half of their sentence should be included. Early release is granted in about one-third of all cases. It should be noted that this practice is at odds with the official principle that the treatment of offenders is to lead to rehabilitation. Prisoners are so quickly in and out of custody that no treatment is possible for those who both need it and are entitled to it under the constitution.

The increase in the number of prisoners who are granted early release runs parallel with the increase in the number of long-term prisoners. Between 1980 and 1990, for example, custodial sentences of up to two years dropped from 33 per cent to 28 per cent whereas sentences over two years increased from 29 per cent to 33.8 per cent (Statistische Bundesamt 1993).

Custody remains the core punishment: it is increasingly inflicted on serious offenders and is also used for defendants awaiting the final stages of trial (for example, those awaiting an appeal). Finally, over the last two decades, a marked increase has been observed of non-German prisoners, who are now about 15 per cent of the total prison population, a point we shall also return to below.

In 1990 40 per cent of the prison population was under 30. Those under 18 constituted less than 1 per cent. Altogether just over three-quarters of the population were aged 40 and under. There were 327 prisoners aged between 60 and 64, 142 between 65 and 69, and 72 aged 70 or more.

The prison system

The German prison system is built on a variety of institutions including: those for convicted offenders, those for remand prisoners, those for juveniles, and those providing support for offenders sentenced to non-custodial alternatives. In 1992 there were 194 prison institutions, of which 151 were defined as 'closed', 22 as 'open', and 21 as prisons for juveniles. Of the 59,002 places available, 45,892 (78 per cent) were occupied (Statistische Bundesamt 1994). All institutions are run by the state. It is a strongly held principle that the state should never give up its monopoly in the use of force and the control and treatment of deviance. Hence, examples of prison privatization offered by the United States, the UK and France, for the time being at least, are regarded with suspicion. However, this attitude has been suspended when it comes to other state agencies using force, such as the police and other security services, where privatization is being encouraged.

Legislation introduced in 1976 was aimed at subjecting prison treatment to the control of the judiciary, with judges specifically appointed for the supervision of regimes and the hearing of prisoners' complaints. Eventually, these provisions became part of the Prison Act 1977, a piece of legislation which is often seen as a model to be emulated in the arena of prisoners' rights.

It has been suggested that the Prison Act restored the principle of resocialization which was prevalent during the years of the Weimar Republic. The Act was designed to introduce substantial reform in the nature of imprisonment which all too often was seen as violating human rights. It was therefore aimed at 'extending positive rights, thus providing in effect a mechanism for ensuring minimum standards' (Prowse et al. 1992:116). Prisoners' rights had to be safeguarded against the background of the basic principles of the German constitution, namely the rule of law and the principle of welfare, or the 'social state principle'. The latter principle, which entails a duty on the part of the state to support its more needy citizens, has particular implications for prisoners. For imprisoned citizens, support means rehabilitation, which in a sense can be seen as one of their rights. 'In this constitutional context, the notion of rehabilitation does not spring from a belief that a prisoner can be "reformed" or "treated" . . . the idea of re-socialization inherent in the social state principle is a *basic right* and thus a *citizen's right*' (1992:116).

However, the principle of resocialization is challenged by the 'public defence' principle whereby prisoners' rights can be suspended when it is felt that public safety is at risk. This generates a degree of discretion which in fact undermines the rights of prisoners. Paradoxically, it was after the implementation of the Prison Act, when the nature and limits of the Act itself were clearly perceived, that prison disturbances erupted on a larger scale. These disturbances were partly due to disillusionment on the part of prisoners after their expectations had been unduly raised (Ortner 1990). Expectations were high with regard to a general improvement in prison conditions, and more specifically, with respect to newly established prisoners' committees and boards of advisers. These were allegedly designed to facilitate the participation of the inmates in the running of the institutions, and to develop relationships with the outside world. However, these structures were never given enough power to achieve their purposes, and their influence remained marginal (Prowse et al. 1992).

The Act was also criticized with respect to the regulations regarding prisoners' complaints. Litigation procedures were said to take so long that by the time complaints were heard about the regime or resocialization practices, the prisoner concerned had often served her/his entire sentence (Weber 1990).

Remand prisoners

Detention on remand is not regarded as a penal sanction as such. In this sense remand prisons and remand prisoners are not formally part of the penal apparatus, in that the treatment of offenders cannot start before they have been proven guilty by a court. Nevertheless, remand has a considerable impact on the prison system as a whole. In the late 1980s, for example, between 33 and 36 per cent of prisoners were on remand. Requests for remanding defendants in custody are made by public prosecutors to judges, when it is apparent that the investigation of a case is likely to be protracted. Apart from cases in which very serious offences have been committed, remand can only be applied when specific reasons are given and when these strictly refer to and are included in the Code of Criminal Procedure. It should be noted that remand imprisonment has no time limitation.

Table 6.1 illustrates that between 1986 and 1993, the number of remand prisoners consistently increased. The increase was in both absolute and relative terms, with the percentage of remand prisoners reaching well over 50 per cent.

In 1991, the large majority of remand prisoners (96 per cent) were described as likely to attempt to escape. In the same year, in 25 per cent of the cases the remand period lasted up to 3 months, in 20 per cent it lasted up to 6 months, in almost 13 per cent its

Table 6.1 *Remands in prison, 1984–1993*

Number of prisoners	Sentenced prisoners	Remand
1984	42,140	13,855
1985	41,852	12,598
1986	39,407	11,626
1987	36,987	11,544
1988	36,076	11,813
1989	36,101	12,023
1990	34,799	NA
1991[1]	25,581	14,068
Jan. 1992	30,123	15,480
Sep. 1992	32,606	16,548
Oct. 1993	32,349	19,218

[1] For 1991 the numbers were counted around Christmas, when there are usually fewer people in prison. They are therefore not representative for that year.

Source: Hornle 1994

duration was up to a year, and for the remaining cases it was more than a year. Finally, in 10 per cent of the total cases, the duration of remand equalled or exceeded the sentence eventually given.

People under 21 are more likely to be remanded in custody than those over 21. The following ratios, which have remained constant since the mid 1970s, may illustrate this. If among the adult prison population 1 in 3 prisoners are on remand, the ratio becomes 1 in 2 for adolescents and 1 in 1 for juveniles (Dünkel 1993). Remand in custody has replaced the previous 'short sharp shock' sentences for young offenders.

Recent trends

In the mid 1970s the increase in the prison population became so pronounced that commentators warned that all officially available places would soon be filled. Fears that tension would follow proved realistic, as disturbances erupted in many German institutions. These, as we have seen, coincided with the disillusionment of prisoners with regard to the Prison Act. In the second half of the 1980s, perhaps as a result of unmanageable tensions and disturbances, decarceration policies were put in place.

As a consequence, as already shown in Table 6.1, the prison population in the former West Germany decreased consistently until the early 1990s. During the second part of the 1980s, it declined by more than 8,000. This process took place in all eleven states of the Federal Republic, and encompassed both remanded and sentenced prisoners, juveniles as well as adults (Feest 1991). Initially, the drop mainly affected remand prisoners whose numbers fell by about 1,000 per year to a record low in 1987: a reduction of 28 per cent on 1982. In the city of Bremen 'the historical remand prison . . . was abandoned in 1986 because the city fathers felt that it was too costly to run a prison for so few prisoners. The remaining prisoners and personnel were moved to an empty wing of another prison' (1991:132).

Given that changes in the crime rate could not explain these trends, attempts have been made to interpret the decline of the prison population against the background of economic, demographic or legislative changes (Council of Europe 1985). However, these attempts have all proved unsuccessful. The German economy fared relatively better when the prison population was higher. Unemployment was twice as high in 1990 than during the 1970s, and yet in 1990 the prison population was down by 20 per cent. The demographic explanation of the trend is also only partial, as the decline in the birth rate only accounts for about one-quarter of the prison population reduction. Finally, no relevant piece of legislation was introduced during the course of the 1980s which could account for the apparent decarceration process (Graham 1990). Feest contends that the explanation must lie somewhere within the criminal justice process itself. Data show that while the police processed about the same number and types of individuals, the number of prosecutions, remands and convictions decreased. 'The reduction of the West German prison population is therefore clearly attributable to changes in the behaviour of prosecutors and/ or judges' (Feest 1991:135). On the one hand, prosecutors seem to have failed to bring a number of cases to court, while on the other, judges seem to have dropped a number of cases presented to them. A further explanation may be found when the remand population is examined. As we have seen above, requests for remanding defendants in custody are made by prosecutors. Again, in the period considered, they seem to have failed to do so, or a number of their requests seem to have been rejected. In turn, the decline in the remand population and the corresponding increase in defendants on bail may have acted as a catalyst for the decline in the prison population in general. Many defendants attending trial as free persons (and perhaps even while employed) may have avoided custodial sentences because they were able to persuade courts that their new lifestyle was proof of their rehabilitation.

But why did the behaviour of prosecutors and judges undergo such significant change? According to Feest (1991), something

Table 6.2 *Convictions and sentences, 1986–1991*

Year	Number of convictions	Number of prison sentences (%)
1986	565,675	18.1
1987	NA	18.4
1988	578,044	17.9
1989	582,401	17.2
1990	590,707	16.7
1991	598,492	16.2

Source: Hornle 1994

happened which shook their faith in the usefulness of prisons. Widespread criticism of remand, the persuasive arguments put forward by the movement for alternatives to custody, and the movement against the building of new prisons, all contributed to the sense of disillusionment on the part of criminal justice practitioners. Table 6.2 shows that it was not so much the percentage of convictions as the percentage of custodial convictions which declined.

However, since the early 1990s an opposite trend has been observed, with an increase from 60 to 80 prisoners for each 100,000 population (Hornle 1994). Whether the reversal of the trends is due to a real increase in the crime rate or to other factors should be explored through the examination of specific phenomena and their perceived threat. These phenomena and their perceived threat are associated with the use of illicit drugs, the reunification of Germany, and the growth of asylum seekers. These issues will be examined later. Here, it is sufficient to note that the increase has been in the remand population rather than in the prison population as a whole (Hornle 1994). This may signal that the phenomena just mentioned, or the social panic associated with them, have resulted in the authorities seeking to reassure the public by inflicting some sort of preventive punishment on defendants (Hassemer 1994). Increasingly, therefore, people serve *de facto* sentences before a sentence is given to them.

Drugs and prison

During the late 1980s prisons underwent unprecedented change owing to the influx of prisoners with drug problems (Feest and Stover 1994). Since that time many prisoners have come to be seen as 'offenders with special needs', and their offending is often regarded as a consequence of their drug problem. The nature of the interactions between groups of prisoners and between prisoners and officers are consequently changing, along with the perceptions of the inmates on the part of the prison administrations. The treatment of offenders and the differentiation among them in terms of prison regime have also been affected. Health issues are becoming paramount in the running of prisons, a circumstance which may find officers culturally unprepared and professionally untrained.

It is difficult to establish the exact number of drug addicts serving a prison sentence in German institutions. For Bavaria, estimates indicate that between 10 and 15 per cent of prisoners are drug addicts. Krumsiek (1992) suggests that between 1983 and 1991 the number of drug addicts in prison doubled, and that they now represent 20 per cent of the male and 40 per cent of the female prison population respectively.

In a number of studies, the hypothesis that drug users in prison are more at risk than other users of contracting HIV has been tested. According to Kleiber (1991) prisoners who inject drugs are twice as likely to be HIV positive than their counterparts in free society. About 67 per cent of those who are HIV positive at the moment of arrest continue to inject drugs while serving a prison sentence. Moreover, about 39 per cent of those who are not HIV positive also continue to inject and often share needles. One in five drug users in prison either is infected by the virus or has AIDS. Although one should treat data cautiously, the extrapolation of this figure would suggest that in 1994 more than 1,000 prisoners were HIV positive or had developed AIDS.

Prison administrations are mystified by the drug phenomenon. On the one hand, they tend to minimize the problem, particularly when questions regarding the availability of drugs in prison are posed. On the other hand, they have to face the issue of drug addiction within the prison walls, which requires an ambiguous mixture of punishment and therapy. 'Drug deaths, drug traffic, and drug-related crime and growing brutalization forced a change in the official line. In most prisons it is now freely admitted that there is an active drug scene' (Feest and Stover 1994:22). Furthermore, the fact that both prisoners and prison officers do use drugs adds to the embarrassment and makes responses to the issue all the more contradictory and ambiguous.

The problem is compounded by the fact that identified HIV positive prisoners are frequently denied home leave or day release. 'The reason for this restriction is, presumably, the fear of adverse press coverage' (1994:25). Because needle-exchange schemes are not available in German prisons, high risk practices are likely to occur.

The shortage of needles leads to 'extensive needle sharing or the manufacture of even more dangerous equipment such as sharpened ball point pens' (1994:27). Compulsory testing of prisoners is legal only in the state of Bayern. But even in those states where compulsory testing has not been introduced, the percentage of prisoners tested on a 'voluntary' basis is very high. 'All prisoners are encouraged to take the test. But the principal reason for the high take-up is that those who refuse are treated as if they were HIV positive until tested' (1994:23).

Women in prison

In 1991 there were 1,575 women in prison, 110 of whom were serving a sentence in the female sections of institutions for young offenders. Almost all institutions for female offenders are sections of institutions for males, and are usually devoid of training or social facilities, let alone work opportunities. In these appendices of male institutions, women are mainly required to perform traditional tasks assigned to them such as cooking and sewing (Fischer-Jehle 1991). The absence of institutions specifically designed for female offenders, and the fact that their treatment takes place within institutions for males, echoes forms of socialization in operation for women in a patriarchal society. These usually hinge on the learning of passive roles, while episodes of women's deviance are often interpreted as an escape from this passivity (Einsele and Rothe 1982). Problems are therefore individualized, and deviant women are deemed to 'individually' fail to conform (Funken 1989). In this way, women's social background is overlooked, while the development of an individual sense of guilt is strongly encouraged.

Trends show that, between 1975 and 1991, the female prison population more than doubled (from 750 to 1,575). It should be noted that the incidence of short sentences (up to nine months) also declined substantially (from about 60 per cent to about 40 per cent) (Greive 1992). Women offenders are therefore more harshly treated than in the past, with about 60 per cent serving sentences above two years. The increase in drug offences committed by women between the early 1970s and the early 1990s does not account for this increased harshness, as almost one third of women in custody have committed 'simple theft' (Greive 1992).

Alternatives

Throughout the 1970s and 1980s, the debate on crime policy centred on three aspects: the effectiveness of rehabilitation programmes, diversion from custody, and the discovery of the victim. As the effectiveness of rehabilitation was questioned so the development of alternatives to custody was pushed to the top of the agenda (Deichsel 1991). Alternatives were intended to remain part of the criminal justice system rather than sanctions diverting offenders from that system completely. In this sense, alternatives should be understood as ways of rationalizing the criminal justice system, rather than examples of its partial or slow abandonment (Albrecht 1990; Kaiser et al. 1991). This interpretation of alternatives to custody is still valid in the 1990s.

All alternatives to custody share some ambiguous traits. This ambiguity is due to the fact that they are supposed to encapsulate aspects of both welfare and punishment. More specifically, this ambiguity is found mainly in the following aspects. First, because alternatives do not appear to be overtly punitive they are often used for petty offences. If alternatives were not available judges would drop charges which were either trivial or difficult to prove. In this sense, alternatives play a role in rationalizing the criminal justice system rather than resocializing offenders. They contribute to the decongestion of prisons and therefore to their smoother management. Second, because they are part of the penal system, alternatives can hardly avoid labelling offenders, thus affecting, if in a more 'humane' manner, their future criminal career. Finally, alternative punishments do not rule out the possibility of inflicting punishment *par excellence*, namely custody, a possibility which arises when alternative treatment allegedly fails. This is the case, for example, with alternatives such as restitution orders, where the inability of offenders to abide by the orders results in imprisonment. Equally, this happens for victim–offender reconciliation orders with respect to juvenile offenders.

Probation

Since 1975, probation orders may be combined with other forms of penalty. In these cases they are termed 'conduct supervision orders', and require that offenders report to *ad hoc* offices located in district courts. Between 1971 and 1990, there was a constant increase in the number of probation orders given by courts: 44,537 in 1971, about 61,000 in 1975, more than 90,000 in 1980, about 125,000 in 1985, and finally 131,381 in 1990 (Kaiser et al. 1991). During the same period (1971–90), the ratio of probation officers to probationers remained almost unaltered (1 to 60), while the number of breaches of orders slightly declined (from about 8 per cent to about 6 per cent). The percentage of probationers under the age of 21 simultaneously decreased (from 36.6 per cent to 20 per cent), which, considering the total increase of probation orders at the national level, indicates a willingness to deliver this punishment also, and increasingly so, to adult offenders (Statistische Bundesamt 1992). Probation officers are required to help offenders lead an honest life and prevent them reoffending. They hold an officially recognized certificate of social work, and their function is limited to the period after sentence.

Community service

Alongside restitution and reconciliation orders which we have already referred to above, community service is also available in Germany (Kaiser et al. 1991). This consists of up to 240 hours of unpaid work for the community, and can only be granted to fine defaulters. Although doubts are often expressed over its educational function, this alternative is used across the states of the German Federation (Dürr 1990). However, its role seems to be limited to the avoidance of the negative effects of imprisonment on offenders, and the decongestion of prison institutions (Deichsel 1991).

The debate on alternatives, in as much as it involves notions of restitution, is intertwined with that on the victims of crime, who remain a neglected party within the German criminal justice system as a whole. The system remains strongly offender oriented and obsessively concerned with punishment (Messner 1994). The Code of Criminal Procedure does not attribute any special role to victims, and their opinion is not heard even when compensation and restitution are discussed.

It should be noted that in the former East Germany the victims of crime played a more significant role. The decisions of the courts were linked to the demands of victims and their willingness to negotiate with offenders. Thiel has described the disappointment of victims from former East Germany who have become involved in criminal proceedings since Germany was reunited. Among victims the feeling prevails that their role is a passive one. 'They have to sit for hours and wait . . . and finally nothing happens' (Thiel 1993:9).

Exceptions to this neglect appear to be conflict resolution programmes set up in a number of cities (Dünkel and Rössner 1989; Pelikan 1991; Messmer 1992). But these programmes mainly involve juvenile offenders. The main reason for this is that legislation regarding juveniles is based on the principle that educational goals should have priority over punishment. 'This reflects the view that juvenile offenders should not be regarded as fully responsible for their norm-violating behaviour' (Messmer 1992:177). The selection of cases is made by public prosecutors, and cases of robbery and assault are included. The young offenders and their victims are contacted to ascertain their readiness to participate in the programmes. The willingness of both offenders and victims to co-operate is usually high. 'The same holds true for the rate of settlements agreed upon and also for the rate of their reaching a successful conclusion' (Pelikan 1991:167).

Supplementary measures
The German Penal Code draws a distinction between proper penalties and 'measures'. The latter are supplementary sanctions inflicted as a response to the characteristics of the offenders rather than the nature of offences. Psychiatric treatment, drug treatment, preventive imprisonment, but also a driving ban and a temporary or permanent debarment from a profession or public office, are all examples of these measures. They may either replace custody or supplement it: for example, they can be added to a prison sentence and be extended after the sentence expires. However, there is a tendency to combine custody and additional measures in most cases where drug offenders are involved. In these cases, imprisonment and some other specific requirement are parts of the same sentence (Kaiser et al. 1991).

The effects of reunification

It is part of the official rhetoric that the reunification of Germany has caused a tremendous increase in crime. Moreover, it is a common assumption that 'immigrants' and foreigners play a central role in the 'unprecedented rise in crime'. Close examination of the statistics indicates otherwise. It may also suggest that the problems associated with the reunification need to be placed in the context of developments in German society as a whole. In 1993, offences recorded by the police across the old Federal Republic of Germany were 5.35 million, an increase of about 2.7 per cent on the previous year. However, the bulk of the increase was caused by petty offences such as: bus fare dodging, theft of less than 100 Deutschmarks, and violation of the asylum legislation. If we leave these offences aside, the increase in crime corresponds to 0.3 per cent.[1] Furthermore, if we consider the crime rate in relation to the increase of the overall population, crime in fact dropped by 0.9 per cent (Klingst and Pfeiffer 1994).

But these figures should be considered cautiously. After reunification, problems arose as to the interpretation of statistics. The police did not seem able to interpret data relating to East Germany, and when these data were aggregated with statistics for West Germany, there was considerable confusion over their meaning and interpretation. This was the result of differences in statistical methods and criteria for accounting in the two countries. So, for example, there was a strange claim that homicides had risen alarmingly between 1984 and 1994. Official figures are inexplicable unless statistical categories are examined in detail. Figures regarding homicides include deaths caused by the very existence of the Berlin Wall, namely incidents which occurred at the border between the two Germanies. Many victims of murder, in other words, were killed by the border police. Figures also include controversial deaths in the prisons of the former East Germany (Klingst and Pfeiffer 1994). If we exclude these 'incidents', the figures tell us that the risk of being murdered in Germany has constantly declined between 1984 and 1994, and that the homicide rate is now at its lowest point in history.

Public opinion surveys show that in Germany two-thirds of the population of the East and half that of the West put violence at the top of their fears. One in six in the East and one in ten in the West feel in danger of being attacked. It is true that, over the last two decades, armed robberies rose significantly, but the risk to ordinary citizens of being robbed or attacked decreased by 1 per cent (Reuband 1992). In other words, violence and robberies increasingly seem to target large businesses rather than random individuals. Among ordinary citizens, those whose fears are indeed well founded are marginalized groups or individuals such as immigrants, asylum seekers, and the homeless. The victimization of these groups, along with the apparent rise of domestic violence, seem the real new features of crime in the reunited Germany (Wahl 1989; Frehsee 1992).

Statistics regarding violence against foreigners are at variance with each other. However, police statistics issued in 1992 showed that 'up to the end of November 1992, a total of 4,587 "xenophobic indictable offences" had been perpetrated as against a total of 2,426 the previous year' (Atkinson 1993:154). Figures released by the Ministry of the Interior showed that violent attacks carried out by right wing extremists amounted to 2,285 in 1992. Of these, 1,953 involved foreigners as victims, and 686 involved arson or the use of explosives. Seventeen people had been killed and 542 wounded. 'In any case, the real toll of attacks is probably higher since not all attacks are reported and then again not all racist attacks are treated as such by the police' (1993:155).

As Table 6.3 indicates, in the former East Germany the rate of imprisonment dropped from 187 to 29 per 100,000 of the population during the period 1989–93. This trend can be explained by the extreme severity of the old regime, but also by the fact that

Table 6.3   *Prisoners in the former East Germany, 1989–1993*

Period	Number of prisoners	Per 100,000 inhabitants
October 1989	31,000	187
March 1990	6,903	43
November 1991	3,223	20
January 1992	3,262	20
September 1992	4,491	28
October 1993	4,598	29

Source: Hornle 1994

many East Germans may now be serving a sentence or be remanded in custody in the West. In turn, judges of the former East Germany are said to be overwhelmed by work because they are still unable to cope with a criminal justice system that they do not understand completely (Thiel 1993). In other words, the decline of the prison population in the former East Germany has not resulted in a reduction in the workload for judges. They are extremely busy in adapting to the new system, and while they may be dealing with fewer 'political' offences than in the past, they are now processing an increasing number of property offences. Thiel (1993) argues that the judges of the former East Germany now have to conform to the practice of prosecuting petty offenders, a practice which in the past was rare because it was deemed too costly.

Ausländer and adolescents

As we suggested earlier the problems associated with reunification need to be placed in the context of developments in German society as a whole. The reunification of the country has caused not an increase in crime, but rather the increased victimization of more vulnerable groups. If we stretch the concept of victimization to include variables such as poverty, a parallel process becomes apparent with regard to foreigners (*Ausländer*) and adolescents.

During the course of the 1970s and 1980s the issue of foreign offenders was high on the agenda. Police and court data suggested that immigrant minorities committed more crimes than the majority of the population. It was argued that these figures were biased because they did not take into account variables such as socio-economic status and the discriminatory treatment of foreigners by institutional agencies. Critics such as Albrecht argued that relative deprivation was to be regarded as central in explaining crime within foreign minorities. He also suggested that 'decision making in the fields of pre-trial detention and imprisonment should be rethought in order to avoid differential and disadvantageous treatment of foreign offenders' (1987:285). However, guest workers being charged with an offence were likely to receive exemplary punishment consisting of the loss of their residence permit. In 1991 the proportion of foreigners in the prison population was about 15 per cent for men and 10 per cent for women (Statistische Bundesamt 1993). There are no specific institutions for foreign prisoners awaiting deportation.

It is now officially claimed that the 2 million 'guest workers' resident in Germany, and German citizens above the age of 25, do not represent problems. Younger people, particularly children of asylum seekers, are officially said to be the real problem. Why is this so? And why are these young people criminalized? These groups have a common characteristic: both young German citizens and second-generation immigrants are increasingly poor. Between 1986 and 1993, the number of individuals receiving support from welfare agencies grew by almost two-thirds. In the same period the rich have also become richer, with 57 per cent of general wealth owned by one-third of the population (Klingst and Pfeiffer 1994). While in the past the elderly were the major recipients of welfare benefits, it is now young people who mainly rely on welfare to survive.

Numerous reports published by the trade unions and charity organizations indicate that in Germany two children in eleven are brought up in a family surviving on welfare support. In the meantime, one-third of those living below the poverty line in the old West Germany are non-German. Homelessness is also increasing, with a peak 60 per cent rise in the region of Nordrhein-Westfalia (Klingst and Pfeiffer 1994).

In conclusion, both the reunification of Germany and the issues associated with the new immigrants and asylum seekers need to be examined outside the framework provided by the mass media and the fear of crime that they inevitably foster. Police statistics show that two-thirds of those charged with theft are German citizens born in the West, three-quarters are adult, and the large majority are not drug users. This notwithstanding, according to widely shared perceptions, crime is associated with foreigners, the reunification of Germany, young people and drug users. As we have tried to argue, it is the poverty of these groups and their visibility which foster the fear of crime. This fear thrives on the sentiment of insecurity which is spreading among the German population, and is also associated with the belief that such visible poverty is a potential generator for the increase in crime.

Conclusion

Between the early 1980s and the early 1990s there has been a substantial decline in the prison population in Germany. We have attempted to demonstrate that this decline was due less to a corresponding reduction of the crime rate than to the scepticism of judges with regard to custody. Despite the increase observable since 1991, the rate of imprisonment is lower in reunited Germany than it was throughout the 1980s in the former West Germany. As we have seen, this increase has been in the population on remand. This may be the result of increased fear of crime and the subsequent higher demand for custodial punishment. At the same time, it seems that the more vulnerable are both more exposed to crime and more likely to receive a prison sentence. We have mentioned the high risk of victimization run by asylum seekers and immigrants. It is also worth mentioning that the number of offenders with no fixed abode more than doubled between 1989 and 1993 (Klingst and Pfeiffer 1994).

The German penal system presents us with two apparently distinct faces: repression and welfare. The combination of the two renders it ideologically powerful, and unlike systems inspired by pure retribution, it also provides an aura of justice and fairness. Perhaps it is this combination which protects the German penal system from widespread criticism, and even makes it 'a model' to copy in the eyes of reformers of more punitive countries. However, as we have tried to argue, repression and welfare are not mutually exclusive. Moreover, the use of both is subject to discretion and depends on public fears, contingent scares and the general socio-political climate.

At the beginning of this chapter we pointed to the severity of the criminal justice system during the course of the 1970s, when emergency legislation was introduced to tackle the real or perceived threat of political armed struggle. It has to be noted that such legislation was never repealed, and is still used as a Damocles sword to be activated whenever contingent fears emerge. For example, this is the case with drug trafficking and organized crime, which according to agencies such as the police require the use of the special legislation still in existence, including harsher penalties, longer remand periods, and the use of extraordinary investigative and surveillance means such as phone-tapping (Hassemer 1994). One might wonder why the same legislation is not activated to respond to 'the appearance on a massive scale of gangs of thugs' (Enzensberger 1994:142) who contribute to the victimization of the more vulnerable that we have tried to describe in this chapter.

Perhaps one of the answers lies in the 'rising German nationalism which has been given a massive boost by reunification and which has also given a dubious legitimacy to many arguments of the extreme Right' (Atkinson 1993:155). In discussing the attacks of neo-Nazi gangs on foreigners and asylum seekers, Enzensberger recalls how during the 1970s 'beating, kicking and shooting were carried out with considerable vigour' to tackle political unrest created by left wing groups. By contrast, he argues, categories such as unemployment, immaturity and cultural disorientation are heavily mobilized when dealing with the neo-Nazis. However, empirical evidence from court cases suggests that 'young, the practitioners of violence certainly are. Unemployed and from "bad" family background, they certainly are not' (Atkinson 1993:163).

Note

1 This argument is based on official criminal statistics in relation to reported and recorded crime. The problem of unrecorded crime still remains. Violation of the asylum legislation may be regarded as a petty crime although, from the perspective of the authorities in Europe, this appears to be an increasingly significant 'crime'.

References

Albrecht H-J (1987), 'Foreign Minorities in the Criminal Justice System in the Federal Republic of Germany' *Howard Journal* 26, 4: 272–86

Albrecht P A (1990), *Informalisierung des Rechts. Empirische Untersuchungen zu den Grenzen der Opportunität im Jugendstrafrecht* Berlin/New York: de Gruyter

Atkinson G (1993), 'Germany: Nationalism, Nazism and Violence' in T Bjorgo and R Witte (eds) *Racist Violence in Europe* London: St Martins Press

Council of Europe (1985), *Economic Crisis and Crime* Strasbourg: Council of Europe

Deichsel W (1991), 'Überlegungen anlässlich des Hamburger Diversionmodells' *Monatsschrift fur Kriminologie und Strafrechtsreform* 74, 4: 224–35

Dünkel F (1993), 'Heranwachsende im (Jugend-) Kriminalrecht' *ZstW* 105, 1: 137–65

Dünkel F and Rössner D (1989), 'Law and Practice of Victim/Offender Agreements' in M Wright and B Galaway (eds) *Mediation and Criminal Justice* London: Sage

Dürr K (1990), 'Zwischenmenschliche Konfliktlösung statt Bestrafung' *Soziale Arbeit* 39, 5: 162–73

Einsele H and Rothe G (1982), *Frauen im Strafvollzug* Reinbek: Rowohlt

Enzensberger H M (1994), *Civil War* London: Granta

Feest J (1991), 'Reducing the Prison Population: Lessons from the West German Experience?' in J Muncie and R Sparks (eds) *Imprisonment: European Perspectives* New York: St Martin's Press

Feest J and Stover H (1994), 'AIDS in Prisons in Germany' in P Thomas and M Moerings (eds) *AIDS in Prison* Aldershot: Dartmouth

Ferrajoli L and Zolo D (1977), *Democrazia autoritaria e capitalismo maturo* Milan: Feltrinelli

Fischer-Jehle P (1991), *Frauen im Strafvollzug. Eine empirische Untersuchung über Lebensentwicklung und Delinquenz strafgefangener Frauen* Bonn: Forum

Frehsee D (1992), 'Die staatliche Förderung familiärer Gewalt an Kindern' *Kriminologisches Journal* 1: 37–49

Funken C (1989), *Frau-Frauen-Kriminelle. Zur aktuellen Diskussion über 'Frauenkriminalität'* Opladen

Graham J (1990), 'Decarceration in the Federal Republic of Germany: How Practitioners Are Succeeding Where Policy Makers Have Failed' *British Journal of Criminology* 30, 2: 150–70

Greive W (1992), *Frauen in Haft* Rehburg: Akademie

Hassemer W (1994), 'The Current German Scene' paper presented at *Punishment and Politics: A British-German Seminar on Criminal Policy* Goethe Institut, London, 9–10 June

Hornle T (1994), 'The Level of Punitiveness within the German Criminal Justice System' paper presented at *Punishment and Politics: A British-German Seminar on Criminal Policy* Goethe Institut, London, 9–10 June

Kaiser G, Kerner H J and Schöch H (1991), *Strafvollzug* Heidelberg: Müller

Kleiber D (1991), 'Die HIV/Aids-Problematik bei i.v. Drogenabhängigen in der Bundesrepublik Deutschland' in M Busch, W Heckmann and E Marks (eds) *HIV/AIDS und Straffälligkeit* Bonn: Forum

Klingst M and Pfeiffer C (1994), 'Tatort Deutschland' *Die Zeit* 20 May

Krumsiek R (1992), 'Das Drogenproblem im Strafvollzug' *Zeitschrift. Strafvollzug* 5: 306–8

Messmer H (1992), 'Victim–Offender Mediation in Germany' in G Davis (ed) *Making Amends: Mediation and Reparation in Criminal Justice* London: Routledge

Messner C (1994), 'Recht, Vernunft, Gewalt und die Frage nach dem Ursprung' *Archiv für Rechts-und Sozialphilosophie* 80, 2: 252–73

Ortner H (1990), 'Rätselhafte Revolte?' *Neue Kriminalpolitik* Heft 3: 11

Pelikan C (1991), 'Conflict Resolution between Victims and Offenders in Austria and in the Federal Republic of Germany' in F Heidensohn and M Farrell (eds) *Crime in Europe* London: Routledge

Prowse R, Weber H and Wilson C (1992), 'Rights and Prisons in Germany: Blueprint for Britain?' *International Journal of the Sociology of Law* 20: 111–34

Reuband K H (1992), 'Kriminalitätsfurcht in Ost und Westdeutschland-Zur Bedeutung psychosozialer Einflussfaktoren' *Soziale Probleme* 3, 2: 211–19

Seelmann K (1981), 'Una tendenza attuale nello sviluppo delle teorie della pena in Germania' *La Questione Criminale* VII, 3: 425–37

Silvi R (1977), 'Assassinio socialdemocratico nella Repubblica Federale Tedesca' *Senza Galere* 1: 1–4

Statistische Bundesamt (1992), *Fachserie 10: Rechtspflege 1990* Wiesbaden

Statistische Bundesamt (1993), *Fachserie 10: Rechtspflege 1991* Wiesbaden

Statistische Bundesamt (1994), *Fachserie 10: Rechtspflege 1992* Wiesbaden

Thiel K (1993), 'Reorganization of the Authorities of Penal Control in the New Federal States of Germany' paper presented at the *XXI Conference of the European Group for the Study of Deviance and Social Control* Prague, 28–31 August

Wahl K (1989), *Studien über Gewalt in Familien* München: DJI

Weber H (1990), 'Rechtsverweigerung durch Vollzugsbehörden bei Lebenslänglichen' *Zeitschrift fur Rechtspolitik* 23, 2: 65–70

7

The Spanish Attempt to Build a Democratic Criminal Justice System

Roberto Bergalli

In the literature on contemporary European criminal justice systems, there is a dearth of information on the Spanish penal system. This can easily be understood when it is recognized that it was only in 1982 that Spain, together with Portugal, became a member of the European Community, and only four years before that, in 1978, that the Spanish constitution (CE) came into being introducing the rule of law in Spain. These two historical developments only became possible after the death of the dictator Francisco Franco in November 1975, which saw the beginning of the period called 'transition to democracy'.

Prisoners of the dictatorship

Until that time the Spanish criminal justice system had developed under the rigid political control that the Franco dictatorship had established in Spain at the end of the Civil War in 1939. Repressive measures used by this regime included the indiscriminate application of the death penalty, with or without reasons being given, and secondly imprisonment, which in the majority of cases took the form of solitary confinement.

It is therefore possible to argue that during this long period of dictatorship many institutions of the Spanish criminal justice system were mainly dedicated to the political control of dissidence. For example, even though the courts had a degree of autonomy when dealing with ordinary offences, a tribunal of public order dealt with the prosecution of offences against the state. Similarly, the different police forces which were in existence during the dictatorship devoted much effort to the prosecution of political dissidents. Torture was commonplace. Meanwhile, the main role of most custodial establishments was to accommodate the prisoners of the regime. The Model Prison in Barcelona is a case in point. It was, and still is, situated in the capital of the autonomous community of Catalonia, where much of the resistance against the Franco regime developed, so much so that Barcelona was one of the last bastions to fall during the Civil War. The prison was built in 1888, with a capacity for 750 inmates, but in the year immediately following the end of the Civil War (1939–40) it housed 12,745 prisoners (Marin Rodriguez 1986).

Prisons were the instruments of oppression used by the victorious party against the defeated (Bueno Arus 1978). It could not have been otherwise, as immediately after the Civil War the elaboration of penal policies was the preserve of sections of the army. In the initial years of the dictatorship there were more than 300,000 prisoners sentenced for political offences (Lurra 1977; Marti 1977). However, this situation changed as a consequence of international pressure including the diplomatic boycott promoted by the United Nations (Carr 1988). During the 1950s the prison population dropped to 30,000, although the political component remained pre-eminent. During the 1960s different political prisoners started to populate Spanish prisons, namely the new activists of democratic and left wing parties, who had begun to reorganize. Among the common prisoners few were professional criminals, the majority being petty property offenders (Draper Miralles 1984).

The late 1960s saw the rebirth of the prisoners' movement, with the political inmates leading a number of disputes. These political leaders of the prisoners' rights movement had credibility in the eyes of large sectors of society, and were regarded as 'good' as opposed to the common prisoners who were deemed 'bad' (Lurra 1977). This separation within the prison population was the result of the political prisoners' effort to describe themselves as completely different from those 'who committed crime' (García Valdés 1977). In this way a section of the prison population was marginalized by the very politically conscious people who should have supported the underprivileged both inside and outside the prison system (Garrido Guzmán 1983). For this reason, common prisoners set up their own organizations in Burgos, Seville, San Sebastian, Barcelona and Valencia, where disturbances erupted during the early and mid 1970s.

The democratic transition

The transition to democracy had three distinct periods. The first runs from the death of Franco to the free elections of the constitutional courts in July 1977. During this phase Arias Navarro became head of government. This phase was characterized by a flurry of activity generated by the various political groups opposed to Franchismo, and to any continuation of it by means of secession. Working-class struggles also characterized this phase. The next phase started with Adolfo Suarez as head of government, and produced a truly coalitionist strategy, paving the way for the great politics of consensus which led to the well known Pact of Moncloa (between the government, the various groups of the opposition, the trade unions and the organizations of entrepreneurs). This phase lasted until the attempted coup of 23 February 1981. This date arguably and definitely signified the consolidation of the Spanish political class in favour of the values of pluralism, a system of political parties and parliamentary agreement, all of which were enshrined in the constitution of 1978. The last phase, from 1981 to the present, is said to have come about when a momentous political change in government took place. The middle classes and a large part of the popular classes came to be represented by the Spanish Socialist Party (Partido Socialista Obrero Español or PSOE).

The purpose of this brief politico-historical review is to describe the circumstances surrounding the emergence of a new culture in Spain, which has been called the 'culture of democracy'. It is within this culture of democracy that the evolution of the Spanish criminal justice system (SPE), including the penal system, has to be examined, and it is to this task that the rest of this chapter will now turn.

Framework and procedures

The Spanish constitution establishes a series of principles, including the principles of legality and the proportionality of punishment, through which the criminal justice system operates, and in important respects shares the characteristics of other constitutional states within the rule of law and the continental judicial tradition. The constitution stipulates the abolition of the death penalty and of torture, and supports the principle of the rehabilitation of offenders. It also includes general guidelines as to the circumstances and limits within which the criminal justice system may intervene.

In this respect the Penal Code and the Code of Criminal Prosecution should be mentioned. The Penal Code covers the legal definition of offences and establishes the minimum and maximum penalties for each offence. The Code of Criminal Prosecution lays down how suspected offenders are to be processed, and guarantees certain safeguards such as the suspect's right to be heard and the right to be tried in public. It also establishes the time limit within which the different phases of criminal proceedings must take place.

Profound amendments to the Penal Code have been on the agenda since the beginning of the democratic period. In 1980, proposals for a new Penal Code were rejected by Parliament; this was followed by proposals for a new Penal Code in 1983, which were partially introduced in that year. In 1992 there were further proposals to introduce a completely new 'democratic' Penal Code. This code may be implemented in the near future, although other priorities emerging during the course of 1994 and 1995 make it difficult to predict whether it will be approved before the end of the current administration. The new code under discussion in 1994 stipulates the shortening of maximum sentences for each offence, the introduction of alternative punishments and the expansion of the competence of prison judges in the treatment of individual prisoners (Ministerio de Justicia e Interior 1994). The role of such judges will be described in more detail below.

Police organization

Following the territorial and administrative division effected by the constitution in the Spanish state, there are three types of police force: state, regional (for each of the 17 autonomous communities) and municipal police forces. They also play a role within the penal system. In Catalonia, for example, apart from traffic offences, the regional police also deal with juvenile offenders and are involved in the external vigilance of prison institutions (*El Periodico de Catalunya* 18 October 1994).

Confusion as to the functions of these different police forces may arise, as overlap between them is not always easy to avoid. But the true dilemma of police activity in Spain is the relationship between the police and the courts. In Spain, unlike in Italy and France, there is no police branch working in partnership with prosecutors and undertaking investigations under their direction. In this respect, the provisions of the constitution and the Criminal Procedure Act are vague, and this has so far prevented the formation of a specific police force working under the direction of the judiciary (Recasens i Brunet 1985). This situation creates great difficulties in the control of the investigation of offences, the gathering of evidence and the identification of offenders because no clear statutory demarcation of the competencies of the different police forces is in place.

Criminal jurisdiction

Spanish courts have very strictly determined areas of competence. At the same time the constitution grants them real judicial power.

Procedural guarantees contained in natural law such as the right to counsel, due process and the presumption of innocence are central to the operations of the courts.

Some of these consist of 'courts of first instance' (*tribunales de primera instancia*) with one judge sitting. These courts deal with minor offences and are entitled to impose fines. They pass more serious cases upwards. Provincial courts act as *tribunales colegiados*, that is to say they are staffed by several judges. They act as courts of appeal to the former, but also as courts of first instance for more serious offences. There is also a court of first instance with an exclusive jurisdiction over matters of national interest – the Audiencia Nacional – which has competence to carry out both investigation (instruction stage) and judgement in cases of political violence and organized crime. It must be said that the unique nature of the Audiencia Nacional, which is based in Madrid, has been questioned. The arguments put forward which question its legitimacy come in two categories: first, that the Audiencia Nacional is the direct descendant and continues the work of Franco's tribunals of public order (because it could be seen as an agency geared to the control of political dissidence); and second, that its 'central' position is incompatible with the principle of the natural judge, which says that an accused person, his/her behaviour and the results thereof must be judged by a court or tribunal with the appropriate competence in the area where the crime took place (Gimeno Sendra 1981).

There are parliamentary commissions of investigation, which deal with cases of political corruption and, between 1992 and 1994, investigated a number of episodes of illegal funding of political parties. These commissions can hear defendants and witnesses but cannot return verdicts, as the material they gather is passed over to public prosecutors who then may establish penal responsibilities and initiate criminal proceedings.

There is also a specialized jurisdiction which deals with imprisonment itself. The law governing this jurisdiction was introduced in September 1979 and is concerned with the application of the relevant constitutional principles to the prison system from the deprivation of liberty to the running of the institutions. Such principles also run through the concept of prevention and particularly rehabilitation, as stated in Article 25.2 of the constitution ('Custodial sentences and other means of security aim at the re-education and the social reinsertion of the individual, and should not therefore take the form of forced labour'). In line with what happens in other (continental) European justice systems, prison judges (*jueces de vigilancia penitenciaria*) are responsible for the custodial environment *per se*, and the treatment of prisoners. They are involved in a range of penal areas including the resolution of disciplinary matters where prisoners are sentenced to more than 14 days in solitary confinement. They are concerned with conditional release, parole and the classification of prisoners. Finally, they answer queries and complaints of prisoners concerning custodial regimes, and approve all home visits exceeding two days.

The administration of custodial establishments

Custodial establishments are managed by two large public administrations. The first operates at state level, within the Ministry of Justice and Interior, and is known as the Secretariat of State for Custodial Establishments (SEAP). SEAP has authority over the Dirección General de Asuntos Penitenciarios, which in turn is responsible for actually administering and running prisons establishments. There are 76 such establishments in Spain.

Certain aspects of penal policy are dealt with at regional level. One region – Catalonia – has assumed responsibility for custodial matters. Article 11 of the Statute of Autonomy of Catalonia, passed in 1979, granted the community of Catalonia authority in custodial matters. To fulfil this aim the relevant competencies were transferred to the autonomous community, through Decree 3462 of 28 December 1983, that is to say all relevant resources and personnel were transferred to the community on 1 January 1984. It is now the Catalan Department for Prisons and Rehabilitation (DGSPR), run by the Department of Justice of the community of Catalonia, which is responsible for the management, organization and inspection of the custodial establishments and services in the whole of the territory of Catalonia. I shall explore the question of Catalonia in greater depth below.

The Spanish prison system: some characteristics

When studying the features of any custodial system, its relationship with society at large must be taken into account. The prison system is affected by the nature and state of the labour market, the structure of the social welfare system, and the ethnic structure of the population as a whole.

This chapter does not privilege any of these aspects. But it is important to remember that in the short period during which the Spanish criminal justice system has been studied – which coincides with the 'culture of democracy' – Spain has incorporated a system of social democratic values, both political and ideological, using other social democracies as a model. It has also undergone socio-economic change of a structural nature. The latter involved attempts to improve output and the regulatory mechanisms of the labour market, to amend the principles and structures at all levels of the education system, to increase the benefits of and expand the health system, and so forth. Generally speaking all areas of economic and social life have been transformed, in order to comply with the requirements brought about by the accession of Spain to the European Union and the need to 'catch up' with other social democracies.

As for the criminal justice system, and in particular the custodial system, change has been particularly difficult. The process of reform has been hampered by a number of factors including low productivity, the late accession of Spain to the process of European consolidation, the remaining differences between the north and the south of Europe, and the historical and imperial relationship of Spain with North Africa, the Philippines and Latin America. Other factors include the Spanish support of, and at the same time responsibility for, the failing economies and the aberrations of the political systems of these countries, whilst receiving their migrant populations. Finally there is the geographical configuration of Spain, which acts as the southern border of Europe, as a result of the rigid implementation of the Trevi and the Schengen agreements.

Trends in the adult prison population

The Spanish penal system has been under pressure since the mid 1980s, as was detailed in a series of reports from the Ministry of Justice between 1985 and 1991. This period coincides with the end of Spain's economic expansion, the rise in unemployment, and an increase in immigration from North Africa and Latin America. These problems are compounded, as in the rest of Europe, by an increase in drug use, dealing and trafficking and the emergence of forms of organized crime related to the drug business. These phenomena have dramatically altered the features of the prison population.

In order to illustrate some significant trends we compare some relevant data from 1985 with data from 1991.

The situation in 1985

Because at the time of writing figures on the application of the fine are not available, in the following sections we shall focus on imprisonment only. In 1985 there were 73,058 receptions into custodial establishments (67,013 men and 6,045 women). This

Table 7.1 *Percentage of convicted prisoners by type of crime and gender, 1985*

Crimes against	Men (%)	Women (%)
Property	66.9	48.0
Persons	11.7	21.1
Public health (drugs)	7.0	13.7
Security of the state	5.2	10.6
Decency (sexual freedom)	5.1	1.7
Others	4.1	4.9

Source: Ministerio de Justicia 1986

constituted an increase of 13.7 per cent over 1984. On 31 December 1985 the average daily prison population reached 22,396 (21,392 men and 1,004 women). The increase over the previous year was 26.4 per cent (Ministerio de Justicia 1986). The rate of incarceration of 57.8 per 100,000 people was the highest for twenty years.

Almost half of the prisoners were on remand. This proportion was identical to that of 1984. Data also showed that the prison population was younger, with 47 per cent of prisoners under 26 years of age (36.6 per cent between 21 and 25) compared with 35.1 per cent in 1984. As Table 7.1 illustrates, with respect to convicted prisoners, the most common crimes were property crimes, followed by crimes against the person, drug offences, and crimes 'against decency', which include sexual offences. The remaining crimes did not exceed 5 per cent.

It is interesting to note that in 1985 a higher percentage of women than men were serving a prison sentence for violent offences. Perhaps a partial explanation of this can be found in the other interesting data in the table. Twice as many women as men were serving a prison sentence for crimes against the security of the state, namely political violence. But a more complete explanation of this 'anomaly' is perhaps to be found in the harsher institutional response to women's violence in general, and in the tendency to classify women who step outside their traditional roles as 'violent deviants'.

Among all those receiving a prison sentence 52.4 per cent were given sentences up to 6 months. The number of reoffenders increased slightly compared with the previous year, and constituted 58.9 per cent of the prison population. Among women convicted prisoners only 15.7 per cent were reoffenders (Ministerio de Justicia 1986).

One aspect of the Spanish prison population which began to be of some concern in 1985 was the relative increase of foreigners in Spanish jails. In 1966 the total prison population was 10,765, with only 365 foreigners (354 men and 11 women), 3.4 per cent of the total. In 1985, when the total prison population was 22,396, there were 2,590 foreign prisoners (2,390 men and 200 women), some 11.6 per cent of the total prison population. Of these non-nationals 46 men were imprisoned for offences against the security of the state.

The situation in 1991

Six years later – in 1991 – the prison population in Spain reached a total of 33,274 (30,370 men and 2,904 women). This included 10,719 men and 1,471 women on remand (Ministerio de Justicia 1992). Among convicted prisoners 4.9 per cent of men and 5.1 per cent of women respectively were in the age range 16–20.

Data on sentenced prisoners for 1991 indicated that property offences had dropped to 50.2 per cent for men and 34.5 per cent for women, and political violence from 5.2 per cent and 10.6 per cent to 2 per cent and 3 per cent respectively. The most interesting data related to men and women serving sentences for drug offences. These were respectively 22.4 per cent and 51.5 per cent (more than a threefold increase for men and more than a fourfold increase for women on 1985) (Ministerio de Justicia 1992). I will return to this aspect when discussing the issue of drug addiction in prison.

In 1991 long custodial sentences (between 12 and 20 years) accounted for 11.4 per cent. In December of the same year 55.8 per cent of men were reoffenders, as opposed to 29.6 per cent of females (Ministerio de Justicia 1992).

Out of a total of 33,274 in November 1991, the percentage of foreign prisoners was 15.4 per cent for men (4,657 prisoners) and 24.8 per cent for women (719 prisoners). These prisoners experienced harsher treatment than their Spanish counterparts. For example, they were rarely given conditional remission because they lacked support outside and therefore they were deemed unlikely to be rehabilitated. Moreover, current legislation stipulates that foreigners without a permit to stay who commit an offence are to be repatriated after serving a prison sentence. They are literally taken by the police when exiting prison, and deported after a period in police custody which must not exceed 40 days (Rule 1993).

In December 1991 the total population of *sentenced* prisoners was 19,283, of whom 3,057 were serving a sentence of between 1 and 6 months, 13,940 between 6 months and 6 years, and 2,286 more than 6 years (Ministerio de Justicia 1992). Prisoners are held either in male prisons, of which there are 32; or in male prisons which have a women's wing, of which there are 41; or in one of the three institutions for women, one of which has a male wing.

Table 7.2 *Classification of convicted men and women, 1991*

Class	Men (%)	Women (%)
A (1st grade)	3.7	3.6
B (2nd grade)	59.7	53.6
C (3rd grade)	17.5	23.9
No classification	19.1	18.9

Source: Ministerio de Justicia 1992

Although in 1979 prison legislation introduced the notion of 'differential treatment' into the custodial system, it was only in the mid 1980s that a precise classification of prisoners made an appearance in official statistics. Table 7.2 illustrates the classification of convicted men and women in December 1991.

Differential treatment entails the individualization of prison regimes, which are 'closed', 'ordinary' or 'open' for categories A, B and C respectively. Closed regimes imply the isolation of prisoners for 23 hours per day, while ordinary regimes allow inmates to participate in educational and other internal activities. These include cooking and cleaning duties inside the institution or working for external firms. Although work is regarded as part of the rehabilitation programme, very poor wages are paid to prisoners (Rivera Beiras 1994). Open regimes offer category C prisoners the possibility to work outside the prison establishment and return in the evening. Prisoners can apply for reclassification, for example they may claim their eligibility for shifting from category B to C. Applications are examined by the prison administration in partnership with a consultative body formed by social workers, psychologists and criminologists who work inside the institution.

Prison regimes for women are the same as for men, a circumstance which is challenged by women pressure groups. These groups point to the fact that prison institutions are conceived by men for men, and unless imprisonment for women is abolished altogether, the planning of prison establishments should take into account the specific needs of women, including women with children (Covisa Villa 1992).

Custody in Catalonia

Trends in Catalonia, which as we saw earlier is the only region which has acquired autonomy in penal affairs, are broadly in line with national trends (Generalitat de Catalunya 1992).

In October 1991 there were 5,473 persons of both sexes in Catalan prisons. This represented an increase of 59.3 per cent on 1985. The number of women was 450, an increase of more than 100 per cent since 1985. The only decline was observed for prisoners within the age range 16–20. The most striking figures concerned prisoners serving sentences for drug offences, with a sixfold increase for men and a fivefold increase for women. The number of foreign prisoners trebled between 1985 and 1991 (Generalitat de Catalunya 1992).

The increase in the number of foreign prisoners also occurred in other Spanish regions. In Catalonia, this phenomenon can be partly explained as follows. Firstly, the industrial and commercial development of the autonomous community has made it an attractive place for immigrants. Secondly, its location on the edge of the Mediterranean makes it accessible, as does its proximity to North Africa and its extended border with France. The increase in foreign prisoners mirrors both the social deprivation of immigrants and the punitiveness of the criminal justice system in dealing with them.

Patterns of recidivism in Catalonia have been studied more closely than elsewhere in Spain. A study carried out between 1987 and 1990, for example, investigated whether convicted prisoners had committed the same offences for which they had previously received a prison sentence. About 38 per cent had committed more serious offences than in the past, while 7.1 per cent had committed the same offence. The study also showed that individuals returning to serve a prison sentence within three years represented just under 45 per cent of the total prison population. Furthermore, the highest incidence of recidivism was in the 18–19 age group. Out of a sample of 475, 75 per cent of persons in that age range served a further prison sentence within three years of their release: hence the concentration of young people in Catalan prisons (Redondo et al. 1993).

In a study conducted in 1992, whose findings may partly but cautiously be generalized to the national level, and whose title was 'incarcerating poverty', the social composition of prisoners was found to be as follows. Almost 70 per cent of the inmates were in the age group 18–27; 17 per cent were illiterate; 34 per cent were semi-literate; 75 per cent were habitual drug users; 40 per cent injected drugs; 49 per cent had drug related illnesses; 56 per cent were immigrants from other Spanish regions; 60 per cent had previous experiences of institutionalization; 59 per cent were unemployed before arrest; 89 per cent did not receive money from their families (Rivera Beiras 1993).

This overview of the Spanish penal system between 1985 and

1991, including the Catalan system, reveals that there has been a general increase in the prison population, in terms of both remand and convicted prisoners. The most dramatic increase was observed in those individuals (in particular women) convicted for drug offences.

The prison crisis

Clearly, the official statistics furnished by the central prison administration and from Catalonia are not sufficiently up to date to offer a more detailed, critical analysis of current and future trends. However, with the help of the plan for the prison building programme, put forward by the Secretariat of State for Custodial Establishments (SGAP) and the Ministry of Justice and approved by the Council of Ministers in June 1991, it is possible to gain a clearer perspective of what might be happening to the Spanish custodial system.

This report extrapolates the trends in prison population in the 1990s in Spain, and thereby justifies its proposals for the building of new prisons. Its predictions are based on the annual average increase in the prison population, which is about 1,777. Since 1985 juveniles are no longer the major group of incomers. These data reflect the changing age structure in Spain: in 1977 the birth rate was 2.66, in 1988 it plummeted to 1.44. At present the birth rate is on its way to being the lowest in Europe. In contrast, the increase in the female population in Spanish prisons is significant and seems set to continue. During the course of 1991, for example, there was a clear ascending trend with regard to women in prison. In January there were 2,342, by July there were 2,561 and by December 2,805. Between the beginning and the end of 1991 the percentage of women in prison increased from just under 8 per cent to 8.7 per cent (Ministerio de Justicia 1992). This was due to the fact that an increasing number of women were charged with drug offences.

On the basis of these figures, the report of the SGAP described the prison situation as one involving a 'chronic shortage of places'. It noted: 'Our custodial system is experiencing the worst shortage of places for the past five years, having reached 6,000 at the beginning of the year. Although we are providing 830 extra places a year, the increase in persons accommodated in the custodial environment has been of 1,777 a year. This leads to an average shortage of 947 places per year' (Ministerio de Justicia 1992:1). It is estimated that in 1997 the shortage will be of 11,000 places, with all the social and economic consequences this entails.

In 1991 prison inspectors found that four, five or even six prisoners were housed in less than 8 square metres of cell space. Medical units were found to fall short of legal requirements in terms of staff and equipment (Terradillos Basoco 1994). 'Another unsatisfactory feature of Spanish prisons is that there is no strict separation of remand and convicted prisoners. The reality of overcrowding and the frequent moving of inmates from prison to prison makes this impossible' (1994:100).

It is pressures like these which have prompted the plan to build 18 new prisons, creating a total of 20,500 new places. The cost would be 160,000 million pesetas, each prison costing some 9,000 million pesetas. These new prisons will be macro prisons, covering hundreds of thousands of square metres, each able to hold an average of 1,000 inmates.

This project has raised objections from the prisoners' rights movement. The movement objects to this outdated project of *modernization* which consists in endlessly reproducing carceral structures by building more closed prisons, increasing the number of incarcerated individuals and the length of their sentence. This has the effect of promoting carceral segregation as the only possible response to crime and its social causes (Salhaketa 1992).

The central prison administration is not the only body to recognize the shortage of prison places; official authorities and international organizations have also commented on it. Constant references are made to the increase in the prison population and the use of old buildings with limited capacity. The Ombudsman (Defensor del Pueblo) has repeatedly denounced the overcrowding of prisons in various reports. The first, in 1987, provoked a great public debate and led to the sacking of the then Ombudsman. Another similar report published in 1990 made specific references to health and hygiene in Catalan prisons. The Spanish Human Rights League, the Association of Judges for Democracy, the Episcopal Commission of Pastoral Care, the Union of Public Servants in Custodial Establishments, the Organization against Torture, and Salhaketa, have all campaigned at national level against the various deleterious effects of prison overcrowding. The reports by Amnesty International in 1986 and Helsinki Watch in 1990 were also important in generating a public debate on all aspects of prison conditions for those affected by HIV/AIDS. At regional level, the Ombudsman of Catalonia has publicly criticized the conditions in Catalan prisons. Similar criticisms have also been voiced by the Commission of Human Rights of the Parliament of Catalonia, the Office of the Public Prosecutor of the Supreme Court of Catalonia, the Working Group on the Administration of Justice of the

Barcelona Council, the Bar Council of Barcelona, the Catalan Association of Democratic Lawyers, and prisoners' support groups.

The question of overcrowding highlights three wider themes which are matters of constant debate in Spain. These concern alternatives to custody, the treatment of prisoners with HIV/AIDS, and the treatment of those who are drug dependent.

Prison, parole and remission

While the proposed reform of the Penal Code may change things, there is presently an absolute scarcity in the provision of alternatives to custody properly defined, that is sentences which divert offenders from any risk of imprisonment. A less stringent definition might include the use of conditional suspension of sentences for serving prisoners. This possibility is provided by Article 92 and sections of Article 98 of the Penal Code concerning conditional liberty.

The sentence can be suspended by the same court which imposes it, for a period of two to five years. The length of suspension is calculated taking into account the circumstances of the offence and the length of the sentence, and is dependent on whether the prisoner is a first-time offender. Suspension can be applied to offenders sentenced to less than a year (two years in exceptional cases). As long as the offender actually completes the suspended sentence without reoffending, the sentence is treated as having been served; it is considered to have been completed.

Similarities have been drawn between the Spanish conditional suspended sentence and the British system of probation. However, there are some marked differences. The suspended sentence entails no duties or obligations, apart from the condition not to reoffend. Furthermore, no mechanisms or institutions of surveillance or control are involved during the period of suspension, nor does the convicted person receive any form of assistance.

Parole has two characteristics in common with the conditional suspension of sentence. It reduces the time in custody and is dependent on the condition not to reoffend. However, there are some obvious differences between the two. To be granted parole prisoners must be serving a sentence of more than one year and must have completed three-quarters of it. Should they reoffend or misbehave while on parole, they will return to custody.

To complete the exposition of measures which mitigate the deprivation of liberty, a number of 'benefits' which are separate from parole and other conditional provisions should be mentioned. These benefits are secured within prisons themselves, where individuals have already been deprived of their freedom. Remission through work can be granted to convicted prisoners. After approval by the prison judge, prisoners are given remission of one day for two days worked. In view of the historical antecedents relating to the Franco period, this scheme suffers from a lack of legislative clarity, although it constitutes one of the few mechanisms which potentially shorten custodial sentences.

The classification of prisoners – which is based on so-called scientific individual differentiation – allows for a series of benefits of a progressive character during the period of custody. Category A prisoners (*primer grado*) are situated in 'closed' regimes because they are considered dangerous or unsuited to the mainstream custodial regime. These prisoners are denied all benefits. Category B (*segundo grado*) or 'ordinary' prisoners, who constitute the majority, can be given leave permits for up to 36 days per year. These permits can only be given after prisoners have served a quarter of their sentence. Category C prisoners (*tercer grado*) have access to a wider range of activities within 'open' regime prisons and can be given leave permits of up to 48 days per year, after having served a quarter of the sentence. Weekend permits are also obtainable, and are a feature of the open regime.

All of these permits are granted by the prison administration, on request from the assessment team (*equipo de observación y tratamiento*). In the case of category B prisoners a permit for more than two days must be authorized by the prison judge. However, the procedure necessary for the granting of such permits frequently generates conflict between prison managers and the prison judge – particularly in Catalonia. Such conflicts usually occur when prisoners convicted of sexual offences or offences involving political violence are dealt with. In such cases, the absence of criteria for the granting of permits has led to judges granting permits to convicted prisoners who have reoffended. Although this has not happened on a great scale, the moral panic relating to such reoffending has caused great tension and has led to proposals for legislative reforms to toughen the rules governing sexual offenders and those involved in political violence. However, by the end of 1994 no such changes had been made.

Drug use in prison

The mounting problem of drug dependency in prison has affected the whole of the custodial system in Spain. A number of studies carried out by penal and other authorities have shown that the incidence of drug dependence in the prison population is generally very high. In 1985 a governmental study estimated that 48 per cent of Spanish prisoners were using some variety of illicit drug. Independent research has indicated that between 60 and 80 per cent of the prison population use illicit drugs regularly (de la Cuesta Arzamendi 1988; Beristain Ipina 1985; Reeg 1992). Many are said to become drug users while serving a prison sentence.

In view of this evidence, the prison authorities have discussed the possibility of introducing various programmes of treatment and prevention. Nevertheless, for individuals in prison who find themselves in urgent need of drug rehabilitation, there are no measures which really solve the problem. Legally, the only way to obtain access to treatment outside the prison, thus removing the addict from an environment where drugs are readily available, would be the use of a suspended sentence. But the eligibility criteria for this measure are difficult to satisfy. This causes lengthy discussions in the courts where drug abusers are tried, and where the urgency of the cases dealt with would instead require fast decisions.

It is for this reason that a piece of legislation was introduced in 1983 to allow the early release of prisoners who are considered to be drug dependent. Article 93 of the Penal Code allows for the conditional remission of a sentence but imposes such conditions that this alternative punishment is in fact less appealing than custody itself. These conditions include forms of curfew and a prohibition on meeting individuals and frequenting areas regarded as part of the drug scene. Moreover, non-compliance with one of these conditions reactivates a custodial sentence.

The discretionary use of this provision has stimulated much discussion. This is due to the fact that the judges' propensity to grant conditional remission is based on their own opinion as to whether the drug users are likely to comply with the conditions that such provision entails. Conditional remission for these types of offenders remains therefore a small escape valve which does not go any way towards tackling the thorny problem of drug dependent prisoners.

Prisoners with HIV and AIDS

The conditions of overcrowding which characterize the majority of Spanish prisons, together with the great problem of drug dependence, have led to the rapid spread of HIV and AIDS.

In 1989 a study by the prison authorities revealed that amongst a sample of 19,946 prisoners who consented to be tested 30 per cent were HIV positive (Martinez Sánchez 1990). In 1990 93 per cent of those infected by AIDS were male and 7 per cent were female (Terradillos Basoco 1994). In the same year the number of deaths in prison from AIDS represented half the total number of deaths, with the principal risk factor being the intravenous use of drugs (de Miguel 1991). In Catalonia, the regional prison authorities admitted that the number of prisoners with AIDS was between 160 and 170 (*El Periódico de Catalunya* 18 October 1994).

This situation triggered a debate concerning the level of responsibility of the state and/or the prison authorities for the spread of the virus in prison. The dominant view was that, as far as civil and penal responsibilities were concerned, the state should be held responsible for failing to halt the spread of the virus. Judges should therefore deal with all cases brought before them in which prison administrations were charged with dereliction of duty or lack of care (Silva Sánchez 1993). This principle has been upheld by the courts, although at the time of writing few such cases have been heard.

While the Penal Code through the application of Article 93 allows terminally ill patients to be granted conditional release, and Article 60 of the Penitentiary Regulation of Sentences permits seriously ill patients to be cared for in ordinary hospitals, AIDS sufferers endure endless delays before judges are prepared to release them into the community.

Conclusion

This overview of the Spanish criminal justice system has had two aims. The first has been to set out the practical measures taken in order to carry out the process of democratization in areas where traditionally there has been a lack of accountability. It is not possible for agencies which have powers to curtail the liberty of citizens to be untouched by the culture of democracy which underpinned the political transition. The second objective has been to examine certain trends, making use of official data. We have focused on the changes in the prison system and the way in which this system seeks to further its compliance with the constitutional principles.

Only recently has the study of the social realities of the penal system in Spain entered the agenda. However, this study still reflects the primacy of the legal culture over other modes of approach to the problems which social control poses (Bergalli 1992).

The priority accorded to the production of order has meant that studies of the Spanish criminal justice system previously had to remain within the tightly defined perimeters set by the state. This situation did not differ all that much from the experience in other European countries immediately after the Second World War. Owing to the late introduction of sociology and anthropology as disciplines into this area of research, it was not possible to approach the study of social and institutional realities other than through their legal norms.

It follows from this that the accounts we have had of police activities, or of the way judges assess situations which come to their attention, are always located within a strictly legal space. The Spanish criminal justice system is at present undergoing self-examination of the functioning of its various parts. However, this type of development is ridden with contradictions and, characteristically for a process of democratization, proceeds in fits and starts. Meanwhile, in Spain the range of conceptual frameworks has increased: nowadays psychological, psychosocial, anthropological and other approaches are more readily accepted, and in fact are going through a phase of academic institutionalization. A *rapprochement* with the legal disciplines is drawing near, and areas which were previously the undisturbed preserves of legal culture are now being analysed from a range of different, more critical perspectives. The efforts to democratize the criminal justice system in Spain, and to comply with the legal requirements of the European Union, must therefore be acknowledged, even if problematic areas remain.

The manifest tendency of democratic societies to make excessive use of the penal system as a means of resolving all manners of conflicts has led to 'punitive inflation'. The constant use of the penal route to resolve situations which have found no solutions in the civil or administrative spheres has had the effect of literally choking penal systems, by overwhelming them with a constant flux of social problems. Political inefficiency, court delays and the overcrowding of prisons are all part of this configuration. In this sense, the Spanish criminal justice system is an expression of the general state of affairs.

Note

This paper was drafted in collaboration with Iñaki Rivera Beiras (University of Barcelona).

References

Bergalli R (1992), 'Il sistema penale spagnolo come ambito meno conosciuto del controllo sociale' *Dei Delitti e delle Pene* II, 2: 7–23

Beristain Ipina A (1985), 'Delitos de tráfico ilegal de drogas' in M Cobo del Rosal (ed) *Comentarios a la legislación penal* Madrid: Edersa

Bueno Arus F (1978), 'Las prisiones desde la guerra civil hasta nuestros dias: evolucion, situación actual y reformas necesarias' *Historia* 16, VII: 123–42

Carr R (1988), *España (1808–1975)* Barcelona: Ariel

Covisa Villa S (1992), *Menores encerrados en centros de reclusión con sus madres* Madrid: Ministerio de Justicia

de la Cuesta Arzamendi J L (1988), 'Spanish Drug Crime Policy' paper presented at the *Conference on Drug Policies in Western Europe* Tilburg University, the Netherlands, 30 May to 2 June

de Miguel J M (1991), 'El problema social del SIDA en España' *Revista Española de Investigaciones Sociológicas* 53: 75–6

Draper Miralles R (1984), *De las prisiones de Franco a las cárceles de la democracia* Barcelona: Argos Vergara

García Valdés C (1977), 'El sistema penitenciario español: pasado y presente' in C García Valdés (ed) *El preso común en España* Madrid: Ediciones de La Torre

Garrido Guzmán L (1983), *Manual de Ciencia Penitenciaria* Madrid: Instituto de Criminología de la Universidad Complutense de Madrid

Generalitat de Catalunya (1992), *Estadística básica de la Justicia a Catalunya* Barcelona: Generalitat de Catalunya

Gimeno Sendra V (1981), *Fundamentos del Derecho Procesal* Madrid: Civitas

Lurra M (1977), *Rebelión en las cárceles* San Sebastián: Hordago

Marin Rodriguez J F (1986), *La Modelo: 1939–47. Diseño para un estudio etnohistórico* Barcelona: University of Barcelona

Marti O (1977), 'La copel: historia de una lucha silenciada' *El Viejo Topo* 13: 25–63

Martinez Sánchez M (1990), 'Programa de prevención y control de enfermedades transmisibles en institutiones penitenciarias' *Revista de Estudios Penitenciarios* 1: 51–67

Ministerio de Justicia (1986), *Informe General 1985* Madrid: Secretariá General de Asuntos Penitenciarios

Ministerio de Justicia (1991), *Plan de amortización y creacion de centros penitenciarios* Madrid: Ministerio de Justicia

Ministerio de Justicia (1992), *Informe General 1991* Madrid: Secretariá General de Asuntos Penitenciarios

Ministerio de Justicia e Interior (1994), *Anteproyecto de Ley Orgánica de Código Penal* Madrid: Ministerio de Justicia

Recasens i Brunet A (1985), 'Transición política y justicia penal en España' *Sistema. Revista de Ciencias Sociales* 67: 123–38

Redondo S, Funes J and Luque E (1993), *Justicia penal i Reincidencia* Barcelona: Generalitat de Catalunya

Reeg A R (1992), 'Drugs and the Law in Post-Franco Spain' in H H Traver and M S Gaylord (eds) *Drugs, Law and the State* Hong Kong: Hong Kong University Press

Rivera Beiras I (1993), 'Criminalización de la pobreza', MA thesis, University of Barcelona

Rivera Beiras I (ed) (1994), *Tratamiento penitenciario y derechos fundamentales* Barcelona: Bosch

Rule E (1993), 'Spanish Nationality Law in Outline' *Immigration & Nationality Law & Practice* 7, 4: 119–22

Salhaketa (1992), *Plataforma por las alternativas a la construcción de macrocárceles* Vitoria/Gasteiz

Silva Sánchez J M (1993), 'El SIDA en la cárcel: algunos problemas de responsabilidad penal' in S Mir Puig (ed) *Problemas jurídico-penales del SIDA* Barcelona: Bosch

Terradillos Basoco J T (1994), 'AIDS in Prisons in Spain' in P Thomas and M Moerings (eds) *AIDS in Prison* Aldershot: Dartmouth

8

The Normalization of Swedish Prisons

Karen Leander

While there has long been ambivalence in Sweden as to whether law breakers were to be seen as downtrodden losers in society whose resources would be further diminished by imprisonment, or as parasites on the welfare state (Tham 1995), Sweden has both deservedly and undeservedly been acclaimed for its humane penal policies (Serrill 1977). Short prison sentences and liberal regimes – with, of course, some glaring contradictions – were the cornerstone of this acclaim prior to and following the 1974 Correctional Reform Act. The 1980s, however, witnessed a shift towards a more restrictive and, in some cases, repressive policy, a shift which was reinforced in the 1990s with the election of a right of centre bloc in the autumn of 1991 which had based its campaign against criminals on slogans such as 'Keep them locked in, so we can go out!' The new Minister of Justice published a brochure emphasizing her determination 'To Restore a Degenerated Criminal Policy' (Justitiedepartementet 1993), a critical reference to the perceived failure of successive Social Democratic governments between 1982 and 1991 to halt the general rise in reported crime, and the continued expansion in drug use, a failure which Conservative politicians argued was partly attributable to conscious neglect. Between 1991 and 1994 the Conservative government used the media to articulate a tough and unambiguous message on crime and punishment. What the Social Democrats, returned to office in the autumn of 1994, will do in the light of the changes already implemented in the criminal justice system and the continuing economic crisis in Sweden remains to be seen.

Perhaps in response to this shift in penal policy, to the increasingly managerial style of the correctional system, or to the hottest July since 1756, the summer of 1994 witnessed a demonstration at the maximum security Tidaholm prison for long-term male prisoners. This was triggered by the isolation of an inmate which was perceived as unfair. The prisoners refused to return to their cells after exercise and instead set fire to parts of the prison.

Damages to the tune of tens of millions of Swedish kronor were said to have been incurred. Many of the inmates at this prison were serving long sentences, and many had not been born in Sweden. Less than a week passed before the relatively progressive *Dagens Nyheter* newspaper published a piece by a columnist associated with the Social Democrats in which he suggested that it might be advisable to imprison foreign offenders in slightly less humane conditions as the relative slackness of Swedish prison regimes probably invited crime (Schein 1994). The publication of this column on the editorial page – in spite of Thomas Matheisen's timely reminder in March 1994 in another daily that changes in penal practice rarely have much influence on crime rates – was a clear illustration of just how far to the right the debate on penal policy had shifted.

However, it has to be acknowledged that the greater use of imprisonment in Sweden, from 13 per cent of all sentences in 1975 to 20 per cent in the early 1990s (Ahlberg and Dolmén 1992:27; SCB RSÅ 1993), even though the number of those actually receiving criminal sentences had dropped, was a trend well in place before the centre-right bloc came to power. Furthermore, the picture is not entirely bleak. The overall prison population itself has remained fairly stable through the 1980s and the risk of being sentenced for some crimes, serious drunken driving for example, has actually decreased or at least fluctuated. Such a development in different directions has characterized post-war Swedish criminal policy, that is, a process of 'push and pull', where specific steps taken to liberalize the system are often neutralized by tougher developments elsewhere (Leander 1986).

Sanctions and dispositions

Custody
In 1993, fines (police, prosecutorial and court) constituted 85 per cent of all criminal dispositions, followed by prison (4 per cent), waivers of prosecution (4 per cent), conditional sentences (3 per cent), probation (2 per cent) and other sanctions (1 per cent). Of a total of around 75,000 court dispositions in 1992, 17,714 involved custodial sanctions.

Several sanctions exist in Sweden which imply a deprivation of liberty. These range from the minimal sentence of imprisonment, normally 14 days (prior to 1981, one month) to a maximum of 10 years (12 or 16 years in special circumstances), to life imprisonment; compulsory residential forensic psychiatric care (until recently indeterminate); some probation provisions; and finally custody which is ordered when an offender serving community service commits further crimes. Other indeterminate sentences were abolished in the early 1980s, primarily youth prison (for 18–20 year olds) and internment (to prevent *future* serious criminality). While some voices have been heard in favour of the reintroduction of indeterminate sentences, all imprisonment sentences in late 1994 are finite. Over 86 per cent of all custodial sentences awarded were traditional imprisonment sentences, which will be the sentences discussed below unless otherwise indicated. Under the law, 15–17 year olds may only be sentenced to prison under extraordinary circumstances. Sentencing practice for 18–20 year olds is also restricted but less so, partly depending on the gravity of the offence or other 'special reasons'.

Alternatives to custody
Apart from the fine, conditional sentences and straightforward probation, which are widely used, several other alternatives to prison are being experimented with for some groups of offenders. While some of these alternatives may have certain advantages, they will unquestionably serve to further segregate the 'prison community' to an even greater degree than today, serving as an acknowledgement that mainline prisons are reserved for the hard core – with appropriate regimes.

Community service (samhällstjänst) In 1990 an experiment was begun with community service within five district court areas. This sanction, intended here primarily for 18–25 year olds, was expanded to cover the entire country on 1 January 1993. During 1993, 336 such sanctions were ordered, of which 3 per cent were for women (SCB SM 9401 1993; KOS 1993–4:38).

Contract treatment (kontraktsvård) This sentence introduced in 1988 is now available for some drug abusers instead of a prison sentence. The judge here sentences the offender to probation with instructions concerning a specific treatment or care plan. In many cases, the judge will indicate how long a prison sentence the substance abusing offender would have been given. During 1993 658 such sentences were ordered, of which 11 per cent were for women (KOS 1993–4:37).

Intensive supervision (probation) A study is being made into the possibility of introducing intensive supervision to take the place of prison sentences of 1–2 months. In essence, the offender would be in 'house arrest' during this probation. Control will be effected by means of electronic aids, such as electronic tagging/monitoring. Intensive supervision was implemented on an experimental basis in six aftercare districts in August 1994 and will continue for two years. A report (Straffsystemkommittén) is expected in the autumn of 1995 with recommendations concerning the introduction of tagging into Sweden. These offenders will be expected to pay 50 kronor a day into the victims' fund, so that no economic advantage is incurred over inmates.

The introduction and design of most of these alternatives has had Social Democrat support.

Various provisions also allow prisoners to serve the latter part of their sentence in work, treatment or studies on the outside, though for some prisoners the use of these alternatives threatens to become more restrictive.

Prisons

Administration, structure and admissions

The national government authority responsible for the correctional system is the National Prisons and Probation Administration (Kriminalvårdsstyrelsen). The seven regional offices administer non-custodial sentences and aftercare (*frivården*), remand prisons (*häkten*), and both local and national prisons (*fängelser*). Prisons can be either open or closed. (Plans to abolish the distinction between local and national prisons and to reorganize the entire prison system around a fourfold security classification have been floated.) On 1 July 1994, in addition to the 55 probation and aftercare bodies, the correctional system consisted of the prisons given in Table 8.1.

By law, custodial correctional care must be designed to promote the (re)socialization of the inmate to the outside world and to counteract any deleterious effects of incarceration. Preparations for the inmate's ultimate release are to begin preferably upon admission.

In Table 8.2 we see the average institutional (prison and remand prison) and non-institutional ('aftercare' including probation) populations for certain years between 1970 and 1992. The average daily prison population (including remand) in 1992 was over 5,000 persons. This figure was similar in the early 1970s but dropped closer to 4,100 and 4,200 in the mid 1970s in response to the 1974 Correctional Reform Act and policy proposals to 'empty the prisons'. The figures gradually increased to reach nearly 5,000 by

Table 8.1   *Prisons and remand prisons, 1 July 1994*

Prisons	Number	Capacity	% in open prison
National	18	2,056	31
Local	56	2,855	48
Remand	30	1,541	–

Source: KOS 1993–4:15

Table 8.2   *Admissions to prison and to remand prison as well as daily institutional and non-institutional populations, 1970–1992*

	Persons admitted to prison	Persons admitted to remand	Average daily prison population	Of which on remand	Average aftercare population
1970	10,546	37,109	5,250	787	23,078
1975	10,109	31,644	4,140	691	16,691
1980	12,054	35,911	4,564	818	14,530
1985	13,535	31,807	4,330	743	11,781
1992	13,836	34,899	5,233	1,066	12,500

Source: SCB RSÅ 1977:Tables 3.5.1, 3.5.2b; 1983, 1989, 1990, 1993:Tables 3.5.1, 3.5.2

the late 1980s. The average occupancy rate rose from 70 per cent in 1976 to 94 per cent in the 1990s, thus violating the standard set in the early 1980s of a maximum 85 per cent occupancy rate (adopted in an effort to allow for reasonable differentiation among inmates as well as to provide a buffer during seasonal fluctuations in the population). Throughout this period the aftercare population decreased substantially owing to changes in the length of required supervision by a probation officer (from 3 to 2 to 1 year).

The prognosis is for a future strain on occupancy rates owing to the repeal of 'half-time' conditional release (see below) and the rise in the number of inmates serving long sentences (Somander 1994:12). Changes in the sentencing of drunken drivers will also add to the prison population. Thus, the construction of additional cells seems an inevitability unless policies are altered or abandoned. As if to reinforce this point, the Prison and Probation Administration has indicated that the average daily prison population had risen substantially to 5,664 by late 1994 (personal communication January 1995).

Trends in prison sentencing
In 1992, a report published by the National Council of Crime Prevention (BRÅ) on trends in prison sentences 1975–91 (Ahlberg

and Dolmén 1992) showed a general upswing in the number of prison sentences during this period, with peaks reached in 1981–3 and 1988–9 and dips in 1984–7 and 1990. This report explains the first peak by intensified police efforts against street sales of drugs. The second peak is explained by increased police efforts against drunken driving. However, the dip in 1990 was caused by a temporary change in the law extending the discretion of judges to use sentences other than prison. In general, the rise in prison sentences over the last two decades has been described as dramatic (Tham forthcoming).

The average prison sentence awarded in 1973 was 4.5 months compared with 6.9 months in 1993 for all crimes (SCB SM 9401 1993) and 8.4 months if traffic crimes are excluded (SCB KR 1993). Sentences for foreign citizens increased from 5.7 months in 1973 to 9.4 months in 1992, with the 1992 average length reflecting a 40 per cent longer sentence for foreigners than for Swedish citizens. Explanations given for this discrepancy are that foreign citizens are convicted of fewer traffic crimes than Swedish citizens (they drive less in general) as well as of crimes that lead to longer prison sentences (SCB 1994).

The proportion of long sentences has also increased among the prison population in Sweden. Eleven per cent of prison sentences in 1993 were for more than one year: half of the crimes involved violence or drugs (SCB SM 9401 1993). The absolute number of prisoners starting sentences of five or more years nearly tripled between 1984 and 1993. Between 1973 and 1993, 91 people were sentenced to life imprisonment. The number of prisoners incurring the heaviest (security) restrictions during their incarceration (limited communication with the outside world, restricted furloughs, etc.) has risen dramatically since 1990. The majority have been convicted of drug crimes (KOS 1993–4:61).

The upswing in prison sentences began immediately after the sharp dip in the mid 1970s following the Correctional Reform Act, and in a report authored by von Hofer (SCB 1983) it was claimed that the increase was due in large part to a special focus by the police and criminal justice system on certain crime categories, such as drug abuse and white collar crimes. The same author refutes the argument that the rise in the use of imprisonment was a consequence of a real increase in crimes (except perhaps crimes of violence). Instead, he identified as a partial reason for the upswing, and also for the then much discussed increase in long prison sentences, the abolition of indeterminate sentences for 'habitual' offenders whereupon courts started handing down longer determinate sentences. He observed a growing 'polarization' of the sanctioning system, with

Table 8.3   *Average prison term served (months)*

1965	1970	1975	1980	1985	1990	1992
4.9	4.5	3.7	3.5	3.2	3.0	3.0

Source: SCB RSÅ 1993:120

less use of probation for first-time or occasional offenders (in favour of conditional sentences) and a higher rate of imprisonment for highly active recidivists (SCB 1983).

Sweden has long been known for its comparatively short sentences, many of which are between one and two months for serious drunken driving offences. But parallel with the above described increase in long prison sentences has been a corresponding substantial drop in short sentences: whereas 45 per cent of all prison sentences were for one month in the mid 1970s, this proportion was 32 per cent in 1993. Similarly, sentences for two months or under dropped from 62 per cent to well under 50 per cent (SCB SM 9401 1993; SCB RSÅ 1993:120).

While sentences have for the most part become longer, the average time served has not increased. It is rare for anyone with a sentence longer than two months to actually serve the entire term. One of the main reasons for this is the relatively 'generous' rules regarding conditional release (parole). The required proportion of a sentence that needed to be served before parole could be awarded was shortened three times during the 1980s. The 'half-time' rule was applied from mid 1983 to mid 1993; prisoners serving sentences between four months and two years were eligible. This policy was adopted partly to relieve prison overcrowding. As Table 8.3 indicates, in 1992 the average prison term actually served was three months (four months when drunken drivers are excluded).

What crimes lead to prison?

Most prison sentences are for rape, murder, manslaughter, aggravated robbery, and aggravated drug and smuggling offences (SCB SM 9401 1993). In 1973, 11 per cent of all custodial sentences were for 'crimes against the person' (homicide, assault, threats, other harassment, sexual crimes, and crimes against the family). This figure had risen to 19 per cent by 1992. The proportion of custodial sentences for drug and smuggling offences almost doubled, from 5 per cent to 9 per cent. The proportion of property crimes (including robbery) remained stable at around one-third.

The prison population: what rates and which groups?
In 1992, the average daily prison population was 5,233, composed of 1,066 remanded and 4,108 sentenced prisoners (plus approximately 60 detainees charged with immigration violations: see Table 8.2). According to the Council of Europe, the rate of imprisonment in Sweden in 1990 was 60 per 100,000 of the population, which was lower than the average for those states in the Council. However, for women (4 per cent) and foreign citizens (17 per cent), the average was similar to the other countries. As for Scandinavian comparisons, figures for 1991 suggest that Sweden had the lowest rate of imprisonment, below Norway, with Denmark and Finland the highest (SCB RSÅ 1993:122–3).

Yearly estimates are made within the correctional system of the number of *drug abusing prisoners*, which is operationally defined as those inmates who claim to have used drugs at some time during the two months prior to admission. The number of drug users in the daily population doubled from about 800 in 1975 to about 1,600 in 1992. In recent years, the proportion of new admissions who abuse drugs has ranged between 40 and 42 per cent, with another 20–25 per cent who claim alcohol abuse. This is a much higher proportion today compared with 10 years ago. An overwhelming majority of all drug abusing prisoners are defined as serious abusers, that is, daily or as good as daily users. Drug abuse is clearly less common among those with short sentences. Of those who used drugs two months before incarceration, 75 per cent were between 25 and 44 years of age. The proportion of drug abusers among newly admitted prisoners is rising, and women in prison are more likely than men to have drug related substance abuse (KOS 1993–4:49).

The number of reported HIV-infected prisoners has remained fairly constant, though there is a reported decrease in offenders on probation or receiving aftercare (Table 8.4). The latest budget proposal prepared by the Swedish Prison and Probation Service indicates that special resources are to be devoted for the development of programmes for the struggle against HIV infection (KOS 1995–6:2).

Research findings show that Swedish prisons contain groups that are resource weak, or resource deficient. That is to say, many prisoners have suffered difficult childhoods, have rarely been educated beyond compulsory school level, have often been unemployed and/or have lacked housing, and as we have seen, display high levels of alcohol and drug addiction. In addition, half of the inmates had prior prison experience (SCB RSÅ 1993:121).

A client study (Krantz et al. 1994) showed that half of the

Table 8.4　*HIV-infected persons in correctional care, 1 April 1990–1994*

	In probation and aftercare	In prison	In remand prison
1990	102	27	5
1991	99	22	7
1992	89	18	6
1993	88	25	5
1994	68	28	6

Source: KOS 1993–4:40, 67, 87

prisoners released in 1992 had been unemployed prior to imprisonment, with another 10 per cent being actual or potential disability pensioners. Barely one-third had steady or temporary work. At the time of release, over a third continued to be unemployed, and a majority lived on state benefits, unemployment insurance, disability pensions and other forms of welfare. Only around three-quarters had access to regular housing at the time of admission though this increased somewhat by the time of release. This survey also reveals that imprisonment is largely a big-city phenomenon. About half of those sentenced to prison in 1992 came from the three metropolitan areas in Sweden.

It is widely felt among prison staff that the proportion of inmates with *psychiatric problems* is increasing. Crimes that would have ended in compulsory psychiatric treatment 10 or 20 years ago now result in imprisonment. In percentage terms, prison and psychiatric treatment sentences for murder and manslaughter have essentially changed places; in 1976 the ratio was roughly one-third to two-thirds; by 1992 this ratio was almost reversed (SCB RSÅ 1977; 1993). Media reports revealed that conditions for these groups in some of the tougher prisons are appalling. Many inmates are kept isolated from the general population and there is a serious lack of resources to deal with psychiatric problems.

Another delineated group, often the topic of criminal policy debates as we have seen, is *foreign citizens*. (It is possible in some statistics to distinguish between those who are permanent residents in Sweden and those who are not; 'second-generation' Swedes are also delineated in some discussions). Of the 17,714 custodial sentences passed in 1992, nearly 69 per cent were for Swedes, 10 per cent naturalized Swedes, and 21 per cent foreign citizens (three-quarters of these were permanent residents; SCB KR 1993). This proportion of 'foreign' inmates has remained fairly stable since the mid 1970s (Somander 1994:18), but the composition of the group has changed. (It should be noted here that many foreign citizens remain domiciled in Sweden for years and decades without ever taking Swedish citizenship because most benefits available to Swedish citizens are also available to domiciled inhabitants.)

In 1975, 70 per cent of the new 'foreign' admissions to prison were Scandinavians (mainly Finnish citizens), 21 per cent were from the rest of Europe, and 7 per cent from non-European countries. By the early 1990s, less than half of new 'foreign' prison admissions came from Scandinavia while about one-third came from non-European countries, with 'other Europeans' remaining stable (Somander 1994:20). Nevertheless, deportation orders following completion of prison sentences decreased from 36 per cent in 1975 to 15 per cent in 1991, but have increased substantially in number since then.

Women in prison

Since the 1970s, the percentage of women among convicted offenders has increased from 13 to 16 per cent, and of the prison population (and admissions) from 2 per cent in the mid 1970s, 4 per cent in the 1980s, to more than 5 per cent in 1993 (Table 8.5). These proportions reflect more than a quadrupling of the number of women admitted to prison (and to other custodial establishments). Women are largely convicted of crimes such as shoplifting and forgery, general property crimes, fraud, drunken driving, and drug offences. Only 5 per cent of women prisoners serve sentences for violent crimes compared with 17 per cent among men.

The head of the only closed national women's prison (Hinseberg) has claimed in a newspaper interview that whereas in 1988 only five women were serving sentences of six years or more at Hinseberg, the figure at the end of 1993 was 30 (*Dagens Nyheter* 12 July 1993). The same source also claimed that women first-time offenders were receiving longer sentences than were thinkable in the late 1980s. From nearly always receiving shorter sentences than their male counterparts, many women are now receiving equally long sentences of up to 10–12 years. This situation is compounded by the large increase in the number of women sentenced to prison in the late 1980s which (despite a decline in 1991) continued into 1992 when the figure broke the 800 mark. While explanations for the rise in criminality (or imprisonment) among women have often been divided into the liberation versus marginalization theses (Box 1983), it is economic and labour market explanations that have received the most serious treatment by some Nordic criminologists (Høigård 1990).

Certain other trends among women prisoners are worthy of comment. First, their average age is increasing. This has been

Table 8.5   *Women admitted to prison, 1974–1993*

	1974	1985	1992	1993
Number of women admitted	169	546	683	758
% of total admissions	1.9	4	5	5.3

Sources: KOS various years; Somander 1993

explained, in part at least, by the imprisonment of middle aged women for taking violent revenge on oppressive partners (*Dagens Nyheter* 12 July 1993). Previously these offenders would have been placed into psychiatric care. (At Hinseberg staff point to a growing problem with psychiatric prisoners generally.) Another important reason why increasing numbers of women are being processed within the criminal justice system (and imprisoned) is that the crimes women commit are those that are being heavily sentenced in Sweden today. The obvious example here is drug offences. The percentage of women prisoners sentenced for drug offences is much higher than that for male prisoners (18 per cent against 9 per cent in 1993; see KOS 1993–4). There may be many partial explanations for this in terms of the gender division of labour in the commission of crimes, but this does show the centrality of drug offences in the rise in women's imprisonment. It is also worth noting here that among foreign citizens charged with crimes in 1993, women constituted around 19 per cent; this is a slightly higher rate than for women in the charged (or sentenced) populations as a whole (SCB SM 9401:Tables 410A, 410B).

Most Swedish prisoners serve their sentences in single-gender facilities. Where smaller prisons are mixed, especially local ones, women usually have around 3 of the 30 places. In the mid 1980s, several commentators from both the drug treatment and correctional fields proposed even greater degrees of gender segregation than had previously been the case. Exploitation and sexual harassment were partial reasons for their proposals, but more recognition also started being given to the subordination of women in drug and criminal circles. The role of gender and gender expectations for women's entry into (and perhaps exit from) drug abuse and criminality began to be highlighted. By the late 1980s, many professionals in newly developed treatment facilities felt that these women needed a refuge for a period away from gender relations 'on the outside'. In an interview study at one of these facilities (Leander 1991), women abusers described lives devoid of contact with other adult women friends. They had contact with women as social workers, probation officers, and drug counsellors, but not as peers. Their experience in the treatment facility was for many the first experience with 'sisterhood'. The low level of intrigues, jealousy and back-biting was in part attributed to the absence of men: in any case, the experience proved startling for many of the women. Parallel discussions with women prisoners at the local facility near Stockholm revealed similar sentiments.

The prevailing view of drug abusers and many offenders in Sweden could be summed up in the terminology often used to refer to them: marginalized, outcasts, downtrodden, excluded, on the edge of society. For women this exclusion is reinforced because of the strong gender roles they have violated, in spite of the fact that women are often committing crimes to support not themselves but others. Furthermore, there is a growing body of evidence that women prisoners' lives resemble women's lives in general to a greater degree than has previously been thought, and that their crimes are largely committed to 'cope' with the care demands they have in their daily lives (Pösö 1989; Leander 1993).

While summarizing penal trends in Sweden is far from easy (Ahlberg and Dolmén 1992), the overall picture seems to be one of changing sentencing practices and harsher prison regimes. There is now greater use of prison sentences, and the number and proportion of those serving longer sentences has increased. Furthermore, national prisons which hold long-term prisoners are changing in character in part because of public concern over drug use which has led to stricter regimes.

The report from the National Prison and Probation Administration in September 1994 into the riot at Tidaholm prison highlighted some of these changes and prisoners' reactions to them (it might be of interest here that this prison was one of three targeted earlier for improvements to security systems in part to curtail escape attempts). Some factors mentioned include full occupancy, less attention to the content of prisoners' daily activities, control priorities taking precedence over rehabilitation programmes and the public's less sympathetic view of prisoners (Orrenius 1994).

However, against the hardening of sentencing policies and the development of more punitive alternatives, it must be kept in mind that Sweden's rate of imprisonment is well below many other Council of Europe countries, and in spite of centre-right rhetoric over a number of years, the overall time served by most prisoners is currently still low. Furthermore many serve their time in open prisons with opportunities for work release, early release, and drug rehabilitation programmes. Although the help prisoners receive is far from sufficient to support them on release, it is at least arguable that their experience of confinement is still largely less painful than in many other European states.

The making and unmaking of a modern criminal policy and penal code

The attack on the alleged complacency of the Social Democrats which has been conducted in the 1990s by the right of centre bloc has been seen by many as the beginning of the end of the Swedish 'model'. However, Thomas Mathiesen (1994) has called it the culmination of a process long under way. Many of the statistics presented in the sections above would lend credence to this argument. In truth, although the twenty year period between the Correctional Reform Act 1974 and the 1993 Commission review on the implementation of prison sentences could be delimited as the 'golden era' of Swedish penal policy, in the second half of the 1970s the pendulum started swinging towards the policies that were to culminate in the restrictions of the 1990s. This key issue is explored in this section.

1950–1970

The first half of the twentieth century saw an explosion of correctional reforms and measures introduced for the promotion of individual prevention and rehabilitation. The legacy was established for a differentiation and individualization of sanctioning. Two highly influential changes were introduced at the end of the Second World War, namely, waivers of prosecution in 1944 and the Implementation of Sentence Act in 1945. The latter marked a radical change in the formal design of custodial sanctions. Solitary confinement was abandoned as a standard form of punishment and open prisons were expanded. It was officially accepted that loss of liberty in conjunction with custodial sentences was to constitute *the* punishment. No further deprivation, suffering, or curtailment of rights other than that linked directly to the coercion entailed in incarceration was to be deliberately inflicted on inmates. And life on the 'inside' was to resemble life on the 'outside' as much as possible. The passing of this law has been identified as the beginning of Sweden's role as a forerunner in progressive corrections (Strahl 1970). More cynically, others have remarked that the law created chaos in the system due to lack of funds, which in turn prompted the enforced policy of placing heavily criminalized inmates in small, open facilities which was later to receive international acclaim (Åmark 1985).

The period between the Second World War and the passage of the 1962 Criminal Code was characterized by innumerable government commissions, reports and innovations. In particular, the introduction of prosecutorial summary fines in 1948 changed the face of the sanctioning system and reduced the workload of the courts. Competing penal philosophical factions, in the context of a sharp rise in recorded crime (especially theft and vandalism among young offenders), vied for domination in the legislative field, setting off a lively debate among jurists. Compromise was reached between more radical factions and social defence ideologists, so that the principle of retribution was officially removed while the stated objective of sanctions under the new Criminal Code became general prevention and individual rehabilitation.

While the new Criminal Code which took effect in 1965 effectively incorporated the idea of treatment into the criminal justice system, it also brought about an expanded 'criminalization' in that many acts formally viewed as 'minor' (especially against the person, such as molestation) were brought within the bounds of the penal law, and imprisonment was to be the standard sanction for assaults. Though some dissatisfaction was expressed with this extended arena of penal intervention among other things, a positive by-product was the increasing importance attached to the protection of individual rights.

In the 1960s, special legislation was passed, especially concerning tax, smuggling and drugs. These crimes remain outside the Criminal Code even today. The 1960s and 1970s also witnessed decriminalization, recriminalization, and depenalization especially of public order crimes, which affected both crime rates and sanctioning figures. Some authors (Nelson 1990; Sveri 1981) have indicated that the accountability of the criminal justice system may have been weakened with regard to the formal establishment of guilt as more *types* of crimes have been dealt with in less formal proceedings and as the *volume of cases* disposed of summarily has increased.

The new code also combined prison and hard labour into a uniform imprisonment sentence, during which the inmates had a duty to work and where the correctional system was obligated to make all efforts to facilitate the resocialization of the offender. Despite the expanded penal arena, the late 1960s and 1970s witnessed a general movement towards less use of imprisonment. Prisoner and various solidarity groups emerged and participated in criminal policy debates, culminating in the 1974 Correctional Reform Act. In 1974, the Minister of Justice called for a reduction in the prison population to under 600 by 1980, whereupon sentencing did undergo a slight shift resulting in a drop in the daily prison (sentenced) population from over 4,000 in 1973 to over 3,000 in 1975. The Correctional Reform Act of 1974 was seen to be a codification of already changed practices as well as an articulation of the 'liberal' face of Swedish criminal policy.

1970s and 1980s

By the late 1970s, the focus was on 'the crime' and its seriousness. Treatment ideology extended into the 1960s and 1970s but came under heavy attack as the principal rationale of incarceration. The 1970s and 1980s also witnessed the abolition of indeterminate sentences, increasingly harsher reactions to drug crimes, growing attention to, and tougher sentencing for, physical and sexual abuse in the 'private sphere' (against women and children), and more active efforts against white collar crime (Tham forthcoming).

A refocus on the gravity of the offence

The Criminal Code clearly reflected the shift over time between theft and assault – or property and crimes of violence – and the seriousness with which they were viewed (Hofer 1985:2.2). The National Council for Crime Prevention published a study entitled *A New Penal System* (BRÅ 1977) which paved the way for a shift in the debate, even though some of its proposals were not translated into law for over a decade and some were never taken up at all. It can be seen as a repudiation of the treatment ideology or, less dramatically, as a cautious reaffirmation of the principles of general prevention. It called for a more simplified sanctioning system and promoted some 'neo-classicist' thinking. The greater role that general prevention was to play during this period, however, was gradually to make way for a form of standardized sentencing; the concept of 'penal value' (*straffvärde*) was introduced into the Criminal Code in 1989 as the guideline courts were to use in the selection and severity of sanctions. (Inevitably, perhaps, this meant that the introductory paragraph to the Criminal Code affirming that general and individual prevention were the legitimizing principles/objectives was deleted.)

A convergence of factors has been seen as having influenced this shift, such as the rise in the number of heavily criminalized individuals, the growth in the use of drugs, and a disillusionment with social engineering as a means of solving societal and individual problems. The developments, although largely, were not entirely one way traffic. So, for example, at the same time as juvenile recidivists were receiving harsher sentences, a very liberal measure, conditional release (parole) after half sentence, was adopted in

1983. This suggests that the 'push-and-pull' tension inherent in much of Sweden's pre- and post-war criminal justice policy (curtailment of intervention in one area and a toughening up in another) extended into the 1970s and 1980s.

Another illustration of this tension was that although a harsher penal ideology (and sanctioning) was being promoted for white collar crimes, drug crimes, and violence against women, two government commission reports since the late 1970s can be said to have reinforced or promoted 'the liberal Swedish model'. In a Social Democratic government bill (1982–3 no. 85) the first report's research was summed up as follows. With regard to *individual prevention*, criminological research has shown us that the notion of rehabilitating a convicted person through incarceration is an illusion. As for *general prevention*, all international and Swedish research has shown that crime trends are in no way affected by the level of custodial sentences or their length. The report instead pointed to family and school policies, labour market and social policies, economic reforms, and the prevailing philosophy of human nature as factors which could have a real effect on criminality. The then newly elected Social Democratic government (after six years in opposition 1976–82) restated its commitment to the centrality of redistribution and the development of social policies around income, housing, education, work environment, and culture.

In 1986 a three-volume report by the Commission on Prison Sentences (SOU 1986) called for more use of fines and a corresponding decrease in prison sentences – including drunken driving – and demanded a cautious, general decline in sentencing levels (by lowering minimum sentences and more fines). Steep fines should replace prison sentences under one month, and first-offence shoplifting should only merit a fine; in addition, more fines should be introduced for drunken driving and non-aggravated theft and assault. However, the new concept of penal value introduced in 1989 meant that crimes against personal integrity should be ascribed a higher penal value (and thus harsher sentences), as should vandalism, environmental crimes, and serious drug crimes. Penalties for property crimes could be made less severe. Nothing was said, however, about lessening the already disproportionately harsh sentences for the middle range of drug crimes. The Commission also argued that since prison did not reduce criminality, it was acceptable to decrease its use without this leading to higher crime rates or a crisis in the public's faith in the criminal justice system. Finally, the Commission noted that incapacitation yielded only marginal effects – especially in individual cases – unless the society was willing to increase the number of prisoners to unreasonable dimensions. This was rejected for both humanitarian and cost considerations (see also Hofer 1993:161–88).

1990s

A Conservative MP, Jerry Martinger (a former prosecutor and member of a police board), articulated the right of centre bloc's criminal justice policy during the election campaign of 1991:

> Respect for law and order will increase only if sentences for serious crimes 'hurt' and if prison is associated with a certain degree of discomfort . . . Sweden's criminal policy has been an unfortunate mixture of treatment/care and punishment, where offenders are treated for the purpose of making them law-abiding citizens . . . This has led to an emphasis on the offender's interests . . . Punishment should be punishment and prisons should be prisons and not facilities for correctional care.

> Half-time release [parole] has been one of the greatest scandals of Swedish criminal policy throughout time. It was a product of the Social Democratic 'flummery'. (R&D 1991:14, our translation)

Martinger's detailed proposals included harsher sentences for recidivists than for first-time offenders; the curtailment of unsupervised leave for habitual recidivists; and limiting escapes by indulging prisoners less. This platform was attacked, partly for its support of a return to retribution principles in sentencing. In response, its proponents claimed to prefer the term 'deterrence' to describe their principle: 'The primary goal of punishment must be to restrain people from committing crimes.' Whether deterrence is in fact the goal or whether the policy is actually based on an 'absolute' theory of punishment though is a matter of contention. One commentator (Tamburrini 1993) discusses this shift from offender centred to offence based sentencing in terms of a Hegelian interpretation of the reintroduced principle of 'retribution' where the punishment is to symbolically cancel out the effect of the crime and invalidate the illegal act, thereby restoring the violated rights of the victim. Here redress to the victim requires a sentence (that entails suffering) 'in just proportion' to the gravity of the offence.

One of the main arguments against half-time release was that it was seen as incompatible with what the public thought was reasonable. The notion that a lax criminal policy violated the public's 'general sense of justice' was a favourite assertion by the centre-right bloc during their reign from 1991 to 1994. In the 1993 brochure *To Restore a Degenerated Criminal Policy*, the bloc claimed to be speaking for the people. In general their programme also entailed a rationalization as well as an expansion of the police; tougher prison regimes; swifter and tougher punishment for young offenders; less use of waivers of prosecution; special intense supervision; and more use of pre-trial detention.

A proactive policy

During the period 1991–4, the Conservative coalition government and the Minister of Justice brought to fruition much of what they campaigned on. They changed the face of the criminal justice policy debate, redefined the issues, and set the tone by introducing a terminology previously felt to be obsolete and contemptuous of human values. They shifted the focus from society and the collective to the individual, in terms of crime, guilt and crime prevention. They made the general public a direct participant in the formation of this public policy.

For example, after ten years of use, half-time release was abolished in 1993. This may eventually contribute to the expansion of the prison system by increasing the length of the average prison term served. (This reform came only a few years after the introduction of 'escalated sentences' in 1989 which authorized the courts to tack on additional time to statutorily specified sentences for recidivist offenders). At the time of writing, the average length of time served for 1993 was 3.5 months, and higher figures are projected for the coming years (Kriminalvården 1995–6). As has been discussed above, drugs continue to be a favourite whipping boy, with the 1988 'criminalization' of the act of consuming drugs, eventually leading to the introduction of the sentence of imprisonment for this crime in 1993.

The pitting (and exploitation) of 'victims' against offenders is increasingly evident in the quest to make harsher policies palatable. While much is being made of the discourse concerning length of sentence and 'liberal' leave practices, thus leaving victims unprotected, much more is being made of gestures that are unrelated to the offenders, such as an increased right to legal support for victims during criminal investigations and at trial (government bill 1993–4 no. 26). Proposals have been forwarded for revenues from the earnings of prisoners to be contributed to the crime victims' fund, women's shelters, and so on.

Many actors – professionals, political parties, grass-roots organizations, victim organizations, the mass media, insurance companies, and the crime control industry – have participated in Sweden's shift 'from a "softer" to a "harder" criminal policy'. Tham (1995) relates this shift to diminished support for welfare state ideologies and stresses that economic, material, political, and other factors stimulating these ideological changes must be examined. He also argues that changes in general ideology will influence criminal policies which then, crucially, in their turn reinforce these general ideologies. In this important sense criminal justice policy must be understood as a pivotal site for political parties in conflict with each other in an attempt to establish central values, and a particular form of hegemonic dominance.

Politicians as servants: what do the people want?
As has been noted, the Conservative regime justified its revamping of the criminal justice system (when the dust clears, it may well be less drastic than the propaganda) in terms of reviving public confidence in the criminal justice system after its neglect by the Social Democrats. Naturally, as many authors have noted, when the gap widens between perceived crime rates and perceived official reactions to crime, demands for a stricter criminal justice policy will rise. There are some, albeit limited, data from the 1980s showing that there was a drop in confidence in law enforcement and a hardening of attitudes towards criminals (Tham forthcoming). Questions however arise. First, how extensive is this evidence, and if these attitudes are so widespread, why does the government bother to spend so much time telling us what the public is supposed to be thinking? Second, how accurate is the public's perception of developments, especially when they are rather contradictory? It is never questioned whether 'the general sense of justice' ought to be the ultimate guiding principle, or indeed, whether we are able to measure it.

It is also argued that if the formal system does not become more responsive to the 'will of the people', people will take the law into their own hands. In an effort to challenge any potential tendencies to vigilantism, 'civil society' is to be mobilized and volunteerism encouraged, and to an extent this has already happened. Parent patrols on streets in the city centre at night and neighbourhood watch programmes are some examples of this process.

It ought also to be pointed out that some of the Conservative bloc's arguments about the ineffectiveness of existing penal sanctions do not hold up against statistical evidence. For example, despite a considerable decrease in the use of prison sentences (from 43 to 38 per cent of all convictions of Swedish citizens for serious crimes), the rate of recidivism decreased between 1966 and 1985 except among persons with at least five prior convictions. Recidivism among 15–20 year olds also declined throughout the 1980s (though it may be rising again in the 1990s). A study by Statistics Sweden monitoring 1.4 million convictions (including prosecutorial decisions to impose fines or waive prosecution) over 13 years found that two-thirds of these 'convictions' involved persons without previous criminal records – and three-quarters of them were not sentenced again during a three-year follow-up period (SCB 1991:2).

A prison system in need of overhauling?

In 1993, the Commission to Review the Implementation of Prison Sentences published its report (SOU 1993:76). The Commission's main efforts concerned adjusting correctional principles to developments since the 1974 Correctional Reform Act. In short, the message was that the 1974 Act had outlived itself, and that some problems in the prisons had become so serious as to warrant an overhaul of the system.

A number of basic principles were reviewed including that of *proximity*, according to which prisoners were to serve their sentences as close to home as possible; and that of *normalization*, under which inmates have the same rights to society's support and care services as other citizens and that these services should be offered by normal outside providers rather than specially designated prison personnel. It is suggested that the latter principle be retained, but that the proximity principle be abolished to accommodate *differentiation* of treatment for the growing numbers of mentally disordered offenders now being sent to Swedish prisons and the greater presence of drug addicts who need to be incarcerated separately from non-abusers.

Another issue which the Commission confronted was whether other existing practices should be abandoned in order to achieve the goal of drug-free facilities. In this vein, it was asked whether intensified control of prison populations (especially drug abusing prisoners) – involving changes to leave, work release, use of telephones, letters, visits, private possessions (to limit trading due to drugs), disciplinary measures and body searches – were necessary to eliminate the drug problems. The Commission clearly acknowledged that the perceived problem with narcotic drugs underlies all its proposals for tougher control measures in prisons and its greater restrictiveness with regard to awarding privileges.

It is claimed by the authors of the report who eventually supported intensifying control that most of the proposed changes had already been introduced in practice during the 1980s. However, when the report was circulated for comment, the Court of Appeals located in Stockholm was highly critical and declared many of the proposals to be inappropriate (Svea Hovrätt 1993).

The 1994 election campaign and the future of the Swedish penal system

The political background in which the 1994 general election was fought is easily summarized. The trend towards a levelling of household incomes in Sweden which began in the 1920s based on a system of redistribution through taxes and transferences was reversed in the 1980s as a result of an overheated labour market which led to higher wages for some, less redistribution through taxes, and high capital incomes and capital gains for households with assets.

Rising unemployment is another factor that has reinforced income differentials. Between 1991 and 1994, more than one-third of all households were affected by unemployment. Sweden thus experienced its worst unemployment for half a century: 500,000 jobs, primarily industrial, were lost, most permanently. The number of working people was at the lowest level since the late 1970s. Young people between 16 and 24 suffered rates of unemployment of about 18–19 per cent. All groups experienced about five times more unemployment in 1994 than in 1987. In 1987, there were 92,000 unemployed, compared to 356,000 in 1994 – 7.1 per cent of the labour force. Many more were outside the regular labour force (R&D 1994:15).

In May 1994, 405,000 people were on disability or sick pensions, compared with under 300,000 in the 1980s. It was mostly women who were awarded new disability pensions (in the mid 1980s, the distribution between the sexes was equal). Finally, there was a dramatic increase in the number of long-term unemployed, from 34 per cent of all unemployed in 1993 to 44 per cent in 1994. Other reports indicated that the number of households near or below the poverty line doubled between 1991 and 1993. The trade unions have highlighted unreasonable levels of employer power, worsening working conditions and weakened union influence.

The slowdown in the Swedish economy began in the 1970s, but artificial measures kept consumption high throughout the 1980s. By 1990, the situation had changed dramatically. The Social Democratic war on inflation led to a record low at 2 per cent in 1992, which resulted in a real interest rise, in sinking real estate prices and in credit losses. In short, a financial crisis was at hand.

Municipalities and counties who supplied health and welfare services were forced to make drastic and extensive cutbacks in their operations, thus weakening the social security backdrop, at the time it was most needed. Public allowance payments were sought by unprecedented numbers of individuals and households. Changes in sick leave rules led to lower compensation levels, fewer short-term sick leaves, but more and longer extended sick leaves. Applicants for jobs were being screened in relation to their prior use of sick leave, and single mothers and divorced women faced a greater risk to their long-term sick leave than other women.

It was said that in Sweden in 1994, there were more than one million disability pensioners, welfare recipients, unemployed, disabled, and long-term sick. One writer commented that the 1994 election campaign would be remembered as the confirmation of the plundering of the welfare state – with no compensatory vision for solidarity or general participation in society's efforts. The lack of faith in the future and in political means for effecting change infected this campaign.

Against this background, and unlike the previous general election, not much time was spent in the campaign of 1994 on issues of law and order and criminal justice policy. What was happening to the welfare state was of more central concern. But also, of course, the Conservatives had done, at least to some extent, what they had said they would do and were simply content to hold their ground.

In response, the Social Democrats issued a party statement on criminal justice policy but without extensive publicity or distribution (Socialdemokraterna 1994). In it, they attempted to couple law and order with wider concerns by arguing that the Conservative government's dismantling of the welfare state posed a serious threat to the possibilities of preventing crime. The widening gaps in society, rising unemployment, growing marginalization as well as cutbacks in support to schools, day-care centres, drug programmes, psychiatric care and increasing social segregation, were all cited as being criminogenic. They stressed instead alternatives to prison, not least because they increased the chances for offenders to compensate their victims economically. Crime prevention (especially at the local level) was a key policy in this statement, with a promise to invest 10 million kronor in crime prevention projects over a period of three years.

Other priority areas identified included tackling violence (primarily on the streets, against women and race related) and white collar crimes. The Social Democrats made it clear that they did not intend to 'liberalize' the admittedly very restrictive stance against drugs (based on the goal of a 'narcotics-free society'). It was acknowledged, however, that cutbacks in drug treatment and full capacity in Swedish prisons made differentiation and sophisticated treatment in this area impossible. In spite of the Social Democratic Party's more progressive approach, it still committed itself to continue with several of the Conservative government's innovations such as maintaining two-thirds conditional release, electronic tagging and harsh drug policies.

Conclusion

Fundamental change is under way in Sweden, and much of what has brought Sweden international status in the field of public policy is being dismantled or weakened. New philosophies are being articulated and new contingencies cited. In a review of the cultural determinants of Swedish drug policy, Henrik Tham (1992:94) identified several crucial elements of the public discourse on drugs: morality, 'the people', consensus, and Swedes versus others. He portrayed a 'scapegoat mentality' and illustrated how drugs are presented as an attack against the Kingdom of Sweden, both culturally and territorially. Drugs – and some types of crime – are viewed not as something indigenous, but rather as something brought in from the outside. He concluded: 'The fight against drugs has therefore been interpreted here to represent drugs as something beyond what they are. They have been perceived as the antithesis of Sweden and as an attack on cherished "Swedish values".' In 1994 a similar analysis could perhaps be applied to the shift from the values of solidarity and inclusion voiced as underlying the acclaimed Swedish model of imprisonment to the punitive and exclusionary philosophy characterizing the debate today.

References

Ahlberg J and Dolmén L (1992), *Fängelsedomar 1975–1992* Stockholm: BRÅ-PM: 5
Åmark K (1985), 'Lagstiftning som reformverksamhet. En historiografisk analys av den modern straffrättens historia' *Rattshistoriska studier* 11, Stockholm
Box S (1983), *Power, Crime and Mystification* London: Tavistock
BRÅ (1977), *Nytt Straffsystem: Idéer och förslag* Stockholm.
Hofer H von (1985), *Brott och straff i Sverige: Historisk Kriminalstatistik 1750–1984* Urval nummer, Stockholm: SCB
Hofer H von (1993), *Fängelset: Uppkomst-avskräckning-inkapacitering* Stockholm: Kriminologiska institutionen, Stockholm universitet
Høigård C (1990), 'Criminality, Sex and Class' in Norman Bishop (ed) *Scandinavian Criminal Policy and Criminology 1986–90* Stockholm: Nordiska samarbetsradet for Kriminologi
Justitiedepartementet (1993), *Att renovera en förfallen kriminalpolitik* September, Stockholm
KOS (various years), Kriminalvårdens Officiella Statistik, years 1992–3, 1993–4, Norrköping: Kriminalvården
Kriminalvården (various years), Anslagsframställning, years 1994–5, 1995–6, Norrköping: Kriminalvården

Krantz L, Somander L and Gustavsson J (1994), *Kriminalvårdens Anstaltsklienter: Utvecklingsperspektiv och Nuläge* Norrköping, Rapport 1

Leander K (1986), 'A Study in Push-and-Pull: Swedish Postwar Criminal Policy' unpublished paper

Leander K (1991), 'Ingenting är omöjligt – intryck från ett behandlingshem för kvinnor' in M Järvinen and P Rosenqvist (eds) *Kön, rus och disciplin: En nordisk antologi* Helsingfors: (NAD) Nordiska namnden for alkohol och drogforskning

Leander K (1993), 'Bortom kriminologi – En annan kunskap om kvinnor i fängelse' *Socialt Perspektiv*

Mathiesen T (1994), 'Slutet för svensk kriminalpolitik', *Aftonbladet* 24 March

Nelson A (1990), *Kriminalpolitik och ingripanden vid brott* Uppsala: Iustus Förlag

Orrenius A (1994), 'Tidaholm – fångvård i ruiner' *Oberoende* 3, Stockholm

Pösö T (1989), 'Kvinnofångarna i Finland – hormoner, emancipation eller en fråga om att klara av vardagen' *Retfaerd* 45, 12

R&D (1991), *Straff i stället for vård i borgerlig kriminalpolitik* Stockholm: Fran Riksdag och Department

R&D (1994), *Större löneskillnader for att få ner arbetslösheten* Stockholm: Fran Riksdag och Department 15

SCB (1993), *Dömda till frihetsstraff 1973-1992* KR info. 7, Statistics Sweden

SCB (1983), *Varför ökar beläggningen på fängelserna?* RS Promemoria, 10, Statistics Sweden

SCB (1994), *Utländska medborgare i kriminalstatistiken* RS Promemoria, 1, Statistics Sweden

SCB (1991), *Återfall i brott 1973-1985* RS Promemoria, 2, Statistics Sweden

SCB RSÅ (various years), *Rattsstatistiska årsbok* Statistics Sweden

SCB (1993), *Kriminalstatistik. For brott lagforda personer, 1993* R11 SM 9401, Statistics Sweden

Schein H (1994), 'Fångvård' *Dagens Nyheter* 27 July

Serrill M S (1977), 'Profile/Sweden' *Corrections Magazine* June: 11–36, Correctional Information Service Inc., Burlington, Vermont

Socialdemokraterna (1994), *Kriminalpolitisk strategi* Stockholm: Politiskredovisning

Somander L (1993), *Kvinnliga fångar* Kriminalvårdsstyrelsen, Rapport 1, Norrköping

Somander L (1994), 'Kriminalvårdens anstaltspopulation – ett utvecklingsperspektiv' in *Kriminalvårdens anstaltsklienter: Utvecklingsperspektiv och Nuläge* Norrköping: Kriminalvården, Rapport 1

SOU (1986), *Påföljder för brott*, Statens offentliga utredninger, 13–15, Fängelsestraffutredning, Justitiedepartementet, Stockholm

SOU (1993), *Verkställighet av fängelsestraff*, Statens offentliga utredningar, 76, Huvudbetankande av Fängelseutredningen, Justitiedepartementet, Lund

Strahl I (1970), *Den svenska kriminalpolitiken: En presentation av brottsbalken och en översikt över den svenska straffrättens utveckling från 1800-talet till våra dagar* Stockholm: Aldusserien, Bonniers

Svea Hovrätt (1993), Court of Appeals, Stockholm, Yttrande 1993-12-15, Dnr 4 58/93

Sveri K (1981), 'Vem forvalter rattvisan?' seminar paper delivered at Nordiska samarbetsradet for kriminologi (NSfK), Oslo

Tamburrini C (1993), 'Upprättelse eller meningslöst lidande? Om vård, vedergällning och den ny fängelseutredningen' *Dagens Nyheter* 19 November

Tham H (1992), 'Narkotikakontroll som nationellt projekt' *Nordisk Alkoholtidskrift* 9, 2: 86–97

Tham H (1994), Personal communication

Tham H (forthcoming), 'From Treatment to Just Deserts in a Changing Welfare State' in A Snare (ed.) *Beware of Punishment: On the Utility and Futility of Criminal Law*. Scandinavian Studies in Criminology 14, Oslo: Scandinavian University Press

9

Imprisoned Ireland

Mike Tomlinson

Britain colonized Ireland for several centuries before it was incorporated into the British mainland through the Act of Union in 1800. This only fuelled republican sentiment and Irish independence was eventually, though only partially, secured with the Anglo-Irish Treaty in 1920 which left Northern Ireland under British rule. Since then the prison system in the South has been run by the Department of Justice in Dublin while the penal system in the North is the responsibility of the Northern Ireland Office, since 1972 under the auspices of the British government in London. While these systems fall under different jurisdictions and are therefore run quite independently, and are likewise distinct from the prison system in England and Wales, the interconnectedness and the parallels between them are many, as the opening quotations illustrate.

> On these occasions we would be stripped stark naked and subjected to the most minute examination of our person – so minute that oftentimes the bull's eye lamp was used. Had this search stopped short at a minute examination of the hands and between the fingers, of the soles of the feet and between the toes, of the mouth and inside the jaws and under the tongue, it would be disagreeable enough; but it went further, and to such a disgustingly indecent extent that I must not here do more than imply the nature of it. (Thomas Clarke, cited in Curtis 1994:166)

> While I was at mass, one of the lads gave me a pen and a few skins to write on. I hid them up my backside and went back to the wing. When I got there the screws were doing a mirror search. When they got me bent over the mirror one of them said he could see something. When I refused [to give them the parcel] they told me to turn and face the wall. I said 'No' so one of them grabbed me by the hair and turned me round. Two more grabbed my arms up my back . . . Then two more screws came and lifted my legs into the air. This left me upside down with my head between my legs . . . I could hardly breathe and I thought I was going to pass out. They were all laughing out loud and then he came with the pliers. I remember him putting them into me and he nipped me two or three times. If I cried out the screws holding me would push me to keep quiet. They got the pen and paper and they all kept laughing at me. (Campbell et al. 1994:90–1)

These two accounts of what are euphemistically referred to in official circles as 'intimate body searches' occurred almost a century apart and on different sides of the Irish Sea. The first was written by Thomas Clarke, serving a life sentence in England for his part in the Fenian bombing campaign in London of the early 1880s. After his release in 1898, Clarke went on to sign the 1916 proclamation of the Irish Republic. He was a key figure in the uprising of that year which led to the withdrawal of British sovereignty from all but six counties of Ireland – the area known as Northern Ireland from 1920 onwards. The second account is by Ciaran McGillicuddy, 17 years of age at the time of the search, who was being held in one of the H-blocks in Northern Ireland's main prison for political offenders. This prison was first used as an internment camp and known as Long Kesh. From the mid 1970s when the H-blocks were built, it was renamed by the British administration as Her Majesty's Prison Maze. McGillicuddy is describing the sort of treatment meted out to republican prisoners over a four year period from 1976, treatment which finally led to the well known hunger strikes of 1980 and 1981.

Clarke and McGillicuddy's experiences illustrate a continuity in the special regimes applied to prisoners caught up in the various military campaigns against Britain's role in Ireland. And they serve to introduce the basic argument of this chapter, namely that since the emergence of modern prison systems in the nineteenth century, penal policies and prison regimes in Ireland have been strongly influenced by the containment of political disorder, specifically militant Irish nationalism and republicanism. While it is quite possible to describe the prison systems of Northern Ireland and the Republic of Ireland in administrative and managerialist terms, emphasizing their 'ordinariness' (Brewer 1991) or 'normalization' (Gormally et al. 1993), this would be to miss the extent to which contemporary prison issues have been shaped by the political struggles of a range of movements concerned with ending British sovereignty in Ireland.

The first section of the chapter examines how and why prisons have been a key focus of protest and resistance with reference to the period leading up to partition (1920–1). This is followed by a review of recent trends in imprisonment in both the Republic of Ireland and Northern Ireland. The third section discusses various attempts to 'modernize' prisons in the two jurisdictions in the wake of counter-terrorist policies in the North and a range of pressures in the South, including prisoners' protests, overcrowding, and an ageing prison fabric. The chapter concludes with some speculative comments on how the Irish prison systems may be affected by the

IRA and loyalist ceasefires, and future negotiations over the governance of the North.

The colonial legacy

While punishment in nineteenth century Ireland was in some respects characteristic of penal policies elsewhere, there were, nevertheless, certain unique features which were tied closely to wider political developments and conflicts. As Farrell (1986:5) records, 'Between 1800 and 1921 the British government brought in 105 separate Coercion Acts dealing with Ireland. Habeas corpus was as often suspended as in force in 19th century Ireland, and it was rare that the country's jails and the penal colonies in Australia did not contain some Irish political prisoners.'

The story of the development of the 'modern' prison is well known. The modern prison and associated regimes were part of the search for new forms of discipline in the wake of the social and political upheavals of the eighteenth and nineteenth centuries, and the emergence of industrial capitalism (Foucault 1977; Ignatieff 1978; Melossi and Pavarini 1981; Rusche and Kircheimer 1939; Weisser 1979). With the new prisons the focus became remoralization and the reform of the mind, not the punishment of the body (Cohen 1977), though the extent of this shift is open to question as the opening quotations suggest (Sim 1990). In practical terms, the old sentences applying to 'serious' offenders, such as hanging and physical banishment by means of transportation to British territories in America, Africa or the Antipodes (Costello 1987; Henry 1994; Rudé 1978; Shaw 1966), were replaced by carefully designed and newly built penitentiaries with highly controlled regimes designed to discipline and subdue.

The first Irish penitentiary was opened in Dublin at Richmond in 1818 as a rather belated response to the 1792 provision whereby sentences of transportation could be converted to terms of imprisonment. This arose partly because of the difficulties of sending transportees to America following the outbreak of the War of Independence, and also because agrarian disturbances (Broeker 1970) meant that greater numbers were being sentenced to transportation, including a substantial number of women (Henry 1994; Costello 1987). By the 1830s, commentators and colonial administrators were complaining specifically about Irish transportees and their political demeanour (Holtzendorf 1860). In Nassau Senior's (1868) words, the transportation of Irish political agitators was 'sowing our colonies with poisoned seed'. Senior was the government adviser on economic affairs to whom Benjamin

Jowett, Master of Balliol College Oxford, was referring when he said, 'I have always felt a certain horror of political economists since I heard one of them say that he feared the famine of 1848 in Ireland would not kill more than a million people, and that would scarcely be enough to do much good' (Woodham-Smith 1991:375–6). According to one estimate, 39,000 people were transported from Ireland between 1787 and 1868, including 9,000 women. About 5,000 of the total can be identified as 'political' (Costello 1987:161–2).

Just as the famine was seen by the British administration of the time as an opportunity for economic and social development – a lesson in political economy with the potential to transform a peasant, subsistence and potato based economy into one based on cash and waged labour – so too it was felt that the new prisons should be places for inculcating the fundamental principles of labour and property relations amongst a rebellious peasantry. Thus prison education included instruction on 'the legitimate relations between the employer and labourer, the grounds on which wages are determined, the influence which the use of machinery exercises in benefitting the labouring classes, the means of earning an honest livelihood, and, finally, all matters referring to the rights of inheritance of each member of the family' (Holtzendorf 1860:60).

In the period 1820–45, 26 new prisons were constructed and over 100 closed. The speed and scale of this modernization owed much to the centralization of British rule under the Act of Union (1800) as well as to growing problems with transportation and continuing political agitations and rebellions (Tomlinson and Heatley 1982). The British established a central inspectorate of prisons in Ireland 13 years before doing so in Britain itself. But it took events surrounding the famine years (1845–9) and the cessation of transportation as a punitive option before the Irish 'convict system' was properly established and placed under central government control (McDowell 1964).

The Irish convict system is well known for one particular 'experiment'. Prisoners were required to graduate through a series of stages, for example, from solitary confinement in Mountjoy, the main Dublin prison today, to hard labour on Spike Island (also still used as a prison), and on to release on licence. While this system differed on minor points of detail from the English equivalent, it incorporated an early form of 'open' prison which was unique at the time to Ireland.

These prisons were known as 'refuges' in the case of women and as 'intermediate prisons' in the case of men – and there were two of each, the female refuges being segregated by religion. Rather like the current 'working out' scheme for life sentence prisoners in the North, these institutions allowed prisoners to do work outside the prison during the day, while returning to the prison at night. Earnings were saved with a view to encouraging released prisoners, especially women, to emigrate. These institutions were closed following several years of heated debate between leading English and Irish prison administrators. The English hard-line view was that such open prisons were pandering to the Irish (Tomlinson and Heatley 1982:240).

The idea that the refuges and intermediate prisons were too 'soft' appears to have informed the policy whereby agrarian and other political offenders were excluded from them. Besides, the rehabilitative notion behind open prisons would hardly change the minds of hardened political activists: they required sterner stuff. Accordingly, the Irish political prisoners who were transported, or who were imprisoned in English jails such as Chatham, Portland and Dartmoor in the 1870s and 1880s, found themselves subjected to special regimes which literally drove some prisoners mad. It is to one aspect of this regime which Tom Clarke is referring in the opening quotation of this chapter (see also O'Donovan Rossa 1991).

Specific agitations over the treatment of prisoners, as well as campaigns for prisoner amnesty, became commonplace from the late 1860s onwards. On occasions, the government's response was to hold an inquiry, such as the 1870 Devon Commission or the 1889 Inquiry on Prison Dress. A common thread in these was the vexed question of whether or not to treat political offenders differently and separately from others, and if so, how. This remains a key concern of prison policy North and South to this day, as shown later on in this chapter.

As the struggles for Irish independence, for women's suffrage and for workers' rights grew in the early years of the twentieth century, prison protests correspondingly intensified. Prisoners explicitly demanded that the authorities recognize their political motives and treat them accordingly as political prisoners. The stakes in this struggle were dramatically raised in the summer of 1912 when two English suffragettes, detained in Mountjoy prison for throwing a hatchet at Prime Minister Asquith's coach as he drove through Dublin, went on hunger strike for political status. They were joined by four Irish suffragettes. Although by no means applied consistently, the government adopted a policy of forcible feeding followed by the introduction of the Prisoners (Temporary Discharge for Ill Health) Act. The latter was quickly dubbed the 'Cat and Mouse Act' because it allowed the authorities to release hunger strikers temporarily, only to rearrest them once they had recovered (Owens 1984).

Notwithstanding this experience of suffragette hunger strikes, the government showed no consistency in dealing with this form of protest when adopted by other political activists. Following the 1916 rising, the political crisis was such that at one moment a person could be sentenced to death and the next released. Thomas Ashe, amnestied after the rising, was later imprisoned in Mountjoy after a mass arrest of republicans in August 1917. Along with a dozen others he embarked on a hunger strike and was forcibly fed, a practice which killed him only a month later. In contrast, when the Mayor of Cork, Terence MacSwiney, went on hunger strike after his arrest under new emergency powers in 1920, he was allowed to die.

Shortly after his arrest, MacSwiney had been taken by warship to London's Brixton prison. This reflected a practice, common for about fifty years up to partition, of removing imprisoned activists from Ireland as a crude policy of isolation. For example, after the rising nearly 1,900 prisoners were dispersed in British and Scottish jails before being housed in Frongoch prison camp in Wales, previously used for German prisoners of war. It was during this period that the Irish prisoners in Stafford jail managed to negotiate free access to newspapers, food parcels and free association by day and night, and were able to create and administer their own rules to govern their daily activities. Essentially, the prisoners were able to acquire the same rights as agreed between Germany and England for prisoners taken in the First World War. These rights were conceded on the condition that the prisoners elected a commandant who was to be responsible to the governor for discipline. A similar regime applied in Reading and at Frongoch (Figgis 1917; McGuffin 1973:27–8). This was the high point of a comprehensive practical recognition of political status until the post-1969 period is reached.

This history provides the sociological context for an understanding of the contemporary penal system in Ireland. The political role of this system in maintaining order was to remain substantially intact in the twentieth century as the colonial conflict was renewed and intensified, engulfing the whole criminal justice system.

Trends in imprisonment

Except where otherwise indicated, all the data on prison trends which follow are taken from the relevant annual reports published by the Department of Justice and the Northern Ireland Office (or its predecessors).

During the civil war which followed partition in 1920, there were a number of mass hunger strikes and other prison protests as thousands were interned and more than 80 executed after sentence by military courts in the newly established free state. In response to a spate of prison wrecking, the authorities in the North transferred any prisoners who had lived in the South to the free state in January 1922. Most political prisoners in both jurisdictions had been released by the end of 1924.

Once the civil war was over, the now divided Irish prison system largely faded from view. Although there were moments when republican prisoners once again brought the prisons into the spotlight, for example, during the Second World War and the late 1950s, 'the issue of prison and of prison reform was not a major one on the agenda of the new state' (McCullagh 1988:155–6). In fact, the administrations in both parts of Ireland showed little interest in developing the prison system such as by improving conditions or providing education and welfare resources. With low crime rates on both sides of the new border, and with the fighting over for the time being, prison populations remained low.

McCullagh points out that in the 50 years between 1878 and 1928 the average daily prison population declined from 3,910 to 728, a figure which makes no allowance for partition, it should be noted. By 1943 the average daily prison population in the South was 740, and from that point the numbers declined until reaching the lowest figure ever of 369, including 55 persons held in places of detention for juveniles, in 1958. Women prisoners accounted for 15 per cent of the total at this time. By 1967, a mere nine years later, the number of prisoners had risen by 66 per cent to 611, or taking the 14 year period up to 1972, the figure almost trebled to 1,035. This rapid increase is partly explained by a 460 per cent rise in the numbers incarcerated in places of detention for juveniles, who comprised 15 per cent of the total imprisoned at the beginning of the period (1958) and 25 per cent by the end (1972). Adult prisoners increased by 250 per cent. The prison population in the South became more male in the post-war period. In 1945, 14 per cent of the adult average daily prison population was made up of women but this figure had declined to 6.5 per cent by 1957, notwithstanding the overall decline in numbers at that time and the fact that women matched men in terms of the numbers imprisoned for drunkenness – 90 women and 99 men in 1955. The masculinization of the prison population continued so that by the early 1980s, women accounted for a mere 2.7 per cent of the average daily total of those imprisoned. This is explained by the dramatic rise in male numbers rather than by any decrease in female numbers: in fact the female daily average increased from 22 to 40 between 1973 and 1983.

The position in the North is in some respects harder to read because of the use of internment without trial. The official figure for the average daily prison population in 1920, for example, is 278 (compared with 652 in the North's prisons in 1912) but in addition there were on average around 550 internees in prison each day. At the end of the 1920s the prison population was 329, rising to 361 by 1939. When internment was introduced during the Second World War, numbers rose to 929 in 1943, but with the release of all internees at the end of 1945 the total fell back, reaching a low point of 279 in 1950. At this stage women comprised less than 8 per cent of the total, a proportion which continued to decline throughout the 1950s and 1960s. The average daily figure for women reached its lowest point in 1969 – 9 only, or 1.5 per cent of the total. While the South's total trebled from the late 1950s to the early 1970s, as noted above, the North's total declined from 1958 to 1965 (403) and had increased to 617 by 1969. With some fluctuations in between, it took from 1950 to 1967 for the North's average daily prison population to double.

From the late 1960s the picture changed dramatically in the North. While the average population rose marginally in the South, from 1,035 in 1972 to 1,196 in 1981, the North's increased by over four times within five years. Numbers peaked just short of 3,000 in 1978. This massive influx of prisoners was entirely due to the intensity of the conflict outside the prisons: half of all those killed between 1969 and 1994 died between 1970 and 1976 (Sutton 1994). A total of 766 were interned in 1971 alone, the vast majority of them republicans since it was the IRA the government was targeting (Spujt 1986). By February 1976, 895 republicans and 581 loyalists were imprisoned in special compounds and recognized as 'special category' (i.e. political) prisoners.

Regarding the sentencing of prisoners in the North, the distribution of short- and long-term committals changed rapidly. In the 1960s long-term committals of women never rose above two in any year: this is out of 120 committals in 1960, declining to 37 in 1969. Amongst men, long-term committals never rose above 2 per cent of the total in the 1960s. By 1977, however, long-term committals had risen to 29 per cent of all committals and a similar change occurred in the case of women (Rolston and Tomlinson 1986:164–6; see also Workers' Research Unit 1982:12). Between 1973 and 1983, 440 men were committed to prison with life sentences. By 1987, lifers made up 28 per cent of sentenced prisoners and about 40 per cent of all the loyalist and republican political prisoners (Tomlinson and

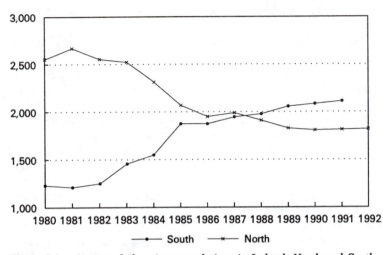

Figure 9.1　*Average daily prison populations in Ireland, North and South*

Sources: Department of Justice *Report on Prisons and Places of Detention*; Northern Ireland Office *Annual Report on the Administration of the Prison Service*

Rolston 1988). This was an unusual prison population by any standards.

By the mid 1980s, a clear pattern had emerged of two distinct prison populations, the one comprising prisoners serving short-term sentences for non-political offences and the other long-term political prisoners (Rolston and Tomlinson 1986:166; ICC/ICJP 1990:26). This assessment is based on official data and legal definitions of offences which are 'scheduled' under emergency legislation because they involve 'terrorism', i.e. law breaking and/or violence for political ends. By June 1985, 90 per cent of all prisoners convicted of non-scheduled offences were serving short-term sentences whereas only 17 per cent of political prisoners were short-termers. This relationship between sentence length and political/non-political prisoners grew stronger for women towards the end of the decade, but weakened for men largely as a result of a reduction in the number of long-term political prisoners (Tomlinson and Rolston 1988:171).

Figure 9.1 compares North/South trends in average numbers of prisoners since 1980. The figure for the South has very nearly doubled in the ten years up to 1991 and is still rising even though the average juvenile population declined by 60 per cent from 1989. Regarding the North, there has clearly been a substantial decline (almost 30 per cent) and a levelling off from 1989. The population

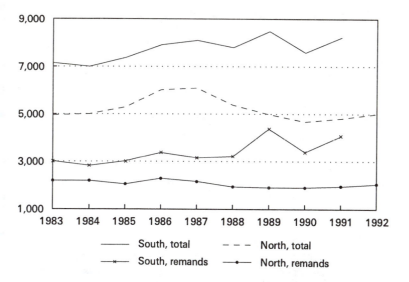

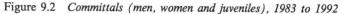

Figure 9.2   *Committals (men, women and juveniles), 1983 to 1992*

Sources: Department of Justice *Report on Prisons and Places of Detention*; Northern Ireland Office *Annual Report on the Administration of the Prison Service*

rose very slightly in the early 1990s because of an increase in remand prisoners. As at 1 June 1994, a total of 4,650 people were imprisoned in Ireland, 59 per cent of them in the South, yielding an imprisonment rate of around 103 per 100,000 population. This compares with Council of Europe figures for February 1990 of 56.0 for the Republic of Ireland and 112.3 for Northern Ireland, the highest rate of imprisonment recorded for member states at that time, although about the same as Hungary's rate for September that year (Council of Europe 1992).

Committal trends between 1983 and 1992 are shown in Figure 9.2. During the 1970s in the South, total committals to prison (sentenced and unsentenced) initially fell from around 6,000 to 5,400 but then climbed steadily to 6,100 by 1981. Two years later they had reached 7,200, climbing to 8,200 in another four years and almost 8,800 in 1989, as the graph shows. There is a similar 1987 peak in the North with committals falling back to 4,700 in 1990. In the early 1990s they rose again.

During the 1980s the proportion of committals accounted for by sentenced prisoners in the North rose from 56 per cent in 1983 to 66 per cent five years later. By 1992, sentenced prisoners accounted for 60 per cent of all prison receptions. Another way of looking at this is to examine the impact of remand prisoners on the average daily figures. In 1981, 19 per cent of the average prison population in the North was made up of remand prisoners, declining to 14 per cent by 1988. In 1992 it had risen to 23 per cent. While there was an attempt to reduce remand periods in the mid 1980s, the time spent on remand for scheduled defendants rose from 1989, reaching an average figure of 54 weeks (from first remand to hearing) in 1991 (Standing Advisory Commission on Human Rights 1993:199–244). In July 1992 an administrative time limits scheme was introduced whereby targets were set to limit the remand times of scheduled defendants. These were set at 38 weeks from first remand to committal, and at 10 weeks from committal to arraignment (the point at which the defendant enters a plea). There is a statutory limit on the latter of 14 weeks. No target was set for the period between arraignment and the actual trial. In the first year of the scheme's operation, the targets were met in the majority of cases and average times between remand and committal decreased significantly. On the other hand, the average time between arraignment and trial (not covered by the scheme) increased noticeably (Standing Advisory Commission on Human Rights 1994:31–2).

The pattern in the South is similar with regard to the proportions of sentenced prisoners among all committals, at around 60 per cent, but there the similarity ends. An unusual feature of the prison population in the South is that, on average, it contains a very low proportion of remand prisoners – about 5 per cent. Time spent on remand in custody is generally very short, a matter of days rather than weeks. As O'Mahony (1993:106) points out, 'a remand prisoner's length of stay tends to be long on the Continent but very short in Ireland. The only Council of Europe countries to approach the low Irish level of remands were Cyprus and Iceland, which both had about 8 per cent [in 1987].' In one way this is not surprising given the 'inquisitorial' nature of many European criminal justice systems: a safer comparison is with the British system. The situation in the Republic of Ireland still stands out, however, when compared with Scotland and England and Wales.

Figure 9.3 shows trends in the committal of male sentenced prisoners with regard to fine default since 1980. At the start of the period, more fine defaulters were being sent to prison in the South than the North, both absolutely and proportionately (15 per cent and 14 per cent of all committals respectively). Within a few years, the position changed radically. While fine defaulters reached 27 per cent of committals under sentence for 1988, the corresponding figure for the North was 55 per cent that year. By 1992, 57 per cent

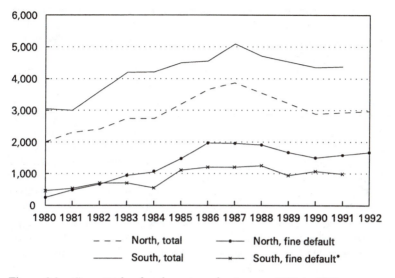

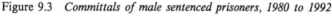

Figure 9.3 *Committals of male sentenced prisoners, 1980 to 1992*

* Includes debtors, default of sureties.

Sources: Department of Justice *Report on Prisons and Places of Detention*; Northern Ireland Office *Annual Report on the Administration of the Prison Service*

of all sentenced prison receptions were for fine default (22 per cent in 1991 for the South). Given that fine defaulters typically serve sentences of around a week on average, however, they contribute less than 2 per cent (1.88 per cent) to the average daily figure in the North, and substantially less in the South. According to one study conducted in the mid 1980s, imprisoned fine defaulters are typically unemployed and unable to pay substantial fines (over £100 in 40 per cent of cases) owing to lack of money. Typical offences were driving without insurance and disorderly behaviour (Jardine et al. 1986).

The trend noted above of declining proportions of women prisoners continued into the 1990s. Taking adult prisoners in the South, for example, women declined from 3.5 per cent of the average daily total in 1983 to 2.1 per cent in 1991. Similarly, in the North women prisoners were 2.7 per cent of the average daily sentenced prison population in 1980 and 1.1 per cent in 1990. This proportion rose to 2 per cent in 1992. For the whole of Ireland, then, the proportion of women prisoners is the lowest of all the Council of Europe countries (Council of Europe 1992:28).

But if, comparatively speaking, Ireland has fewer women prisoners, it has more juveniles and young adults in prison than most Council of Europe countries (using less than 21 years as the defining age). In February 1990, the South's prison population was 27 per cent under 21s, way above all other countries (Council of Europe 1992) although, argues O'Mahony (1993:107), the detention rate of under 21s (numbers detained per 100,000 people) is considerably lower than the British rate. In the North, the equivalent 1990 figure is 21 per cent under 21s. Here, as elsewhere, the proportion of young and juvenile prisoners has fallen noticeably: in 1981 39 per cent of the average daily population was under 21, falling to 19.6 per cent by 1992.

There are very few foreigners in Irish prisons, and some of those recorded as foreigners happen to be from the other side of the border from where they are imprisoned. Two per cent of the North's prisoners were recorded as 'foreigners' in 1990 (Council of Europe 1992), while the corresponding figure for the South was 2.8 per cent or 58 prisoners. But 33 of these were in fact from the North, bringing the figure down to 1.2 per cent.

Many of the above trends reflect a long-term change in the sentences received by adult men. In the South there has been 'a very strong upward trend in the number of relatively long sentences being handed down by the courts' (O'Mahony 1993:110). Between 1973 and 1987 there was a fivefold increase in the numbers sentenced to more than two years' imprisonment, although the numbers declined by nearly one-fifth between 1987 and 1991. In the North, the explosion of long sentences in the 1970s peaked in 1977 although there were 124 life sentences given between 1981 and 1985. The proportion of long-term sentences among committals has declined as a result of the massive increase in fine defaulters, but even so, in the latest year for which figures are available (April 1992 to March 1993) 332 people – 11 per cent of all committed to prison under sentence – received sentences in excess of two years (compared with 429 in 1991 in the South). This included 185 with sentences exceeding four years or with life sentences (there were 11 lifers).

Figures 9.4 and 9.5 compare the distribution of short- and long-term prisoners North and South. The North's prison population remains dominated by a high proportion of long-termers, particularly lifers.

In summary, Ireland as a whole has seen a rapid expansion in the numbers imprisoned over the last thirty years. In the South, the overall committal rate has become very high. More people are being sent to prison both as fine defaulters (and therefore for very

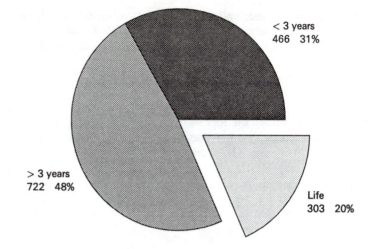

Figure 9.4   *Composition of sentenced population, Ireland, North, March 1993*

Source: Northern Ireland Office *Annual Report on the Administration of the Prison Service*

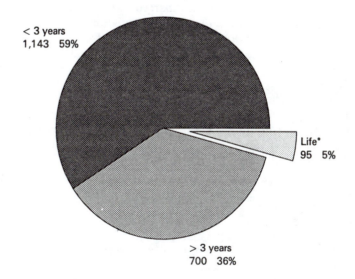

Figure 9.5   *Composition of sentenced population, Ireland, South, January 1991*

* Includes 40 years penal servitude.

Source: Department of Justice *Report on Prisons and Places of Detention*

short periods of time) and as longer-term prisoners. The lengthening of sentences cannot be attributed to changes in the crimes being committed, argues O'Mahony (1993:118). Judges appear to be sending a smaller proportion of those who appear before them to terms of imprisonment, but they are lengthening the sentences of those they do decide to send to prison. In both jurisdictions, there has been a relative masculinization of the prison population, although the average number of women prisoners has been rising in the North recently, mainly due to an influx of political prisoners: there were 21 women IRA prisoners in the North in 1992. By the early 1990s, the North and the South had a very similar average number of women adult prisoners (40). Ireland imprisons high numbers of young people and yet the under 21s constitute a declining proportion of the average daily population over time.

In the North, the political conflict has led to a prison population which expanded rapidly in the 1970s and which is skewed markedly towards long-termers. In the 1980s there was an expansion of a different kind: the imprisonment of fine defaulters rocketed. The short-term/long-term divide in this case closely approximates to a non-political/political prisoner divide. Political law breakers dominate the system. Eighty per cent of remand prisoners in 1992 were awaiting trial having been charged with scheduled offences. Seventy-five per cent of the prison population at September 1990 comprised political prisoners and 72 per cent of the average daily population in 1992 was political (Northern Ireland Office 1993:35–8). The South's prison population is becoming more long-term, but this is less attributable to political prisoners, or 'subversive' prisoners as the Department of Justice prefers to call them, than to sentencing. The number of political prisoners – including one woman, held in Limerick prison – stood at around 60 in 1994 compared with about 200 in 1980 (Council for Social Welfare 1983:17).

Managing crisis and crisis management

The transformation of prison populations in Ireland over the last few decades has unquestionably raised the profile of penal issues and policy, as have the many sporadic and sustained protests by prisoners and their supporters. In both jurisdictions, prison policies have been remote and resistant to influence from pressure groups, campaigners, the churches and even widespread international pressure such as occurred during the hunger strikes in the North in 1980–1. While it can be argued that such secrecy, immunity and non-accountability is an inherent part of the statecraft of prison management in the late twentieth century, this would be to ignore the centrality of political prisoners and the role of prisons in relation to the violent conflict over British sovereignty in the North. This may seem self-evident, except that the denial of this very point has been at the heart of official policy for much of the period under discussion and, arguably, will remain so while British sovereignty prevails.

Nor is this point only relevant to the North. Both the broader political relations between Britain and the Republic of Ireland over the North, and the presence of political prisoners in the South itself, have had their effects on the sluggish pace of penal reform and the modernization of the prison system. As has been observed, the reactionary political climate after partition hardly gave encouragement to the intellectual discussion of criminal justice issues: 'Neither Unionists nor Nationalists, with their strong religious and social doctrines, required the services of a secular sociology to tell them what to do with deviants, inadequates and rebels' (Tomlinson 1988:12).

In both jurisdictions, the aftermath of partition saw the introduction of special legislation to curb republican resistance to the new constitutional arrangements. Isolating prison protest or even authoritative comment on prison conditions (Irish Labour Party 1946; Prison Study Group 1974; Mac Gréil 1980; MacBride 1982) became part of the defence of the state itself. There were a succession of hunger strikes and other protests in the South's prisons from the late 1920s to the mid 1940s (Workers' Research Unit 1982:43). In 1946, a prisoner who had been given the death sentence (later commuted to life) for an assault, died after 23 days on hunger and thirst strike. Two months later, a delegation from the Irish Labour Party publicized conditions in Portlaoise where political prisoners had been held naked in cells for four years, refusing to wear prison uniform and demanding political recognition. The delegation was especially critical of body searches and the extensive use of solitary confinement. New prison rules were introduced the following year (1947) but they proved to be a statement of good intentions rather than the basis for policy implementation until the 1960s (McCullagh 1988:156–7). The two inquiries of 1974 and 1980 cited above were met with a hostile reaction from the Department of Justice. The 1970s were very troubled years in the South's prisons, with regular riots and pitched battles with prison staff, hunger strikes, escape attempts and the buildup of a well organized group of political prisoners. But not until the Church added its weight to the growing criticisms of prison policies and conditions (Council for Social Welfare 1983) did the Department of Justice begin to thaw. Although a judge was asked to carry out an inquiry into protests at the Curragh military detention centre in 1980, the first full-blown official inquiry into the South's prison system did not get under way until 1984 – the first in the history of the state (Whitaker Report 1985).

Whitaker was given a wide brief. This included exploring whether a reduction in committals and a shortening of periods spent in prison could be achieved, a review of existing and planned accommodation, particularly for women and juveniles, and an examination of 'all aspects of the regimes' including aftercare facilities. Whitaker was also asked to look at more managerialist concerns, notably costs and the recruitment, management and training of staff with regard to improving staff/management relations (1985:4).

Essentially, Whitaker followed a reductionist agenda (Rutherford 1986). His report argued that the use of imprisonment could be curtailed by getting the courts to shorten sentences and to commit fewer offenders to prison, and by reducing the time spent in prison through more remission of sentences. The former required the development of a range of alternative disposals for the courts; the latter meant reviewing indeterminate sentences more frequently and encouraging earlier release for good conduct for other long-termers. The standard remission was a quarter of sentence and Whitaker recommended an increase to one-third, plus a liberal approach to early release. Whitaker also recommended that the prison system be taken over by an independent Prisons Board, answerable to the Minister for Justice, thereby loosening the hold of the notoriously conservative civil servants in the Department of Justice.

With the passing of the Criminal Justice (Community Service) Act in 1982, the alternatives to prison were broadened beyond probation orders and supervision during deferment of penalty. Between 1987 and 1990, supervision of criminal cases by the Probation and Welfare Service rose from 2,909 to 3,987. Community service orders, available from 1984, had risen to 1,731 by 1990 and there was also a clear trend during this period of a rise in the average number of hours of work required – 83 hours in 1985 and 142 in 1990 (Department of Justice Report of the Probation and Welfare Service 1989–90). These provisions match those of the North except that the latter has attendance centre orders which declined in use by 60 per cent between 1984 and 1992. The North, however, shows no marked trends in either direction in the use of probation and community service orders between 1982 and 1992. Another difference worth noting regarding the management of alternatives to prison is that, following the Black Report (1979), the North has had a Probation Board (since 1982) which, although financed directly by the Northern Ireland Office, is nonetheless separate from it. Supervision services in the South, in contrast, come directly under the Department of Justice.

The 'diversion' aspect of the Whitaker strategy – providing alternatives to prison and a wider range of non-custodial sentences – has been strongly criticized by McCullagh (1988). He argues that: 'It is the increased punitiveness of the judiciary that has caused the crisis in prison [. . .] it is this wide range of judicial discretion which enables the current punitive climate to exist. The unhampered operation of judicial discretion has produced a penal crisis' (1988:164–5). In a more qualified argument, O'Mahony agrees that diversion may not help matters much because imprisonment is still used as the sanction of last resort when fines are not paid or community orders are breached. Yet it is clear that the South 'over-imprisons', albeit for very short periods, many petty offenders, given the relatively low crime rate compared with other European countries. The prison crisis will only be eased, however, by reducing sentences at the heavier end of the tariff, claims O'Mahony (1993:220–1).

The Whitaker Report was largely ignored by governments and the Department of Justice until 1993 when the Fianna Fáil/Labour Party coalition (which collapsed in November 1994) made a commitment to implement it. Quite what implementation means now that the system has expanded out of reach of the Whitaker guidelines is difficult to gauge. The apparent lack of any urgency in governmental response to Whitaker is perhaps hard to read. At the root of it, however, lies the institutionalized refusal of what at times appears to be a chaotic and inefficiently run Department of Justice to relinquish executive discretion (O'Mahony 1993:240).

There is no shortage of problems to act on. The level of self-destructive behaviour in the South's prisons is alarming. Between 1975 and 1990 there were 23 suicides and 10 deaths from drug overdoses or 'natural causes'. The Republic has double the England and Wales prison suicide rate, and a rate which is 85 per cent higher than the Scottish one (Department of Justice 1991). In the early 1990s there was an average of 4 suicides per year. In 1992 a further 34 lives were saved by the intervention of prison officers (O'Mahony 1993:194). In 1993 24 prisoners attempted to hang themselves, 61 slashed themselves, 22 swallowed blades or batteries and 4 burnt themselves (Centre for Research and Documentation 1994). But the Department of Justice response has been characteristically piecemeal: minor building modifications in an attempt to 'design out' suicide.

The Department's day-to-day activity is dominated by the

Table 9.1   *Prisoners granted 'full temporary release' in advance of normal release date, 1982–1991*

Year	Number
1982	1,982
1983	1,088
1984	2,604
1985	1,320
1986	1,653
1987	1,771
1988	1,504
1989	1,418
1990	1,979
1991	1,619

Source: Department of Justice *Report on Prisons and Places of Detention* various years

exercise of the power of 'full temporary release' under the Criminal Justice Act of 1960, a power which effectively makes civil servants the arbiter of sentences. As Table 9.1 indicates, during the 1980s and early 1990s between 26 and 50 prisoners per week were released early, that is prior to the date of release based on the rules of remission. In fact, the Whitaker proposal of increasing remission to one-third would have almost no impact because of this practice. One minor change worth noting is that 50 per cent remission for people held in the three 'open' prisons (Shanganagh Castle, Loughan House and Shelton Abbey) was introduced in 1991.

If early release epitomizes the crisis management of the Department of Justice, there are few signs of a more forward-looking approach in other areas of policy. By way of example, an important issue for many years now is the problem of repatriating Irish prisoners in foreign jurisdictions, Britain in particular. According to the Irish Commission for Prisoners Overseas (ICPO), there are about 1,200 Irish-born prisoners abroad, most of whom are in England. This question of prisoner transfer from Britain is a long-running one in the North also, but one which is shaped by different legal and constitutional frameworks. The governments of Britain and the Republic have both proven reluctant to transfer a relatively small group of mainly political prisoners from Britain to Ireland, but for different reasons. The ICPO argues that only between 30 and 40 of the Irish-born prisoners wish to transfer to the Republic from Britain in the first instance, and that from then on there would be just a handful of applications each year. Besides, repatriation to the South from Britain and other countries is likely to be offset by transfers to the North (ICPO 1993). The Department of Justice, however, has always adopted the excuse of prison overcrowding as the reason for not moving forward on the issue. Although the Republic signed the European Convention on the Transfer of Sentenced Persons in 1986, it has failed to ratify. The Fianna Fáil/Labour coalition finally promised legislation on the matter in the autumn of 1994, but collapsed before anything more was done. This new-found enthusiasm for the issue was linked to the republican and loyalist ceasefires in the North and the wider peace process.

Transfer of prisoners

The movement of prisoners, whether sentenced or not, between Britain and Ireland has been a high level policy question for as long as there have been political prisoners involved. Nor is it simply a matter of Anglo-Irish relations because the movement of prisoners has become a European concern (Tomlinson 1993:98–102). At the root of the problem of transferring political *suspects* – the problem of extradition – has been Britain's concern to deny the political nature of the actions for which suspects are being held. This is coupled with a more immediate concern that some European countries cannot be relied upon to convict Irish political suspects, or will treat them more benignly than they would be treated under the British criminal justice system (1993:98–102). For instance, there was particular annoyance that a Dutch court only agreed to extradite Gerard Kelly, one of 38 who escaped from the H-blocks in 1983, on condition that the British dropped his life sentence because the court judged the offence 'political': the British complied with this. This is the same Gerard Kelly who conducted secret talks with the British on behalf of the republican movement between 1991 and 1993, and who was part of the Sinn Féin delegation which formally met British government officials at Stormont for the first time in December 1994.

Successive British governments have applied pressure to the Irish government (Farrell 1985), as well as at the European level, to redefine the traditional notion of the 'political exception' to extradition, i.e. the refusal to hand over political fugitives to the requesting state. By the early 1990s, the British government was urging that the already weak safeguards in the European Convention on Extradition should be scrapped altogether (Tomlinson 1993:100). In the 1980s, most of the extradition traffic between

European Union countries and the UK involved Irish political offenders and this was the driving force behind the British policy of pushing for further relaxations in extradition procedures.

The approach to the transfer of *sentenced* prisoners, however, has been to restrict the movement of some and to facilitate the movement of others. Again, it is political prisoners who have experienced most of the restrictions – in this instance, prisoners in England seeking to be transferred back to Ireland – although the stated reasons for blocking transfers have changed over the years. The reluctance of the authorities to address this issue in anything other than an obstructive manner is illustrated by the fact that it took until 1992 for a formal policy review to be conducted (Ferrers Report 1992), notwithstanding two deaths on hunger strike over transfer and a period of forcible feeding of two women prisoners in the 1970s.

Until 1985, governments consistently refused to provide information on prison transfers (Tomlinson and Rolston 1988:187–8). Then information was made available for the 1979–83 period and subsequently for the period 1973 to 1987. Since 1989, more parliamentary questions have concerned transfer policy than any other issue to do with the North's prisons. Most of these questions seem to have been posed with a view to testing the fairness or otherwise of transfer policy regarding loyalists, republicans and members of the British Army. Many of the answers have been evasive, particularly regarding the type of prisoners (political or otherwise) and their affiliation, and some answers have been contradictory (for instance, compare the data given in *Hansard* 26/ 11/91, WA col. 434 with 16/11/89, WA col. 451). So the published data make it difficult to judge if, as is suspected by campaign groups, republican prisoners in Britain have their requests for transfer treated less favourably than others. Certainly, very few of these prisoners were transferred until 1994. From 1973 to 1987 only 5 category A prisoners succeeded in a permanent transfer back to the North (*Hansard* 9/11/87 WA col. 62). A further 6 prisoners convicted of scheduled offences were transferred from 1988 to 1992 (*Hansard* 27/7/93 WA col. 62). Five prisoners (undifferentiated) were transferred between September 1992 and 1993 out of 50 who applied (*Hansard* 21/10/93 WA col. 270). Only 4 out of 33 scheduled offenders serving life sentences in Britain at May 1993 had been transferred to the North – and they had been convicted as long ago as 1973 and 1976 (House of Lords, Debates 26/5/93, WA col. 28). Between 1985 and 1990 only 14 per cent of all applications for transfer from Britain to the North succeeded (Tomlinson 1993:101).

Those applying for transfer from Scotland to the North, most likely loyalist prisoners, seem to have had more success. Between 1985 and 1992, 10 were transferred out of 21 requests (*Hansard* 19/1/93, WA col. 224). Transfers from the North to Britain have also been more fluid. Out of 23 applications for permanent transfer between 1982 and 1992, 10 were successful, and of the 20 applications for temporary transfer, 14 succeeded (*Hansard* 19/1/93, WA col. 171–2).

It was widely anticipated that the Ferrers Report 'administered in a humane way', as the Standing Advisory Commission on Human Rights (SACHR) put it, would begin to ease the conflict over transfer. The report was very cautious and did little to reduce British Home Office discretion over transfers, other than remove from the transfer criteria a clause stating that transfers could be refused in cases of 'crimes undeserving of public sympathy'. Although the government adopted the recommendations immediately, the anticipated movement of prisoners did not materialize. Meanwhile, the European Court of Human Rights ruled in favour of the British government that, amongst other things, it was legitimate not to move prisoners on grounds of national security: they might escape during transfer (Livingstone and Owen 1993:174).

The flaw in the Ferrers Report was that it stuck to the legalism of the principle written into the 1961 Criminal Justice Act (which governs transfers), namely that the 'integrity of the original sentence' must be upheld in any transfer. By recommending temporary transfer and supporting the refusal of permanent transfers if there is a possibility that prisoners will serve shorter sentences, Ferrers ensured that the British Home Secretary would continue to have control over any life sentence prisoners transferred to the North. As SACHR has pointed out, one implication of this policy is the (racist) notion that 'terrorist activity in the rest of the United Kingdom is somehow more heinous than terrorist activity in Northern Ireland' (Standing Advisory Commission on Human Rights 1993:197). The Ferrers Report did, however, also recognize that the 1961 Act should be amended so as to facilitate the permanent transfer of prisoners between Britain and Northern Ireland.

The case of Ronnie McCartney illustrates just how much of a contested area of policy this is. McCartney was convicted of the attempted murder of three police officers after a shoot-out in Southampton in May 1974. None of the men died and all are still serving with the police. McCartney's tariff was eventually revealed by Home Secretary, Michael Howard, as 25 years: in 1983 Leon

Brittan (as Home Secretary) decided that whole categories of offenders serving life sentences should not be released for at least 20 years, including 'murderers of police or prison officers, terrorist murderers, sexual or sadistic murderers of children and murderers by firearm in the course of a robbery' (*Hansard* 30/11/83 col. 506). McCartney was transferred to Northern Ireland in 1992 on a 'temporary' basis, meaning in effect that he remains under the British Home Secretary's jurisdiction. After a protracted legal battle Howard's insistence on a 25 year tariff was overruled in 1994.

When in the late summer of 1994 there was at last some movement on transfers, a political storm blew up with the Prime Minister ordering an investigation into why they were taking place at the same time as the IRA declared a ceasefire. Well before the transfers actually took place, there was widespread coverage in the Irish media that a decision to move eleven prisoners had been taken. Instead of defending the albeit delayed implementation of the Ferrers Report, Major argued an essentially unionist position that the transfers would be seen as a gesture to the IRA and should therefore have been prevented.

Criminalization

The prisoner transfer issue, whether concerning convicted prisoners or not, has been examined in some detail above because it illustrates the tenacity of the policy of political denial. Britain clearly wants to treat Irish political prisoners specially – in terms of the resources devoted to extradition cases, security regimes and by blocking the transfer of sentenced prisoners – and yet it does so through a denial that these prisoners arise from a political conflict of which Britain itself plays a major part. The shorthand for this policy is 'criminalization' and, as is by now well known, its origins lie in the implementation of the Gardiner Report (1975).

As Hillyard notes (1987:296–9), Gardiner argued that the recognition of political prisoners through the introduction of special category status had been a 'serious mistake'. In practical terms, the special category regime meant that loyalist and republican prisoners were held in self-governing compounds according to organizational affiliation. The prisoners did not have to work, could wear their own clothes, cook for themselves and were free to organize their own activities (see Adams 1990). Crawford points out that the government essentially abdicated responsibility for the allocation of political prisoners: 'Once found guilty of a scheduled offence, the prisoner was offered to the compounds. Whichever accepted him got him' (Crawford 1982:156).

Gardiner made the case that the compound system should be abolished because it encouraged a commitment to terrorism. What was required, therefore, was a regime which would replace the collectivism and autonomy of the compounds with an highly rule-bound, individualized cellular system, under which prisoners would be compelled to do prison work and wear prison uniform. Prisoners would be housed in the rapidly built H-blocks at Long Kesh near Belfast and at Magilligan near Derry. These H-blocks were single-storey, low ceiling, concrete constructions housing up to 100 prisoners, 25 in each leg of the H.

In adopting the Gardiner Committee's report, the Labour government of the day decided that scheduled offences committed after 1 March 1976 would attract sentences to be served in the new H-blocks. Neither the Gardiner Committee nor the Labour government appeared to consider that the withdrawal of special category status and the vindictive enforcement of the H-block cellular system might have quite the opposite effect than that intended. They also swept aside the obvious managerial advantages of the compounds which were cheap to build and required very few staff to run – four prison officers per compound of 80 prisoners compared with an H-block staffing of one-to-one (Crawford 1982:157). As subsequent events proved, it was the Gardiner Committee's policy of criminalization which reinforced solidarity among the various prisoner groupings, particularly the republican prisoners who played the lead role in challenging the H-block regime. From the authorities' point of view, and in the long term, the Gardiner policy and its enforcement proved to be more of a political miscalculation than the introduction of internment.

Prisoners sentenced to the H-blocks challenged the new regime by refusing to wear the prison uniform. For disobeying prison rules they were then isolated in cells for 24 hours a day with just a blanket to wear. For the next four years the 'blanket men', with full medical approval, endured calculated deprivation and brutality during a stand-off between themselves, the prison officers and the Northern Ireland Office under the direction of Labour's Secretary of State for Northern Ireland, Roy Mason (Coogan 1980). It is not always appreciated that the hunger strikes which followed this protracted protest were not so much a deliberate political tactic as a last, desperate attempt to resolve an unbearable situation (Campbell et al. 1994). By 1980 the conflict had escalated to such a degree that the protesting prisoners were living in cells with walls covered in their own excrement and had not washed for over two years, although for a period they were occasionally dragged out of the cells and scrubbed with disinfectant.

The enforcement of this regime was well rewarded. As the May Report (1979) recorded, there were just 292 prison officers in 1969 but 2,339 by 1978. In the three years from 1975 to 1978, the number of prison officers doubled. By 1979, the powerful Prison Officers Association had managed to negotiate no less than nine special allowances, including two specifically associated with the refusal of prisoners to accept the post-1976 regime – a special daily allowance for all officers on the protest H-blocks and a steam-cleaning and drying operators' allowance for those hosing down the cell walls.

By the summer of 1994, the H-block regime was unrecognizable. Prisoners were wearing their own clothes (permitted within days of the ending of the 1981 hunger strike), were no longer being punished for not undertaking prison work and had a free run of the wings with no night-time lock-up. According to one analysis (Gormally et al. 1993), the mid 1990s H-block regime is the practical outcome of a change in the Northern Ireland Office's prison management policy from 1981 onwards. The new policy is summed up by the term 'normalization'. It is not clear from this account at what level the new policy was formulated but the thrust of the argument is that normalization adds up to good management: following the hunger strikes, prison management became less confrontational, more pragmatic, and therefore more satisfactory for both prisoners and staff.

Gormally et al. discuss normalization at some length because they see the post-1981 prison management as quite different from the period of criminalization: 'A clear consequence of this policy [of normalization] is the abandonment of the principle of criminalization, at least in a pure form' (1993:87). As they themselves acknowledge, their use of the terms 'criminalization' and 'normalization' is quite different from their established meaning (see Hillyard 1982; 1987; Hall and Scraton 1981; Tomlinson 1980). Other commentators discuss these concepts as ideological processes which at times have been at the centre of political conflict, whereas Gormally et al. are principally concerned with characterizing styles of management.

It is not surprising that the hunger strikes had an impact on prison management and government. Notwithstanding the huge resources devoted to news management during the strikes, the British government's inflexibility and the rigid loyalty of prison managers became internationally renowned (Beresford 1987). But the generally more tender-minded managerial approach of subsequent years was the direct outcome of that conflict and the need to claw back some international legitimacy – to put the H-blocks in the shade and the new prison at Maghaberry, open from 1986, in the light. This did not, however, involve a rejection of either the rhetorical principle or the policy of criminalization. On the contrary, that policy lay behind every point of conflict within the prisons during the 1980s and early 1990s, and has dominated the British contribution to the amnesty debate following the ceasefires of autumn 1994.

As Gardiner demonstrated, criminalization involves more than simply labelling and treating political prisoners as if they were ODCs – 'ordinary decent criminals'. In the context of the Northern Ireland conflict it means seeking to reduce the commitment to military methods of struggle, demotivating collective political action and weakening belief systems. More specifically, criminalization is concerned with 'fragmenting the prisoners' social and political solidarity, and with destroying their systems of communication, discipline and authority' (Tomlinson and Rolston 1988:176). Criminalization, for example, was central to the analysis and proposals of the inquiry into the mass breakout from the Maze H-blocks in 1983, which recommended breaking up groups of prisoners on a regular basis (Hennessy Report 1984). Hennessy gave full support to the policy of integrating loyalist and republican prisoners because 'prisoners in segregated Blocks are generally better able to plan and execute subversive activities of all kinds [and] integrated Blocks are easier to control' (1984:56). Eight years later, the Colville Report supported the integration policy for Crumlin Road prison Belfast (housing mainly remand prisoners) using a similar rationale: 'all the lessons from history suggest that segregation facilitates escapes, and escapes will give freedom to paramilitary fanatics, of both factions, who will kill and maim outside any prison' (Colville Report 1992:29). The integration policy finally broke down in July 1994 following a riot in which 68 cells were wrecked. The NIO responded by transferring 200 remand prisoners from Belfast prison to the Maze (some 15 miles away) and by introducing a Temporary Order whereby prisoners can be remanded without an appearance in court.

Women political prisoners have also been subject to criminaliz-ation, but in their case the pressure came in the form of sexual violence – the authorities' insistence on strip searching by force any prisoners who refused to comply with this 'security' measure. The introduction of strip searching in Armagh prison (now closed) from 1982 was less to do with security than with power, as the National Council for Civil Liberties concluded: 'we think that the intro-duction of routine strip searches amounted to an ill-considered attempt to maintain authority in the prison following years of unrest in the prison community' (NCCL 1986:29–30). In the first four months of the new policy, over 700 strip searches were carried out. Then the practice declined as the searches became random. An uneasy truce on the issue emerged not long after women prisoners were transferred to the new female prison at Maghaberry (which is on the same site as the much larger male prison). From this point on, searches were mainly confined to occasions when prisoners were first admitted to the prison or were leaving it either finally or on pre-release home leave. The number of women searched and the total number of searches carried out, therefore, reflected the flows of prisoners to and from the prison. Even so, both the numbers of searches and individual women searched were at a consistent level from the mid 1980s (*Hansard* 5/3/90 WA col. 422–3; Standing Advisory Commission on Human Rights 1993:39). For the years 1989 and 1992 the average number of strip searches of women prisoners was 375 per annum (the average daily number of women prisoners was 25 in 1989 and 41 in 1992). In 1992, however, there was a major confrontation between the IRA prisoners and the authorities over the decision to strip search every female prisoner in Maghaberry, supposedly on security grounds. It took the prison officers more than ten hours to carry out the searches (see *Statewatch* May/June 1992:10). Nothing was found.

Criminalization has been a significant factor in life sentence review policy and in the prison service's use of Maghaberry male prison. It is clear from the published policy statements concerning lifer review that every opportunity is used to place a negative interpretation on the prisoners' political identities (Tomlinson and Rolston 1988:180–6). Nowhere is it actually stated that early release will be given if there is a ceasefire outside the prison, or if prisoners give up their political beliefs, accept an integrated regime, move from the H-blocks to Maghaberry – at one stage, posters were put up in the H-blocks advertising the benefits of Maghaberry (which include Sky TV in each cell in the lifer unit) – or move from the special status compounds (which are now closed). That, it seems, would be to go too far in recognizing the political nature of the prisoners. But it is implied at every stage of lifer review. The Chief Inspector of Prisons, Judge Tumin, has even concluded, on the basis of an inspection of Maze prison in June 1993, that the Northern Ireland Office was deliberately allowing conditions to deteriorate below those at Maghaberry as an incentive for prisoners to transfer, cutting their political links in the process (*Irish News* 25 February 1994).

The outcome of this type of 'nods and winks' tactic is very hard to gauge. There is some agreement that the conduct of prisoners in relation to the above measures of depoliticization seems to have little or no effect on release dates – with the possible exception of the small number of Official IRA lifers, all of whom were released some time ago and who served on average about seven years (the Official IRA declared a ceasefire in 1972) (Gormally et al. 1993:97–8; Tomlinson and Rolston 1988:184–5). As of the beginning of 1990, a total of 467 people had been given life sentences (not overturned on appeal) since 1974. Of these, 379 were still in prison, comprising 191 loyalists (mainly from the Ulster Defence Association and Ulster Volunteer Force) and 151 republicans (of whom 136 were IRA) (*Hansard* 21/2/90, WA col. 774). Ninety-two per cent of the lifers at that time were convicted of murder. By March 1993 the number of lifers was down to 302.

In addition to the setting up of the Lifer Review Board, there were two other developments affecting sentence length during the 1980s. The first involved reducing the remission of determinate sentenced prisoners from one-half to a third in 1989. Fifty per cent remission had been introduced to entice conformity when the H-blocks first came into use in 1976. Secondly, a system of home leave was developed which now allows lifers and, after a judicial review challenge, other long-termers two periods of home leave per year – a week at Christmas and another in the summer. To qualify, prisoners must have served 12 years.

The home leave scheme has mitigated to some extent the politics surrounding sentence length. Although it is difficult to be precise from the available data, it is evident that the average time served by lifers grew in the late 1980s and early 1990s. By May 1988, 85 lifers, including 36 SOSPs (under 18s at the time of offence, held under children and young persons legislation at the Secretary of State's pleasure), had been released. The released loyalist and republican SOSPs had served 10.6 years on average (*Hansard* 12/5/88, WA col. 203–6). The 18 loyalist released lifers had served 11.8 years and the 19 republicans 11.1 years on average. (The latter figure includes the released Official IRA prisoners.) The 12 listed as 'others' had served an average of 10.1 years. By the early 1990s, the average had crept up to between 12 and 13 years. At the beginning of 1992, there were 176 lifers (still in prison) who had served 10 years and over, but 103 of these had served 13 years or more.

Conclusion

Both jurisdictions in Ireland are heavily committed to the use of imprisonment. Much of this stems from the violent political conflict since 1969, though obviously less so in the South. Yet even here, British sovereignty past and present continues to shape responses to crime and punishment. As O'Mahony (1993:239) puts it, 'most of the Irish legal and penal structures date from the time when Ireland was ruled from Westminster and are based on models which probably never were particularly suited to the local conditions and certainly are not now.' In the North, the defence of the Union over the last 25 years has meant a virtually unquestioned budget for the Royal Ulster Constabulary, the Northern Ireland Prison Service, the Court Service and those sections of the military and the intelligence agencies deployed on Irish affairs. In the 1990s, however, there has been a growing sense that the counter-terrorist policies of the 1970s and 1980s are no longer sustainable economically (Tomlinson 1994). Coupled with the Conservative government's agenda of privatization, there is now considerable pressure to introduce a new element of business management into penal policy and its most expensive part, the prisons.

At the time of partition it cost £94 to keep an ordinary prisoner for a year and £63 for an internee (Ministry of Home Affairs 1921). In 1993 it cost an average of £64,606 to keep someone in prison in the North and £79,711 if held in the Maze/Long Kesh. This compares with £39,868 in the South for the year 1991. If the ceasefires hold and the peace process does not break down, the lack of new long-term customers for the prisons will begin to have a significant impact in a few years. Well before the ceasefires, however, the Northern Ireland Office had withdrawn its blank cheque for the prisons. Its main target for savings is the number of prison officers whose average pay in 1993 was £27,000. In 1994, the plan was to replace around 700 of the 3,200 staff with civilian, administrative workers at less than half the cost of uniformed prison officers.

The peace process offers a much more dramatic change to the prison service, however: the release of hundreds of long-term political prisoners. At the time of writing (December 1994) there is a clear expectation in both loyalist and republican circles and in Irish society more broadly that, whatever happens politically at the negotiating table, the ending of conflict must involve law reform, the reconstitution of policing and the release of prisoners. The latter was recognized by both governments which held office in the South during 1994 and was marked by an albeit cautious release of nine IRA prisoners in December. But the response of the British government to the ceasefires was altogether much more mean-spirited. With regard to prisoners, the popular feeling was that official attitudes had hardened, as shown by the clampdown against IRA prisoners in Britain and by the lower number of prisoners in the North given Christmas parole. Furthermore, security Minister, John Wheeler, responded to the amnesty campaign by saying: 'I can help them on that one. There are no political prisoners.' But as the historian Charles Townshend observes, this attitude of strict legalism will, just as before during the hunger strikes and at other critical moments in Anglo-Irish relations, expose the huge gulf between British and Irish public opinion: 'British people – the Cabinet included – have never been able to understand what is at issue for either side in Ireland' (Townshend 1994). Britain plays safe, he goes on to point out, partly on the grounds that if unionist sensibilities are too deeply wounded, they will launch a full-scale civil war. This is the true meaning of the unionist veto which has been respected by the British ever since the abandonment of Irish home rule in the face of unionist intransigence before the First World War. 'If history tells us anything about this,' Townshend concludes, 'it is that as long as Britain plays safe, there will be no Irish settlement.'

The prison system in the South has also been under economic scrutiny, raising similar spectres of civilianization and privatization. The release of the remaining political prisoners would not contribute much by way of savings. In fact until the fundamental issues of penal policy and the control of prisons are sorted out, crisis management will remain the order of the day. The triangle of conflict between the Department of Justice, prison managers and the Prison Officers Association, whether over how to manage the HIV positive prisoners in Mountjoy (52 in March 1994) or the high proportion of drug addicts and ex-psychiatric patients, is unlikely to be resolved by civil servants occasionally looking over their shoulders to Britain. The South's penal crisis will not be addressed until policy-makers and judges discover alternatives to prison and an accountable, independent prisons board is established.

O'Mahony (1993:239) provides a fitting conclusion:

> The history of the Irish criminal justice system since independence indicates that very few if any original initiatives have been taken by the Irish authorities. Our system still very much resembles the British system and any new provisions or approaches, such as the community service order, have usually been imported from Britain after a suitable delay. This is a sorry situation not only because it reflects on the post-colonialist mentality of the Irish State, but also because it indicates a complete failure to respond creatively to the unique aspects of the Irish situation.

References

Adams G (1990), *Cage Eleven* Dingle: Brandon

Beresford D (1987), *Ten Men Dead: The Story of the 1981 Irish Hunger Strike* London: Grafton

Black Report (1979), *Report of the Review Group on Legislation and Services for Children and Young Persons in Northern Ireland* Belfast

Brewer J (1991), *Inside the RUC: Routine Policing in a Divided Society* Oxford: Clarendon Press

Broeker G (1970), *Rural Disorder and Police Reform in Ireland, 1812–36* London: Routledge and Kegan Paul

Campbell B, McKeown L and O'Hagan F (1994), *Nor Meekly Serve My Time: The H-Block Struggle 1976–1981* Belfast: Beyond the Pale Publications

Centre for Research and Documentation (1994), *Prisons and Prisoners' Rights* CRD Factsheet no. 1

Cohen S (1977), 'Prisons and the Future of Control Systems: From Concentration to Dispersal' in M Fitzgerald et al. *Welfare in Action* Milton Keynes: Open University Press

Colville Report (1992), *The Operational Policy in Belfast Prison for the Management of Paramilitary Prisoners from Opposing Factions, Report of an Inquiry* Cmnd 1860, London: HMSO

Coogan T P (1980), *On the Blanket: The H-Block Story* Dublin: Ward River Press

Costello C (1987), *Botany Bay* Cork: Mercier Press

Council for Social Welfare (1983), *The Prison System* Dublin.

Council of Europe (1992), *Prison Information Bulletin* no. 16

Crawford C (1982), 'The Compound System: An Alternative Penal Strategy' *The Howard Journal* XXI: 155–8

Curtis L (1994), *The Cause of Ireland: From the United Irishmen to Partition* Belfast: Beyond the Pale Publications

Department of Justice (1991), *Report of the Advisory Committee on Prison Deaths* Dublin: Stationery Office

Department of Justice (various years), *Report on Prisons and Places of Detention* Dublin: Stationery Office

Department of Justice (various years), *Report of the Probation and Welfare Service* Dublin: Stationery Office

Farrell M (1985), *Sheltering the Fugitive: The Extradition of Irish Political Offenders* Cork: Mercier Press

Farrell M (1986), *The Apparatus of Repression* Derry: Field Day Pamphlet no. 11

Ferrers Report (1992), *Report of the Interdepartmental Working Group's Review of the Provisions for the Transfer of Prisoners between UK Jurisdictions*

Figgis D (1917), *A Chronicle of Jails* Dublin: Talbot Press

Foucault M (1977), *Discipline and Punish: The Birth of the Prison* London: Penguin

Gardiner Report (1975), *Report of a Committee to Consider, in the Context of Civil Liberties and Human Rights, Measures to deal with Terrorism in Northern Ireland* Cmnd 5847, London: HMSO

Gormally B, McEvoy K and Wall D (1993), 'Justice in Northern Ireland Prisons' in M Tonry (ed) *Crime and Justice: A Review of Research* vol. 17, Chicago: Chicago University Press

Hall S and Scraton P (1981), 'Law, class and control' in M Fitzgerald et al. *Crime and Society* Milton Keynes: Open University Press

Hennessy Report (1984), *Report of an Inquiry by HM Chief Inspector of Prisons into the Security Arrangements at HM Prison, Maze* HC 203, London: HMSO

Henry B (1994) *Dublin Hanged: Crime, Law Enforcement and Punishment in Eighteenth Century Dublin* Dublin: Irish Academic Press

Hillyard P (1982), 'Law and Order' in J Darby (ed) *Northern Ireland: The Background to the Conflict* Belfast: Appletree Press

Hillyard P (1987), 'The Normalization of Special Powers' in P Scraton (ed) *Law, Order and the Authoritarian State* Milton Keynes: Open University Press

Holtzendorf Baron Von W (1860), *The Irish Convict System* London: Simpkin, Marshall

ICC/ICJP (1990), *A Study of the Northern Ireland Prison System* Belfast/Dublin: Irish Council of Churches/Irish Commission for Justice and Peace

ICPO (1993), *Newsletter* no. 10, Dublin: Irish Commission for Prisoners Overseas

Ignatieff M (1978), *A Just Measure of Pain: The Penitentiary in the Industrial Revolution 1750–1850* London: Macmillan

Irish Labour Party (1946), *Report on Certain Aspects of Prison Conditions in Portlaoighise Convict Prison, Dublin*

Jardine E et al. (1986), *Fines and Fine Default in Northern Ireland* Policy Planning Research Unit, Occasional Paper no. 11, Belfast: Department of Finance and Personnel

Kelly F (1988), *A History of Kilmainham Gaol: The Dismal House of Little Ease* Dublin: Mercier Press

Livingstone S and Owen T (1993), *Prison Law* Oxford: Clarendon Press

MacBride S (ed) (1982), *Crime and Punishment* Dublin: Ward River Press

McCullagh C (1988), 'A Crisis in the Penal System? The Case of the Republic of Ireland' in M Tomlinson, T Varley and C McCullagh (eds) *Whose Law and Order? Aspects of Crime and Social Control in Irish Society* Belfast: Sociological Association of Ireland, pp. 155–66

McDowell R (1964), *The Irish Administration, 1801–1914* London: Routledge and Kegan Paul

Mac Gréil M (1980), *Report of the Commission of Enquiry into the Irish Penal System* Dublin

McGuffin J (1973), *Internment: The Story of 50 Years Repression of the Irish* Tralee: Anvil Books

May Report (1979), *Committee of Inquiry into the Prison Service* Cmnd 7673, London: HMSO

Melossi D and Pavarini M (1981), *The Prison and the Factory* London: Macmillan

Ministry of Home Affairs (1921–7), *Report of the Ministry of Home Affairs on the Prisons in Northern Ireland* Belfast: HMSO

Ministry of Home Affairs (1927–71), *Report on the Administration of Home Office Services* Belfast: HMSO

NCCL (1986), *Strip Searching: An Inquiry into the Strip Searching of Women Remand Prisoners at Armagh Prison between 1982 and 1985* London: NCCL

Northern Ireland Office (1993), *Digest of Information on the Northern Ireland Criminal Justice System 1992* Belfast: HMSO

Northern Ireland Office (various years), *Annual Report on the Administration of the Prison Service* London: HMSO

O'Donovan Rossa J (1991), *Irish Rebels in English Prisons* (1874) Dingle: Brandon

O'Mahony P (1993), *Crime and Punishment in Ireland* Dublin: The Roundhall Press

Owens R (1984), *Smashing Times* Dublin: Attic Press

Prison Study Group (1974), *An Examination of the Irish Penal System* Dublin

Rolston B and Tomlinson M (1986), 'Long-Term Imprisonment in Northern Ireland: Psychological or Political Survival' in B Rolston and M Tomlinson (eds) *The Expansion of European Prison Systems* Belfast: European Group for the Study of Deviance and Social Control, pp. 162–83

Rudé G (1978), *Protest and Punishment: The Story of the Social and Political Prisoners Transported to Australia 1788–1868* Oxford: Clarendon Press

Rusche G and Kircheimer O (1939) *Punishment and Social Structure* New York: Russell and Russell

Rutherford A (1986), *Prisons and the Process of Justice* Oxford: Oxford University Press

Senior N (1868), *Journals, Conversations and Essays Relating to Ireland* (2 vols) London: Longmans, Green

Shaw A (1966), *Convicts and the Colonies: A Study of Penal Transportation from Great Britain and Ireland to Australia and other parts of the British Empire* London: Faber

Sim J (1990), *Medical Power in Prisons: The Prison Medical Service in England 1774–1989* Milton Keynes: Open University Press

Spujt R (1986), 'Internment and Detention without Trial in Northern Ireland (1971–75)' *Modern Law Review* 49: 712–39

Standing Advisory Commission on Human Rights (1993), *Eighteenth Report of the Standing Advisory Commission on Human Rights: Report for 1992–3* HC 1992–93, 739, London: HMSO

Standing Advisory Commission on Human Rights (1994), *Nineteenth Report of the Standing Advisory Commission on Human Rights: Report for 1993–4* HC 1993–94, 495, London: HMSO

Sutton M (1994), *Bear in Mind These Dead: An Index of Deaths from the Conflict in Ireland, 1969–1993* Belfast: Beyond the Pale Publications

Tomlinson M (1980), 'Reforming Repression' in L O'Dowd, B Rolston and M Tomlinson *Northern Ireland: Between Civil Rights and Civil War* London: CSE Books, pp. 178–202

Tomlinson M (1988), 'Introduction' in M Tomlinson, T Varley and C McCullagh (eds) *Whose Law and Order? Aspects of Crime and Social Control in Irish Society* Belfast: Sociological Association of Ireland, pp. 9–20

Tomlinson M (1993), 'Policing the New Europe: The Northern Ireland Factor' in T Bunyan (ed) *Statewatching the New Europe: A Handbook on the European State* London: Statewatch, pp. 87–114

Tomlinson M (1994), *25 Years On: The Costs of War and the Dividends of Peace* Belfast: West Belfast Economic Forum

Tomlinson M and Heatley P (1982) 'The Politics of Imprisonment in Ireland: Some Historical Notes' in P Hillyard (ed) *Securing the State: The Politics of Internal Security in Europe* Working Papers in European Criminology no. 3, Bristol: European Group for the Study of Deviance and Social Control, pp. 226–50

Tomlinson M and Rolston B (1988), 'The Challenge Within: Prisons and Propaganda in Northern Ireland' in M Tomlinson, T Varley and C McCullagh (eds) *Whose Law and Order? Aspects of Crime and Social Control in Irish Society* Belfast: Sociological Association of Ireland, pp. 167–92

Townshend C (1994), 'The Prisoners of Caution' *The Guardian* 9 November, p. 22

Weisser M (1979), *Crime and Punishment in Early Modern Europe* New Jersey: Humanities Press

Whitaker Report (1985), *Report of the Committee of Inquiry into the Penal System* Dublin: Stationery Office

Woodham-Smith C (1991), *The Great Hunger: Ireland 1845–1849* (1977) London: Penguin

Workers' Research Unit (1982), *Rough Justice: The Law in Northern Ireland* Belfast Bulletin, no. 10

Index